Profiles of
Radical
Reformers

Profiles of Radical Reformers

Biographical Sketches from Thomas Müntzer to Paracelsus

Hans-Jürgen Goertz, Editor

Walter Klaassen, English Edition Editor

HERALD PRESS
Kitchener, Ontario
Scottdale, Pennsylvania
1982

Translated by arrangement with Verlag C. H. Beck München from
the original German edition, *Radikale Reformatoren,* © C. H.
Beck'sche Verlagsbuchhandlung (Oscar Beck), München 1978.

82 83 84 85 86 87 88 10 9 8 7 6 5 4 3 2 1

Contents

Preface to the English Edition

A valuable resource for students of the Radical Reformation is offered in this translation. In order to understand the history and thought of the sixteenth century, we must have some acquaintance with its people. The editor has made a judicious selection of figures who often constitute only footnotes in the histories. They illustrate especially the many and complexly interlacing strands of life and thought in that turbulent time.

The biographies of Karlstadt, Denck, Gaismair, Reublin, Hutter, Marpeck, Rothmann, Simons, Franck, Cellarius, and Servetus were available in English as the authors originally wrote them. All abbreviations of those texts in the German edition have been followed here. The translators of those parts originally written in German are: James M. Stayer, Introduction and Müntzer; Werner O. Packull, Hut and Hoffman; Thomas W. Cunningham, Hubmaier; Leonard Gross, Sattler; Peter C. Erb, Schwenckfeld; Walter Klaassen, Lotzer, Hergot, Grebel, and von Hohenheim.

Authors will occasionally find spellings of places and persons changed. This has been done in the interests of uniformity. Wherever possible, more English titles were added to the bibliographies, as well as new and other literature which will aid the serious reader.

Walter Klaassen
Waterloo, Ontario

Hans-Jürgen Goertz

Introduction

> Despite their suffering,
> their fear and trembling,
> in all these souls
> there glows the spark from beyond,
> and it ignites the tarrying kingdom.
> —*Ernst Bloch*

When we speak of the sixteenth-century Reformation we evoke names that still live: Martin Luther and Philip Melanchthon, Ulrich Zwingli and John Calvin. These men began reforming movements which quickly developed into great confessions with an astonishingly wide historical impact. They have exercised a lasting influence on the development of the cultural, political, and economic life of Europe and North America.

In this book we turn our attention to some figures who are not so well known. They burst onto the historical stage at the outbreak of the Reformation, but after a short period they changed from fellow travelers or sympathizers of the Reformers into critics of a "stalled" Reformation. They brought their own notions of the renewal of Christendom into the noisy debate of those years. They risked their lives for their beliefs, and often enough they died on the scaffold. Thomas Müntzer was beheaded, Michael Sattler, Balthasar Hubmaier, and Michael Servetus were burned at the stake, and Melchior Hoffman died in the damp dungeons of a Strassburg prison. Others were drowned, tortured, or spent their lives in flight before their persecutors. Pain, fear, and trembling set the tone for their existence.

Only a few, such as Andreas Bodenstein von Karlstadt, Pilgram Marpeck, and Martin Cellarius, succeeded in finding peace and rest in their last years. All of them laid down the gauntlet to religious and secular authorities and chose to take paths which perforce led them out of the society of their day, whether temporarily or permanently.

These individuals were not only ostracized by the world of their own day, but were condemned by the world of the future when they did not disappear from the pages of history entirely. Leopold von Ranke, who explored a broad spectrum of these figures from Müntzer through the Anabaptists to Paracelsus, pointedly summarized their deviant and threatening qualities: "The inspirations of Müntzer, the socialistic undertakings of the Anabaptists, and these theories of Paracelsus corresponded very well with each other; together they would have changed the world. They could never have become a principle of authority, they were too confused and excessive for that; they could only have interrupted the great historical development of culture." This insight is no product of dispassionate historical observation. Rather, it articulates the displeasure of a conservative with those historians, philosophers, and politicians who, in the intellectual climate of the French Revolution, were attempting to achieve a historical rehabilitation of the despised and rejected of earlier days by recognizing them as the forerunners of libertarian thought and action.

Some examples of this new trend will have to suffice. Friedrich Schleiermacher, the "church father" of the previous century, was not embarrassed in his *Christliche Glaubenslehre (Christian Doctrine)* to make use of expressions of the Silesian nobleman, Caspar von Schwenckfeld. Karl Marx spoke of the "great" Sebastian Franck; Friedrich Engels followed the *Geschichte des grossen Bauernkrieges (History of the Great Peasants' War)*, written by the radical democrat Wilhelm Zimmermann, and reminded the German people of their "revolutionary tradition," which began with the "unruly, but powerful and unyielding men of the Great Peasants' War." Finally Wilhelm Dilthey made the direction of his sympathies very clear when he wrote, in *Weltanschauung und Analyse des Menschen seit Renaissance und Reformation (World View and Analysis of Modern Man Since the Renaissance and Reformation):* "Although in his classical early writings Luther hoped to reform secular society and its order, when he was confronted with the living fullness of the profound beliefs and radical demands which sprang forth from the genuine gospel of the Anabaptists, the revolutionary peasants and the urban Spiritualists, he had no better response than to invoke a bald standard of Scriptural authority and to call into force the divine right of the ruler." In the opinion of Dilthey the future belonged not to the Wittenberg Reformer but to the most brilliant figures among the Spiritualists.

This rehabilitation of the once rejected figures of history did not go unchallenged, even after Ranke. Indeed, the fact that they were referred to again and again in the struggle between revolution and restoration, radicalism and conservatism, assured their continuing historical interest and prevented any fixed historical judgment upon them. Instead, people reacted to them on the basis of the good and the bad experiences of the nineteenth century. Recently awakened affection is just as questionable a basis for historical interpretation as ingrained hostility. However, after a time the historical and political polemics cooled down and prepared the way for a scholarly study of these untamable spirits of the Reformation era. For instance, Ludwig Keller tried to trace the origins of the Anabaptists back to the period of the original church by way of the Waldensians; Carl Adolf Cornelius worked for a source-based presentation of the Anabaptist kingdom of Münster; and Karl Kautsky searched for the forerunners of modern socialism among the radicals of the Reformation. An important new departure was achieved by the studies of Max Weber and Ernst Troeltsch in the area of sociology of religion. Troeltsch, above all, tried in his *Soziallehren der christlichen Kirchen und Gruppen (Social Teachings of Christian Churches and Groups)* (1912) to take a nuanced and differentiating approach to figures who had simply been labeled "enthusiasts" or "fanatics" *(Schwärmer)* since the days of Luther and Melanchthon. He separated the peaceful Anabaptists from the revolutionary Thomas Müntzer and established the gifted Spiritualists as a distinct group. The several "types" begin to emerge and thereafter become the objects of increasingly thorough scholarly research.

This research developed in several separate directions. Since the 1920s the study of Müntzer developed independently, as did that of the Anabaptists. The Spiritualists were treated individually, Franck differently than Schwenckfeld. The same occurred in the case of figures who could not be classified into any group or movement: for instance, Karlstadt, Cellarius, and Paracelsus. Finally the study of the Peasants' War took its own course. In the meantime these research areas have grown into specialized topics of history and theology. By way of general orientation, however, we can point out some broad characteristics of these research areas.

I. It is striking that all of the figures sketched in this volume are isolated for purposes of study from the general history of the Reformation, although now, in contrast to earlier times, no one seriously denies their inner relationship to the Reformation. The most important expression of this methodological isolation appears in George H. Williams' book, *The Radical Reformation*, in which the "Radical Reformation" appears as an entity set over against the official "Magisterial Reformation" and the Counter Reformation. Its most striking characteristic is the separation between church and temporal power. Williams, to be sure, did not fall into the old error of effacing the distinctions and peculiarities, the linkages and the feuds within the radical camp; but he did try too soon to achieve a summarizing presentation of this camp.

Some of the more impressive detailed studies of the various personalities and movements were begun only since the appearance of his book. They have suggested that the lines between all of the groups of the sixteenth-century Reformation were extremely fluid rather than that there was a clearly delineated "Radical Reformation." This is illustrated in the process by which Karlstadt became an independent Reformer. Karlstadt's departure was precipitated rather by disagreements among the Wittenberg Reformers over church polity than by theological conflict; and when he turned toward the common people he did not at the same time rupture the normal connections between church and government.

Likewise in the prevailing anticlerical mood of the early Reformation, Thomas Müntzer could regard it as consistent with his program to attempt for a time to win the court of Electoral Saxony for his revolutionary theology. Moreover, the same point can be registered about the beginnings of Anabaptism in the Reformed congregationalism of the rural territories surrounding Zürich, where at first the baptist Reformation aimed to include whole communities and only later to "gather" or separate individual believers from their worldly milieu.

In the cases mentioned there emerged no new ecclesiastical form, which renounced the previous connection between church and temporal government and offered a distinct alternative both to the Old Church and to the church of the Reformation. Or, to put it in another way: the distinction between "radical" and "magisterial" Reformation did not reach back into the process by which schisms developed in the Reformation camp. This distinction took shape only gradually, sharper and clearer in some instances than in others, and it cannot be counted among the originating forces of any "Radical Reformation."

II. In the present century, too, defensiveness and veneration have their place among the motivating forces behind the progress of research. Lutheran and Reformed church historians, particularly, tend to assume a defensive stance. Surely they make the effort to rise above the confessional polemic of earlier times; but they still measure the radical Reformers against the theological insights and political concerns of the major Reformers, also accepting as normative the powers that achieved the practical execution of the Reformation. No doubt these analyses from the standpoint of the theological and political victors are sincere enough in their attempts to be fair to the vanquished, but they are successful only to a limited degree.

The free church historiography, which saw in the Anabaptists and Schwenckfelders of the Reformation era the forefathers of their own confessions, naturally took a different position. The "Schwenckfelder Church" undertook the editing of the *Corpus Schwenckfeldianorum* and academics among the Mennonites, occasionally joined by Baptists, began an intensive and widely esteemed scholarly study of Anabaptism. In North America the emphasis was on the biblicistic, peace-oriented currents in Anabaptism, while in the Netherlands the spiritualistic elements in Anabaptism received special attention. In both cases Anabaptist research was applied to the search for the researching group's own identity among the free churches. Thus they increasingly found themselves reproached with trying to jump over the historical chasm separating the sixteenth century from the twentieth, and with favoring only a particular group—be it biblicistic-pacifistic or spiritualistic—as the "genuine" Anabaptism. This partisan approach, with its stress on contemporary relevance, whatever its good intentions, ended by dehistoricizing the Anabaptists. Only in the most recent period has a current of research without confessional commitments begun the process of rehistoricizing them.

Finally, the Marxist researchers should be mentioned. They approached the most radical Reformers, the revolutionaries and the militants, with a venerating fascination. They concentrated on Thomas Müntzer and the events of the Peasants' War; but they also studied Central German Anabaptism, the Anabaptist kingdom in Münster, Sebastian Franck, Johannes Hergot, and Michael Gaismair, all of whom have since the sixties been classified within the "theory of the Early Bourgeois Revolution." As a counterweight to the one-sided stress on historical theology characteristic of both established church and free church historians, the Marxist historians performed a valuable service with their stress upon the entire social context. Up to now, however, no convincing resolution has been achieved between the efforts to understand the radicals through their historical and social milieu and the strong parallel tendency among Marxists towards partisan and modernizing applications of their history.

III. We have already referred to the difficulties of finding a particular unifying conception applicable to these very different figures. Nevertheless, some such general designation is increasingly sought after, although without the systematizing paraphernalia of a Williams. Sometimes the terminology of "marginal currents" of the Reformation (in German, "nebenkirchliche" or "nebenreformatorische" movements) has been employed; in France the term "nonconformists" is coming into general use. However, the concepts of "radical Reformation" (G. H. Williams) and "the left wing of the Reformation" (R. Bainton and H. Fast) have gained the broadest currency. All of these terms were advanced in an obvious effort to supersede the defamatory label of "Schwärmer" (in English, "enthusiasts" or "fanatics"). Each of them has something in its favor, but each is problematic.

"Marginal currents" (or its German approximation: "nebenkirchliche" or "nebenreformatorische" movements) has the advantage of being an entirely formal category, hence with room for a broad scale of the most disparate spirits. It is problematic because it obscures something essential: namely, that these currents and movements were not really "marginal." One can hardly apply such a label to phenomena which originated in the center of things, in the Reformation's original critique of church and society, and which developed further precisely in those areas where church and society were most in need of reform. Besides, many of our protagonists aimed at nothing less than the restoration of the primitive church in its full apostolic purity; they had no intention to found conventicles (Nebenkirchen) even though their efforts at reform frequently could not fail to create such an external impression.

Although at first glance the "nonconformist" label seems very apt, since most of our protagonists did in fact decline to conform theologically and politically, in the last analysis it is not very apt. Luther himself was at first a nonconformist, Roman loyalists were later nonconformists in Lutheran territories, just as Lutherans continued to be nonconformists in Catholic realms. Moreover, there were certain Anabaptists, Balthasar Hubmaier in Waldshut and Nicolsburg, or Bernhard Rothmann, Jan Matthijs and Jan of Leyden in Münster, who were able for a time to establish their nonconformity as a norm.

The designation "left wing of the Reformation" is much more defensible. Heinold Fast defined it in the introduction to a source collection of 1962 which bore that title: "It is derived from the political practice according to which parties arranged themselves from right to left in conservative and radical groups, according to the degree of their readiness to depart from the traditional." Fast does not intend to stress political concerns but solely the "criterion of external rupture with the immediate past." Since ecclesiastical, no less than secular governments, have a "traditional" foundation (so Max Weber), the notion of "left wing" is in the first place and primarily political. A difficulty with the associations of the term is that in the context of parliamentary parties a left-wing opposition is accepted without question as having a legitimate relation to the currently prevailing social structures. According to this analogy it would seem necessary to exclude from the "left wing" those elements which were involved in disturbances, uprisings, and revolutionary activities.

If we are to use a modern political analogy the image of a nonparliamentary or antiparliamentary opposition would seem to be more apt than that of the parliamentary seating order, although this comparison, too, has its difficulties. Moreover, the concept of "left wing" effaces necessary distinctions between a group's background, its actual founding, and its eventual impact. For instance, it is increasingly clear that many figures began their historical prominence in the religious and political crisis of the early Reformation, yet fed on background impulses derived from a tradition of late medieval piety; and that, despite—or sometimes even because of—this "right wing" background, they produced a "left wing" impact on the future. The advantage of the "left wing" concept is that it sketches a loose framework that enables us to focus on the connections and transitions, as well as on the differentiations in the Reformation camp as a whole.

It seems, nevertheless, that the most valuable concept is that of a "radical Reformation"; but we repeat that in accepting the label we do not conceive of it in the same way Williams did. That matter will now be explained separately.

IV. The problems connected with the term "radical Reformation" have already been discussed above. The divi-

sion between a Reformation authorized by the magistracy
and a Reformation free from the magistracy, pinpointed by
Williams, does not lead us to the cause of the schism
between radicals and moderates in the Reformation camp,
nor can all the radicals be convincingly assigned to one side
of that division. Hence Williams finds it necessary to
regard Thomas Müntzer and the Münster Anabaptists as
misguided exceptions, inasmuch as they put their hopes in
the power of "reborn governments." However, there are
many more radicals whom this division does not suit and
who cannot be fitted into the free church objectives which
would later leave their stamp on the religious and social
life of the Anglo-Saxon world. Neither Reublin nor
Hubmaier, Hoffman nor Menno Simons, the Hutterites
nor the Spiritualists showed any interest in this ecclesiological self-conception. And these are not exactly marginal
figures among the radical Reformers!

Certainly Williams did not measure radicality only by
the objective of separating church and state—he believed
that radicality was also expressed in the effort to penetrate
to the roots of apostolic Christianity and to reconstitute the
primitive church. In a strict sense a "reformatio" was not
radical but only a "restitutio" and this radicalized reform
objective was at the base even of the separation of church
and state. But here new difficulties emerge. Once we observe that historically the notion of "restitutio" appeared
primarily in the context of the governmental Reformation
of Anabaptist Münster, which Williams declared to be an
exceptional case, we realize once again how inconsistent his
conception is.

Lastly, he associated with the ideas of separation and restitution commonly shared conceptions of salvation and
history. Salvation is directed more than among the chief
Reformers towards the experienced, inwardly perceivable
transformation of the person, and history was interpreted
primarily as a fall from an earlier ideal. These observa-

tions are accurate, but the common ideas which they underscore are not pertinent evidence for Williams' conceptualization of the "radical Reformation," since the same ideas can be found among humanist reform circles, in the pamphlet literature of the time with its critique of church and society, even among fellow travelers of the major Reformers. The arguments brought forward in support of these shared conceptions of salvation and history would indeed be pertinent to a definition of the "radical Reformation"; but they are so varied and of such heterogeneous derivation that they cast light rather on the differences than on the commonalities in the radical camp. The objections to Williams' definition of the "radical Reformation" are weighty. Nevertheless, it seems to be meaningful to keep the concept of a "radical Reformation."

To begin with, we must acknowledge the ambiguities in the word "radical." The rupture with church tradition may be radical; political behavior may be radical; theological argumentation may be radical. Radical thought or action in one of these spheres does not necessarily mean that it is present in the others. From the standpoint of the theological tradition Luther with his conception of justification by grace alone was more radical than Müntzer, Denck, the Anabaptists, and the Spiritualists. On the other hand, Müntzer, Hans Hut, Sebastian Lotzer, and the Münster Anabaptists were more radical than Luther and Zwingli in their reform plans and actions with respect to the political situation. They were not afraid to act upon bold programs against the resistance of church and government. Müntzer did not surmount the notion of a *corpus christianum* binding spiritual and secular authority. He mentally loosened those ties only in the hope of knotting them still tighter, and in this sense he was less radical than Luther and some Anabaptists, who in their separate manners paved the way for the secularization of political authority. Still, he had a revolutionary impact of the greatest conceivable radicalness in his own time.

It is clear from these examples that radical is a relative notion; it must always be specified in what context someone or something is radical. And these points of reference are so varied, as between Karlstadt, Müntzer, the leaders of the rebellious peasants, the Anabaptists, and the Spiritualists, that it is difficult to find any common denominator. Here, too, Fast's words apply: "The differences are weightier than the connecting factors." If, despite all this, we prefer the concept of a "radical Reformation," it is first of all because the very ambiguity of radicalness is the distinguishing mark of the struggle for the true path to Reformation, especially where the major Reformers encounter critique from within their own camp. Second, radicalness, so difficult to categorize, kept the boundaries open between the religious parties and theological positions of the Reformation, as well as maintaining open channels from the Reformation to the world of late medieval thought.

Formulated in this way, "radical Reformation" is primarily a heuristic model which requires that each personality or movement be investigated with respect to his or its own standard of radicalness. In such an investigation it would ultimately be necessary to bring the various, fluctuating standards of radicalness into some kind of relation with each other, to capture them within a framework. This can be done if a third aim is kept in mind—namely, that radicalness must never lose its connection with the total social context. By this standard any idea or action would be radical to the degree that it shakes the foundations of society, even if its objectives were by no means social objectives. Theological arguments would be radical only when they threaten the structures of authority. Conversely, political positions or activities would be radical even if they were legitimated by traditionalist arguments, to the degree that they appear from an external standpoint as clear cases of revolutionary defiance. Anyone must be recognized as radical who sets out to explode his own time's prevailing norms of life and thought. And that can happen through theology as well as through political action, through attack or through flight, through militance or through peaceful means, through a Thomas Müntzer or a Michael Sattler. Seen in this way radicalness cannot be measured by the criterion of a rupture with the intellectual tradition of the immediate past, but only by the break with the society of the present. In this fashion the historian can succeed in preserving the dialectical relationship between theological ideas and social development, at the same time measuring radicalness ultimately by the social context in which any theology is grounded.

This definition of radicalness is implied, basically, by the figures whose biographies this book contains. They still stand, as is occasionally remarked, clearly in the tradition of late medieval reformation-models, according to which ecclesiastical and secular institutions should be reformed as a whole. On the contrary, the major Reformers—after they received their first fright from the almost unmanageable forces that they had unleashed—strove to keep religious and worldly reforms strictly separate. It was exactly that which brought upon them the reproach of a "stalled" Reformation from those individuals who would not surrender the hope to expand the transformation of men in the sight of God into a transformation of all human relationships—in a word, a transformation of the world. These men wanted to widen the Reformation front both theologically and sociologically and, in the tense eschatological atmosphere of the time, they aroused in themselves the hope of an imminent kingdom of God. Although their illusions about this kingdom were shattered, much that they hoped for did later come to pass in a completely earthly manner, in the arduous and painful processes of historical continuity and discontinuity. But is this a reason to condemn their hope? Ernst Bloch salutes the "tarrying kingdom" of the radicals.

V. Williams divided the "radical Reformation" into Anabaptists, Spiritualists, and Evangelical Rationalists (with further subclassifications), and Fast divided the "left wing of the Reformation" into Anabaptists, Spiritualists, Enthusiasts, and Antitrinitarians. It is entirely reasonable following the lead of Ernst Troeltsch to derive a number of groups as an aid to a summarizing comprehension of the multiplicity of figures whom we must present. In individual cases, however, it will always be dubious whether the proper associations and differentiations have been worked out. In the personal portraits presented in this book there will be no subdivisions. This is appropriate in view of the present stage of research in which intensive attention has been given to individual figures, resulting in some new differentiations in the radical camp.

Just to give one example, the differentiations within Anabaptism are stressed much more than was the case a few years ago (J. M. Stayer and C.-P. Clasen); the difference between Müntzer and the Anabaptists has for some time not seemed so absolute as it once did, and precisely because of this it has been possible to bring many Anabaptists into clearer focus. The polygenetic view of Anabaptism (e.g., J. M. Stayer) has loosened up the terrain, and also, more than previously, set forth the diverse points of contact between peasant uprisings and Anabaptist movements in Switzerland, South and Central Germany.

This book aims to inform about the lives of individual radicals in accord with the best current research, but in a way that departs from the usual mode of academic analysis and reaches out to a wider circle of readers. Naturally, only a limited selection of Reformation radicals can be presented. Many readers will miss a favorite figure or perhaps be astonished at the inclusion of one or the other of our protagonists (for instance, Sebastian Lotzer, Johannes Hergot, or Paracelsus). Our first concern in the selection is to present the most important actors in the radical camp. However, the selection is also dependent on the readiness of authors, often after long years of intensive research on special figures or processes of the Reformation, to produce a "biographical sketch."

There is no intention here to insist upon the biographical medium in contrast to the analysis of trends, powers, and structures, nor to assert the greater importance of the individual than the collectivity, or of personal creative activity over against social and economic determination. Our use of the biographical genre involves no programatic or methodological claims but is a product rather of the state of the research. The time is not yet ripe for a general presentation of the "radical Reformation," but there is an opportunity now to set forth the brilliance and the misery, the fear and the hope of the radicals in a gallery of biographical portraits. Common traits and similarities, cross connections and points of contact will spring into view, and the contrasts will emerge.

The selection begins with the early critics of the Wittenberg Reformation and moves on to the leaders and partisans of the rebellious peasants. It brings in Anabaptists from Switzerland, South Germany and Moravia, Münster and the Netherlands, and in a last group includes Spiritualists, anti-Trinitarians, and some figures close to them but difficult to categorize. This order is intended to be only a loose succession, arranged according to a mixture of chronological, geographical, and theological considerations. It would not be correctly understood if it were taken to be a new proposal for typological ordering of the radical camp. Associations are more important here than definitions.

The biographical sketches have various contours each from each. Aside from differences of style and arrangement, in some the accent is placed more on the history of ideas and of theology, in others more on social history. No one would expect methodological uniformity in a collection of essays by specialists in the "radical Reformation" coming from various countries. Nevertheless, I hope that these sketches will communicate a vivid picture of the intellectual, spiritual, political, and social problems which gradually transformed enthusiastic associates or sympathizers of Luther and Zwingli into embittered critics of church and society, into untiring protagonists of a "radical Reformation."

Sketches are only suggestive and leave a lot of gaps. For those who want to learn more about the radicals an appendix with suggested readings is included. As a rule the primary sources are given first and then a selection from the most important interpretive literature. These selections may sometimes appear arbitrary, because the academic literature has grown so fast that it is difficult even for the specialists to keep up with it. The book is also intended for them, certainly less to provide them with information than to stimulate them to further work on the strokes that are still missing from these sketches.

For further reading:

G. H. Williams, *Spiritual and Anabaptist Writers. Documents Illustrative of the Radical Reformation*, London, 1957.

H. Fast, *Der linke Flügel der Reformation*, Bremen, 1962.

E. Troeltsch, *The Social Teaching of the Christian Churches*, New York, 1960.

G. H. Williams, *Radical Reformation*, Philadelphia, 1962.

C.-P. Clasen, *Anabaptism. A Social History. 1525-1618, Switzerland, Austria, Moravia, South and Central Germany*, Ithaca and London, 1972.

A. Friesen, *Reformation and Utopia. The Marxist Interpretation of the Reformation and its Antecedents*, Wiesbaden, 1974.

J. M. Stayer, W. O. Packull, K. Deppermann, "From Monogenesis to Polygenesis. The Historical Discussion of Anabaptist

Origins," *Mennonite Quarterly Review*, 49, 1975, 83-122.

M. Steinmetz, A. Laube, G. Vogler, *Illustrierte Geschichte der deutschen frühbürgerlichen Revolution*, Berlin, 1975.

J. M. Stayer, *Anabaptists and the Sword*, 2 ed., Lawrence, Kans., 1976.

H.-J. Goertz, *Die Täufer: Geschichte und Deutung*, Munich, 1980.

J. M. Stayer and W. O. Packull (eds.,), *The Anabaptists and Thomas Müntzer*, Dubuque, Iowa, and Toronto, 1980.

The
Reformers

Hans-Jürgen Goertz

1. *Thomas Müntzer*

Revolutionary in a Mystical Spirit

Thomas Müntzer has always been expected to be more than he really was. His enemies made of him a "devil incarnate," his sympathizers a "true and loyal proclaimer of the gospel." Even in his lifetime he became a symbol either for the true or the false way of Reformation. In the process the historical Thomas Müntzer got lost. He made his own essential contribution to the disguising of his person, when he insinuated to his hearers and readers that he should be identified with biblical figures. He volunteered himself to the Electoral Saxon court as the adviser who could interpret the signs of the transformation of the world, just as Daniel had done with Nebuchadnezzar's dream. He wanted to terrify and root out godless rulers, priests, and monks in the spirit of Elijah, who once slew nearly four hundred priests of Baal. John the Baptist was for him the "figure" of all preachers, and he was the "new John" for whom the common people must learn to wait.

Thomas Müntzer knew that people became polarized in response to his person. His name, he said, "was a sweet aroma of life to the needy, and to the lustful an omen of rapid destruction." And so it remained. The malicious judgment of the Reformers, to which Müntzer had once replied with equally aggressive polemic, was handed down for centuries. Only in circles touched by the French Revolution was Müntzer glorified as the courageous leader of the German people's war of liberation. Ultimately he attracted great interest among socialists. Karl Kautsky struggled to interpret him as did many successors, most profoundly Ernst Bloch. Once again Thomas Müntzer became a symbolic figure, this time in the controversies over the "social

TOMAS MVNCER PREDIGER ZV ALSTET IN DVRINGEN.

Thomas Müntzer

question." For some he was still a "murder prophet," for others the "Liebknecht of the sixteenth century." He first appeared carved in stone and poured in bronze in the German Democratic Republic. "The fascination of his person and work permitted no evasion in the response. It had to be either magnetic attraction or shuddering aversion." So Theodor W. Adorno wrote about Walter Benjamin, but the same could have been said about Müntzer. The challenge today is to bring together the attraction and aversion in order to get closer to the historical reality of the man who called himself "the destroyer of unbelievers."

Thomas Müntzer mounted the historical stage at a time when the "Wittenberg nightingale" could already be heard throughout the whole empire. He must have taken the side of the Reformation. At any rate a Catholic polemic of 1519 identified him, together with a friend, as a "Lutheran" in calling him to account for anticlerical denunciations. Here the term "Lutheran" first appeared, not without historical irony. For soon this "first Lutheran" became the first enemy of Luther's who was able seriously to imperil the Reformation. The childhood and youth of Müntzer lie in the dark with little hope that further research will illumine them. The few facts that are known are insufficient to sketch his development, at least without the aid of apocryphal constructions from the time of his fame and notoriety in the Peasants' War. If we choose not entirely to put aside this anthology of biographical phantasy, we are assured that his character developed quite early—whether as an unprincipled conspirator, a profound religious seeker, or a convinced agitator for the cause of the suppressed masses. Not even the year of his birth is certain. He was born around 1490 in Stolberg on the Harz and spent his childhood in Quedlinburg. Certain only is that he began the basic university curriculum at Leipzig in 1506 and appeared six years later at the university of Frankfort on the Oder. Neither university was dominated by the nominalism which, in its conceptualist form, transmitted important impulses to the Lutheran Reformation. Müntzer was educated in the atmosphere of medieval realism. There is a good deal to be said for the importance of the long smoldering nominalist-realist controversy as a background for the confrontation between Luther and Müntzer, if we want to do justice to its theological depth. Müntzer sought new knowledge voraciously; he found the opportunity to deepen his studies above all when he was confessor to the nuns of Frose near Aschersleben and to the Cistercian nuns near Weissenfels. He read some historians of the ancient church, the records of the Council of Constance (which had tried Jan Hus), the German mystics, and the tracts and pamphlets of humanism and the early Reformation. Before he made his own mark on history he was already a man learned in religion and committed to an activist course of church reform.

Müntzer's eye-catching public career began in 1520 in the economically important city of Zwickau. Luther recommended him to fill a vacancy in St. Mary's church, surely with the intention of influencing the local church situation in the direction of the Reformation. Soon Müntzer moved to a permanent position at St. Catherine's church, which supposedly brought him closer to artisans and to the lower class. In reality he found support in all groups of the population including the city council. In inner-city politics Müntzer sided with those disenfranchised groups which pressed for a role in government and with the council members who wanted to free Zwickau from any outside ecclesiastical power in its affairs. The Reformation succeeded in many a city with precisely these political allegiances. The involvement of Müntzer, although a bit too violent for Luther's taste, was nothing extraordinary for those years, certainly not a decision to carry through his own "people's Reformation." He had simply joined in, and perhaps strengthened, the usual anticlericalism which constantly appeared in combination with economic discontent and social protest. After a quarrel with the Franciscans in the city he turned to a theological controversy with Johannes Sylvius Egranus, the humanistic colleague whom he had temporarily replaced a few months previously. He took offense at the humanist's cool intellectualism which dampened zeal for the Reformation, stressing instead a faith inspired by the Spirit and personally appropriated. This quarrel, too, was carried on with much anticlerical abusiveness and an accompaniment of popular rowdiness. It polarized the city. For Müntzer the antitype of the cultivated Egranus must have been an uneducated layman, the clothworker Nicolaus Storch, a spiritually gifted apocalyptic visionary. In Zwickau Müntzer experienced the effect of mystical piety and theology in anticlerical struggle. Hatred of the priests and enmity to Rome, followed by iconoclastic riots and sermon interruptions, brought many persons into the Wittenberg camp, even though they had the most diverse theological allegiances. Anticlericalism provided the climate in which Müntzer began to think about and work for the Reformation; the mystical tradition provided him with theological arguments. Indeed anticlericalism and mysticism have gone together often enough in the history of religion. In Müntzer the rejection of the institutional church latent in late medieval mysticism became manifest.

If Müntzer's future as an original theologian and a Reformation activist was foreshadowed at Zwickau, it came into focus much more clearly in a manifesto which he composed in Prague. He undertook to work for the Reformation there after he had to leave Zwickau in April 1521. The Prague Manifesto is a bubbling mixture of anticlerical sallies and mystical ideas, not a casual pamphlet but a document from which at least the outlines of Müntzer's theology can be reconstructed. Everything that he later wrote and did is basically present here, needing only to be worked out, deepened, sharpened by concrete situations, just as it helped to create those situations. Müntzer, who always went to the core of things, signed the manifesto: "Thomas Müntzer doesn't want to pray to a dumb but to a speaking God." Thus he underscored the idea which justified his anticlericalism and lay at the foundation of his program of Reformation. He rejected the legitimation of the priests of the official church, because they could not hear the voice of God. Proper shepherds watered their flocks with the living voice.

Müntzer supplied anticlericalism with a theological justification from a mystically shaped teaching of Word and Spirit. Anticlericalism is no mere favorable precondition of the Reformation; it is a Reformation program. Müntzer wants to show that claims to authority of the priests are shattered by the experienced authority of the speaking God. The only people who can experience this authority are those who allow themselves to be purified of creaturely attachments and desires through an agitating struggle for existence. This struggle is marked by inner torment and suffering and is the precondition for the birth of the Word of God in the "abyss of the soul." Müntzer's struggle contains revolutionary traits. It is an abbreviated description of the process of salvation which Müntzer brings to discussion again and again, employing the most varied metaphors from the mystical tradition. This process leads through suffering submission to God's work to the "arrival of faith" and places the person within a new order, whose secrets Müntzer has yet to hear "whispered" by any priest. In this conception of order the interiorized process of salvation interacts with the structure of the world. When the person is alienated from his divine origin he perverts the divinely ordained order of the world into power relations such as dependence and suppression. But if the original order within which God is Lord should be restored, then sooner or later, as Müntzer promised the Bohemians, the "kingdom of this world" will be given over to the elect.

Such a perspective had far-reaching consequences. For one thing the human race was divided into the elect and the godless. Those of the one group have experienced faith, the others only imagine it or "steal" it out of the Holy Scriptures. Moreover, the separation of wheat and tares must precede the assumption of government by the elect. Thus a world of apocalyptic images colors the original mystical conception, beginning in the Prague Manifesto but much stronger and more definitely in later writings and letters. It is worth noting that the godless who must be annihilated are not the great "mass of perdition" but at first only the clergy who, obsessed by their false authority, put themselves between God and mankind. Here we encounter the Lutheran slogan of "the priesthood of all believers," with a different grounding and different consequences, to be sure. The grounding is derived from the mystical process of salvation and the consequence is a great confrontation between the godless and the elect, which assumes apocalyptic dimensions. Müntzer does not battle on behalf of a "holy remnant" which will be preserved in the final judgment, rather he battles for the people, a potentially elect people. From such a standpoint he even occasionally scolds the people, for permitting themselves to be "seduced" by the priests, so that they render greater fear to creatures than to the Spirit of God.

Müntzer was unable to remain long in Prague. After a number of failed attempts to locate himself in the Saxon-Thuringian area he finally obtained a pastorate shortly before Easter 1523 in the Saxon farming town of Allstedt. In a short period he was able to build up a broadly based local Reformation which quickly showed distinct deviations from the Wittenberg pattern. He was able to secure the allegiance of the majority of the inhabitants, pastoral colleagues, and for a time, even the local representative of electoral authority, the castellan, Hans Zeiss. With his translation into German of the liturgical offices, psalms, and hymns, people crowded to the Allstedt services from the surrounding territories. His sermons and liturgies became an event. Recently, Siegfried Bräuer has referred to Müntzer as "the father of the German Protestant worship service and congregational song." In this reform of worship Müntzer pursued the goal of educating the people, so as to lead them to the experience of faith and make them the

bearers of the new order. The new worship service clearly
was designed to have not merely an inner, ecclesiastical
function but likewise a world-shaping one. That quickly
stimulated the enmity of the Catholic rulers and officials
in the neighborhood. Moreover, it confirmed Luther in his
distrust of Müntzer.

At the beginning of the Allstedt period Müntzer had not
crossed over into open opposition to Luther. His first two
tracts, "On the Imaginary Faith" and the "Protestation,"
were on the surface only a clarification of his understanding of faith, baptism, and Reformation. Perhaps they were
also designed to deprive the authorities of any basis for dis-
turbing his work of Reformation. In their content,
however, both works indicated a clear rejection of Luther's
theology. Now Müntzer turned that image of the clerical
enemy, which he had shaped in Zwickau and Prague,
against the Wittenbergers. They, too, proclaimed an
"imaginary" faith, which trusted only in the letters of the
Holy Scriptures. As learned "scribes," who claimed a monopoly of interpretation for themselves, they, too, placed
themselves between God and mankind with their glorification of the slogan *sola scriptura.* The Scriptures are there
to initiate the painful process of salvation, not to dissipate
it through a false and easy consolation. It was Müntzer's
belief that the Scriptures convey a "witness" of faith but
not faith itself. In this limited function they are indispensable to him. Baptism, too, is in the service of the
process of salvation. Since shortly after the time of the
primitive church it began to be administered to the imma-
ture, it became "subhuman monkey business as far as
entry to Christendom was concerned," and it was at fault
in the decline of the church. Müntzer synchronized the
outer act of baptism with the beginning of the salvation
process and tried to awaken a new understanding of the
baptismal ceremony in the context of his liturgical reform
in Allstedt. He had no intention to initiate a new baptism

of persons already baptized in infancy, in this respect differing from the later Anabaptists.

This criticism of faith and church is but the logical extension of Müntzer's theological position as already described. Even if the mystical impulse were transmitted to him from Luther's early writings, which is not likely, he would have inherited the mystical tradition in the context of medieval realism, while Luther appropriated it "nominalistically" and later dropped it. Müntzer found in mysticism a device by which to transform the inner spiritual sphere of persons into an external reality, while Luther saw it in the last analysis as a confirmation of his stress on faith as a link between God and mankind. Müntzer's broad alignment with Wittenberg's external program of Reformation disguised the theological difference which was there from the beginning and caused many to call him a renegade pupil of Luther. In fact Müntzer had a different origin and a different destiny than the Reformer of Wittenberg.

As the disorders around Allstedt increased, particularly after Müntzer's supporters destroyed the chapel dedicated to the Virgin at Mallerbach, the court at Weimar found itself obliged to investigate the situation. Müntzer had taken the pastorate without the approval of the court, or so at least Count Ernst of Mansfeld was told in response to his complaint. He would now have to present a "trial sermon" at the castle in the presence of Duke John and his son John Frederick. The first had not yet made up his mind about the course of the Reformation, while the second stood under the influence of the Wittenbergers. Müntzer assessed this situation realistically and quite consciously sketched an alternative program to the Lutheran Reformation. He interpreted the dream of Nebuchadnezzar about the collapse of the world empires in Daniel 2. His prophecy was that while the last empire, comprised of a mixture of ecclesiastical and worldly power, went to its doom a

transformation would be brought about by the Spirit of
God, culminating in the erection of the kingdom of Christ
on earth. He sought to win the princes for this "uncon-
querable" Reformation. They must help it to victory
against the resistance of the godless; otherwise, he
threatened, God would take the government from them
and give it over to the common p ople. This forthright and
bold sermon known as "The Ser on to the Princes" numbers among the most impressive documents of the
Reformation era.

The Saxon court, however, refused the overtures of the
"new Daniel", and the political situation in Allstedt soon
developed in such a way that Müntzer was forced to leave
this town, too, in August 1524. He fled secretly over the
wall. The period between the sermon and Müntzer's new
exile contained the activities of the "covenant," which
Müntzer founded for the defense of his Reformation, and
various measures by the court, including a hearing at
Weimar and the closing down of his printing press. This
was the time of composition of the early version of the "Explicit Exposure of the False Faith," which Hans Hut later
had printed in Nuremberg. In connection with a discussion
of the first chapter of Luke, Müntzer explained anew his
understanding of faith and moved on to an early attack on
the princes. He derived a right of resistance to authority
from the spirit of mysticism. If a ruler gives cause for fear
of the creature instead of making place for fear of God, he
has lost all claim to legitimate authority and will lose his
power to the people. In fact, a government that resists the
Word of God *ipso facto* legitimates the resistance of the
people. Basically, Müntzer transferred his anticlerical
stereotype of the enemy to make it apply to worldly rulers
as well as priests. This turning away from the princes occurred under the impression of events: it appeared that his
persecuted followers who had fled to Allstedt would be
handed over to their Catholic rulers. Müntzer would not

have it said of him that he condoned the delivery of the elect to persecution, so he followed the logic of his anticlerical-mystical path. He must turn away from anyone who obstructed the gospel and side with anyone who was willing to open himself to the gospel and work for the kingdom of Christ. However, this must not be construed as a falling away from legality into a rebellious illegality. Müntzer was on a revolutionary course from the beginning on.

In the meantime Luther published his sharp "Letter to the Saxon Princes about the Rebellious Spirit," in which he anticipated that the sermons preached at Allstedt would lead to violence and urged rigorous intervention by the princes as soon as the violence became manifest. Müntzer reacted to this with his "Much Provoked Defense," published in Nuremberg but largely confiscated before being issued. It directed a merciless polemic against the "Spiritless, Soft-living Flesh at Wittenberg" and placed his critique of the Lutheran teaching on justification within the framework of the political quarrels. It is striking in its coarseness, but also in its foreshadowing of ideology-critique. Müntzer had recognized how easily theology could be abused as a prop for the existing order and foresaw Luther's path into a Reformation which relied upon princely sponsorship. Defiantly, he closed with the famous sentence, which today is often attended to only in its first part: "The people will become free, and God alone will be their master."

After Allstedt an inconstant life opened before Müntzer once again. He cooperated with Heinrich Pfeiffer in trying to initiate a radical Reformation in the Thuringian imperial city of Mühlhausen, but both were soon obliged to leave the city. From there Müntzer headed toward Nuremberg to attend to the publication of the "Defense." He then emerged in the Black Forest region at the beginning of the peasant revolts. Perhaps there are traces of his

presence in the revolutionary camp in the so-called "Draft
Constitution," which was discovered among the papers of
Balthasar Hubmaier. As the disorders spilled over into the
north he was readmitted to Mühlhausen and participated,
in cooperation with a new council, in the organization and
carrying through of peasant marches through Thuringia
and the Eichsfeld. The motto was violence against things,
rather than against people. Müntzer committed himself
totally to the uprising and spurred it on: "Attack, attack,
while the fire is hot! Don't let your sword grow cold or dull.
Strike, cling, clang, on Nimrod's anvil and cast his tower to
the ground." He did not forget to bring out the theological
justification for this as well: "It is not possible so long as
they live for you to be free of the fear of men. It is impossible so long as they rule you to speak to you of God. Attack,
attack, while it is still day! God goes before you, follow,
follow!" Müntzer interpreted the imminent confrontation
with worldly might as the last judgment and joined the
peasant army awaiting the advancing princely army near
Frankenhausen. The rebels were defeated and slaughtered
in a brutal pursuit. Luther's call for the stern punishment
of the peasants was here brought to a shameful realization.
About six thousand peasants were massacred, while there
were only six fatal casualties in the whole princely army.
Müntzer was able to escape the field of battle, but he was
discovered in an attic in the town, interrogated under torture, and executed on May 27, 1525.

Müntzer's path to the rebellious camp in the Peasants'
War and his particular activities while there cannot be
totally clarified by historical investigation. But, in view of
the anticlericalism which conditioned his earlier career and
his obvious receptivity to the revolutionary situation, the
course he took appears consistent and logical. He had the
same enemies as the peasants, priests and rulers, and like
the peasants he worked for a change in the authority structure. The peasants were giving political expression to their

economic and social distress; Müntzer was giving free rein to his mystically grounded anticlericalism. The peasants were a good deal more moderate in their demands; Müntzer was inclined to the most extreme radicalism, a radicalism, however, that originated not in political insight but in a theological outlook. The interior and personal revolutionary transformation meant at the same time a revolutionary overturning of the outer and institutional order, which Müntzer conceived of as a personal relation to authority. It is easy to see that his aims were more fundamental, and, in view of the apocalyptic dimension which he gave to them, more far reaching and emotionally charged than the most radical aims of the peasants. Here the circle of his career was closed. For Müntzer rose into the public eye out of the anticlerical chaos of the Reformation, which brought together the most dissimilar theological spirits, and he perished in the revolutionary chaos of the Peasants' War, in which the most diverse political and theological groups joined in a common front against the ruling powers. He wanted to free the people and put them under the lordship of God, in the sense that he aimed at a radically new orientation of the human person which would abolish the relations of subjection and authority which had developed in a society based on feudal estates. He sought a Reformation in which ecclesiastical and social reform could not be separated one from the other. In that sense he followed the traditional late medieval pattern of reform. Only he gave this traditional approach a distinctive grounding which synchronized the inner and outer worlds. In this way the Reformation became a revolution. Müntzer exemplifies the rare case in which turning inward is not an obstacle to changing the outer world but rather fuels and magnifies the impulse to transcend existing conditions.

With his theological rationale for anticlericalism Müntzer reaches back into the Middle Ages, but, in his theological subjectivism which liberates the individual from clerical and political authority, he is a precursor of modernity. Indeed, he basically belonged neither to the old nor to the new age. He sought completely to liquidate and to reshape the authority structures of his time, which had gotten themselves into a deep crisis. He staked everything on a democratic theocracy or a theocratic democracy. A basic process in the social history of the waning Middle Ages can be labeled the dissolution of clericalism through lay culture. Müntzer made himself a partisan of the laity. But he did this with such theological radicalism and personal decisiveness (also extremely one-sidedly, if one accepts Luther's teaching on the two kingdoms as a standard of measurement) that, fixated by his own stereotype of the enemy, he turned the layman into a priest. He wanted "us fleshly, earthy men to become gods," and had "put the heart into chains"—if we may transfer Marx's famous reproach against Luther to Müntzer, whom it fits better.

To compare Luther and Müntzer, Luther certainly had the more radical conception of the relationship of God and mankind with respect to salvation, in that he proclaimed the total sinfulness of mankind in the sight of God and their unconditional acceptance by God. Müntzer, however, included humanly created social structures in his understanding of sin and the gospel and was therefore the more radical thinker in the context of persons, society, and God. Luther's theological radicalism was compatible with handing over the social sphere to secularization, which was on its way anyhow and was in the interest of the powerful. Müntzer's radicalism tended toward a new clericalizing of the layman and his world; it was an obstacle on the path to secularization toward which the age could have no sympathy. For that matter, when we look at things from the standpoint of those in authority, the age had no sympathy either for the peasant's need for freedom, however much that coincided with the historical trend toward secularization in the way it was perceived by the lower echelons of society. Müntzer was executed because in the last months of his life he put his talent for charismatic leadership at the disposal of his liberation struggle, not because of a theological program understood neither by the peasants nor the princes. His concern was about the "justification of Christendom," i.e., purification in the face of the Judgment, and it could only be realized in a process which banned all religious or social suppression.

The question is still discussed whether Thomas Müntzer was a theologian or a social revolutionary. Jean-Paul Sartre once said of Karl Marx: "It would take a subtle mind indeed to say whether he made his choices first as revolutionary and subsequently as philosopher, or first as philosopher and subsequently as revolutionary. He is philosopher and revolutionary, a single whole." The analogy applies to Müntzer. He is theologian and revolutionary, a single whole.

For further reading:*

G. Franz, ed., *Thomas Müntzer und Briefe. Kritische Gesamtausgabe*, Gütersloh, 1968.

C. Hinrichs, *Luther und Müntzer. Ihre Auseinandersetzung über Obrigkeit und Widerstandsrecht*. 2. ed., Berlin, 1962.

M. Steinmetz, *Das Müntzerbild von Martin Luther bis Friedrich Engels*, Berlin, 1971.

M. Bensing, *Thomas Müntzer und der Thüringer Aufstand 1525*, Berlin, 1966.

H.-J. Goertz, *Innere und äussere Ordnung in der Theologie Thomas Müntzers*, Leiden, 1967.

E. W. Gritsch, *Reformer Without a Church. The Life and Thought of Thomas Muentzer*, Philadelphia, 1967.

W. Elliger, *Thomas Müntzer. Leben und Werk*. 3. ed., Göttingen, 1976.

R. Schwarz, *Die apokalyptische Theologie Thomas Müntzers und der Taboriten*, Tübingen, 1977.

A. Friesen und H.-J. Goertz, eds., *Thomas Müntzer. Wege der*

---

*The biographical resources following each chapter in this book list first the source publications and then the secondary literature.

Forschung, Darmstadt, 1978 (with a comprehensive survey of the history of Müntzer research).

J. M. Stayer and W. O. Packull, eds., *The Anabaptists and Thomas Müntzer,* Dubuque, Iowa, and Toronto, 1980.

H. J. Hillerbrand, *A Fellowship of Discontent,* New York, 1967, 1-30.

Ronald J. Sider

2. Andreas Bodenstein von Karlstadt

Between Liberal and Radical

Andreas Bodenstein von Karlstadt (c. 1480-1541) was first a friend and ally—and then a bitter foe—of the more famous reformer of Wittenberg. As a prominent professor of theology at Wittenberg, Karlstadt promoted Luther to the doctorate in 1512. Because of his discovery of St. Augustine in early 1517, Karlstadt was ready to do battle as an ardent polemicist for the new Wittenberg Theology when Luther's Ninety-Five Theses ignited controversy throughout Europe. It was Karlstadt whom John Eck first challenged to the important debate at Leipzig in 1519. From 1518 through 1521, Karlstadt rushed into print a flood of books developing and defending the new Wittenberg Theology. When the bull of excommunication was published in October 1520, Karlstadt's name appeared along with Luther's as a teacher of damnable heresy. Together they defied the pope.

When Frederick the Wise "kidnapped" and hid Luther in the safe seclusion of the Wartburg castle after the dramatic encounter with Emperor Charles V at Worms, Karlstadt and the young humanist Melanchthon were the most influential leaders left at Wittenberg. As they moved from theological debate to practical implementation in the fall of 1521 and early 1522, however, occasional violence resulted and Karlstadt was—unjustly to a very large degree—blamed for the disorder. When Luther abruptly returned to assume leadership at Wittenberg in March 1522, he reversed most of the reforms Karlstadt had

45

initiated. Karlstadt was disgraced and furious. In 1523, he moved to the important Saxon town of Orlamünde, where he was able to enunciate a theology more oriented toward sanctification and ethics and introduce his more radical program of reform. In 1524, Karlstadt published the first Protestant attack on Luther's doctrine of the Real Presence, thus initiating the important sacramentarian controversy of the 1520s and contributing to the division of Protestantism. Expelled from Saxony, Karlstadt spent his later years teaching at the University of Basel.

Karlstadt reached the height of his influence as a Magisterial Reformer during the Wittenberg Movement (1521-1522). On Christmas Day, 1521, he celebrated the first public evangelical Eucharist of the Reformation. For some time Luther and Karlstadt had polemicized vigorously against the medieval view of the mass. During the fall of 1521, small groups had begun to meet privately to receive both kinds. Both the public services remained the same until Karlstadt defied the elector's prohibition against innovation on Christmas Day.

Advance notice of the historic service and drunken rioting the previous night guaranteed a huge crowd at All Saints on Christmas Day. Dressed in a simple, secular gown, Karlstadt read a simplified Latin mass, omitting all references to sacrifice. For the first time in the Reformation, the words of institution were spoken in German in a public service. Karlstadt declined to elevate the host. The tension and high drama reached its peak when, instead of placing the bread in each communicant's mouth, Karlstadt allowed ordinary laypersons to take the bread and cup in their own trembling hands. This break with centuries-old custom so terrified one frightened layman that he dropped his wafer and was too terror-stricken to pick it up.

Unfortunately, historians have not always distinguished carefully enough between the acts of Karlstadt and those of the Christmas Eve revelers and rioters who wished the conservative priest at All Saints pestilence and hellfire. One act in defiance of an electoral prohibition did not make Karlstadt a raving radical. He was still opposed to riot. The common charge that he forced his way into Luther's pulpit in the parish church without authorization is very probably false. (A contemporary document demonstrates that the one evangelical mass that Karlstadt is known to have conducted at this time at Luther's parish church was done with the consent and assistance of the parish minister.) In January, Karlstadt was entirely engrossed in effecting peaceful reform. He played a leading role as the city councils introduced a new eucharistic mass modeled after his evangelical mass of Christmas, and reorganized the common chest to aid the poor.

Almost immediately, however, political considerations frightened the elector into squelching most of the innovations Karlstadt had helped to introduce. After the imperial government meeting at Nuremberg demanded that he suppress the recent changes at Wittenberg, Frederick ordered a restoration of most of the old customs. Karlstadt was forbidden to preach. And Luther returned home to resume leadership of the Reformation and denounce the recent changes. Painful years of alienation and conflict between the two original leaders of the Reformation followed.

Most scholars have explained the bitter quarrel between Luther and Karlstadt in terms of major theological differences. But careful analysis of Karlstadt's theology in 1521 reveals few significant theological disagreements. Like Luther, Karlstadt strongly affirmed *sola scriptura*, the necessity of literal exegesis and the mediation of grace via the external word. Karlstadt's primary understanding of *justitia* in 1520 and 1521 was that of imputed righteousness which is reckoned to the believer who trusts in Christ's promise. Although Karlstadt employed the words "justification" and "gospel" less than Luther, he certainly believed deeply in forensic justification. By 1521, Karlstadt had rejected his earlier Augustinian notion of eternal life as the reward of divinely bestowed good deeds, and adopted Luther's view that since even the best deeds are tainted with sin, faith alone must be the sole ground of eternal salvation. Karlstadt also adopted Luther's doctrine of the priesthood of all believers. And his eucharistic writings were largely a repetition of Luther's ideas.

To be sure, there were differences. Karlstadt rejected oral confession. He condemned as sinful the communicant who followed medieval tradition and took only the bread. Most important, he believed that the Old Testament was normative for Christians in a way that Luther feared would undermine Christian freedom. But the disagreements were relatively few and they dare not obscure the fact that Luther and Karlstadt were in fundamental theological agreement up to the time Luther returned to Wittenberg in March 1522 to squelch Karlstadt's reforms.

Why then the violent confrontation?

To a far greater extent than has been realized Luther and Karlstadt fell out because of disagreement over strategy, tactics, and timing. James S. Preus has correctly argued that "the fundamental issues in 1521-22 were issues of religious *policy,* and that important aspects of the doctrinal profiles by which Lutheran and 'radical' are identified are as much a *function* of the religio-political struggle and the result of reflection upon the outcome of that crisis, as they are a *cause* of the breakup of the movement. To be sure, the theologies of Karlstadt and Luther were by no means identical in 1521-22, but neither were theological differences the decisive reason for their separation" (p. 2). One cannot satisfactorily explain the break between Luther and Karlstadt primarily in terms of theological differences. One dare not be misled by the fact that both Karlstadt and Luther sometimes expressed their disagreement over strategy and timing in theological categories and buttressed their stances with extensive biblical exegesis. In 1522, they disagreed far more over strategy than over theology and the two dare not be confused.

In eight powerful sermons in March 1522, Luther persuaded a majority of the Wittenbergers that delay and caution were imperative. Publicly denouncing the previous changes, he restored still more of the traditional

Andreas Bodenstein von Karlstadt

practices—not because he preferred the old customs but because he disagreed with the timing and strategy of Karlstadt's innovations. Karlstadt was livid! He wrote a fiery tract denouncing the tyrant's squelching of the innovations. Although ostensibly directed against a Catholic by the name of Ochsenfahrt, everyone realized that the real target of Karlstadt's fury was Luther. The university establishment seized the half-printed work and forbade its publication.

At this point, Karlstadt might have apologized for his excessive zeal and worked behind the scenes as one of Luther's important lieutenants to foster as much change as possible. But he chose another route. After a period of intense introspection, during which he immersed himself in German mysticism, he rejected the educational elite at Wittenberg and turned toward the common people.

In February 1523, Karlstadt announced that henceforth he would have no part in the granting of academic degrees. He appealed to the injunction against calling anyone master in Matthew 23. In a book published a few weeks later, he confessed that formerly he had studied in order to write well and win disputes. Now, however, he saw that it was very wrong to study Scripture for the selfish, competitive purpose of knowing it better than another. More directly, he argued that people seek nothing but the praise of men in the universities. They become masters or doctors and give presents for the sake of worldly honor and arrogantly refuse to sit with those who possess fewer degrees.

Karlstadt preferred to adopt the role of a peasant. Perhaps he realized that one must have external signs of one's rejection of established values and mores. Sometime in 1523 he put aside his academic dress, adopted the felt hat and gray garb of the peasants, and urged his neighbors to call him "Brother Andrew." Disillusioned with the intellectual elite, Karlstadt moved to identify with the lower classes. He disaffiliated himself still further from the elite and strengthened his identification with the peasantry by taking up part-time farming. He was aware that the impoverished lower classes had made possible the pleasant standard of living that he had enjoyed as a member of the privileged professional class. He confessed that he had lived from the labor of impecunious peasants without giving anything in return. Farming was an "honest mortification of the flesh."

In 1523 the opportunity arose to escape his financial dependence on ecclesiastical structures vigorously condemned by the Reformers. He had condemned the corrupt status quo without disentangling himself from its economic benefits. He still earned thirty-four gulden annually from endowed private masses and vigils. And he continued to hold the Orlamünde parish as a sinecure. At the invitation of the people of Orlamünde, Karlstadt moved there to be pastor in the summer of 1523.

Free at last from Luther's supervision, Karlstadt promptly proceeded to introduce his reforms without waiting for official approval or delaying, lest he give offense to the weak. Images were removed from the church. He refused to baptize infants, and interpreted the Eucharist as a memorial of Christ's death rather than a means of grace. He preached to his new parishioners from the book of Acts daily and from the Gospel of John every Friday. In order that laypersons could understand and sing the Psalms, he translated them into German. Undoubtedly, he implemented the liturgical changes which he had introduced and the elector and Luther had suppressed at Wittenberg two years earlier. For a few months in 1523 and early 1524, it seemed as if it might be possible to implement rapid change in one small area and develop a different pattern of Reformation.

Unfortunately for the Reformation in Orlamünde, Luther and the Saxon court mistakenly identified Karlstadt with the revolutionary Thomas Müntzer, who was also busy in the Saale Valley training his League of the Elect to destroy the status quo with violence. That Karlstadt was not a violent revolutionary is indisputable. Both he and his congregation wrote letters rejecting Müntzer's invitation to join the revolution. But when the Saxon princes sent Luther on a tour of the Saale Valley in late August, Luther persistently refused, even though he had seen the Orlamünde congregation's letter rejecting violence, to concede any difference between Karlstadt's spirit which destroys images and removes baptism and Müntzer's spirit which leads to rebellion and murder.

Luther recommended that the princes remove Karlstadt from Orlamünde. The princes decided to go further. Ignoring his pleas for a public disputation, they banished Karlstadt from Electoral Saxony. Driven out, as he complained, without trial or sentence, he vented his rage by polemicizing violently against Luther's eucharistic doctrine and taunting him with defending the gospel with rifles.

The numerous books which Karlstadt wrote after the fiasco of the Wittenberg Movement and before his expulsion from Saxony reveal a creative theologian striving to develop a theology in which discipleship, ethics, regeneration, and sanctification are more central than in Luther. It is hardly surprising that Karlstadt's writings (especially his book on baptism) significantly influenced early Anabaptistm.

Luther's famous charges, developed with such devastating power in *Against the Heavenly Prophets*, that Karlstadt had relapsed into medieval works-righteousness, ignored the objective work of Christ and become a Spiritualist and legalist are either inaccurate or exaggerated. Certainly Karlstadt developed a theology of regeneration which stressed the importance of *Gelassenheit* but insisted that the regenerate life was possible by *sola gratia*. Similarly, it is totally inaccurate to assert that Karlstadt reduced the role of Christ to that of example. He always insisted on the necessity of the external word in the mediation of grace and never claimed any direct special revelation, although a couple statements on the Spirit's role in the task of exegesis justify our thinking that he had very modest "Spiritualist" inclinations. Not even Karlstadt's legalism was as wooden as is often supposed. Gordon Rupp, however, is certainly correct in speaking of Karlstadt's "puritanism" and Ulrich Bubenheimer's recent studies have shown how Karlstadt's legal studies (he had a doctorate in canon and civil law as well as in theology) contributed to his "legalistic" conception of Scripture as "divine law."

In recent years, Reformation scholars have paid increasing attention to the secondary figures who aided and abetted—and sometimes challenged and infuriated—Luther, Calvin, and Zwingli. Andreas Bodenstein von Karlstadt was one of the most influential of these secondary Reformers. One cannot understand the early years of the German Reformation without an awareness of the significant role Karlstadt played.

For further reading:

E. Hertsch, *Karlstadts Schriften aus den Jahren 1523-1525*, 2 Vols., Halle (Saale) 1956-1957.

R. J. Sider, *Karlstadt's Battle with Luther: Documents in a Radical-Liberal Debate*, Philadelphia, 1977.

C. Lindberg, "Karlstadt's Dialogue on the Lord's Supper," *Mennonite Quarterly Review* LIII (1979), 35-77.

H. Barge, *Andreas Bodenstein von Karlstadt*, 2 Vols., Leipzig, 1905.

David C. Steinmetz, *Reformers in the Wings*, Philadelphia, 1971, 175-185.

F. Kriechbaum, *Gründzuge der Theologie Karlstadts*, Hamburg-Bergstedt, 1967.

G. Rupp, *Patterns for Reformation*, London, 1969, 49-153.

J. S. Preus, *Karlstadt's "Ordinaciones" and Luther's "Liberty": A Study of the Wittenberg Movement 1521-1522*, Cambridge, 1974.

R. J. Sider, *Andreas Bodenstein von Karlstadt: The Development of His Thought, 1517-1525*, Leiden, 1974.

U. Bubenheimer, *Consonantia theologiae et iurisprudentia: Andreas Bodenstein von Karlstadt als Theologe und Jurist zwischen Scholastik und Reformation*, Tübingen, 1977.

3. Hans Hut

The Suffering Avenger

We still possess the warrant of arrest with which the Council of Nuremberg pursued him: Hans Hut, a very learned, clever fellow, a fair length of a man, a rustic person with cropped brown hair, a pale yellow moustache, dressed in gray woolen pants, a broad gray hat, and at times a black riding coat. Unfortunately we are unable to give an equally detailed picture of Hut's life. He may have been thirty-seven years of age in December 1527 when the aftereffects of smoke inhalation suffered in an attempt to break jail led to his premature death. Only about the last six years of his life do we possess some scattered information. From the accounts of his followers, rather than from his own few surviving writings, do we gain an understanding of the world of ideas in which he lived. It is not clear whether or not he received an education. Indications are that he was a self-taught man. Similarly we can only infer that it was Hut's concern with the whole Christian social order, rather than the question raised by the monk and professor at Wittenberg about the sinner's standing before God, that brought him into the camp of the Reformation.

For this reason he must have joined Andreas Karlstadt and Thomas Müntzer in rejecting the theology of Luther and his Reformation, when from 1523 onwards their writings appeared in quick succession. For Hut, too, mere trust in the scriptural proclamation of the unconditional acceptance of the sinner by God for Christ's sake must have appeared as in impediment to the necessary transformation

of man and Christian society. As a traveling book peddler—hawker therefore—between Nuremberg and Wittenberg, he may have met with Karlstadt in Orlamünde and
with Müntzer in Allstedt on several occasions. Otherwise it
is incomprehensible why after his expulsion from
Mühlhausen Müntzer entrusted his manuscript of the
"Express Exposee" to Hut for publication in Nuremberg. It
was at this time at the very latest that Hut also met with
Hans Denck, rector of the school at St. Sebald. On the basis
of Denck's "confession" of early 1525, stamped as it was
with ideas of Karlstadt and Müntzer, we may assume that
Hut was the leader rather than the inquirer in his discussions with the headmaster of St. Sebald's.

Karlstadt and Müntzer had stigmatized pedobaptism as
a characteristic sign of an irresolute Christianity that was
neither consciously experienced nor accepted. It followed,
therefore, that Hut shortly thereafter refused baptism for
the last of his three children known to us, and accepted
exile from his native village Bibra. It is also possible that
during the spring of 1525 he had visited Müntzer in
Mühlhausen and witnessed the beginnings of the peasant
uprising in Thuringia. Hut's name appears on the
membership list of Müntzer's "Eternal Covenant." At any
rate, Hut participated personally in the battle at
Frankenhausen, but managed to escape alive. In his sermons shortly before the battle Müntzer identified the
Peasants' War as the last great conflict between the godly
and ungodly before the return of Christ. Hut was so convinced of this that even after the defeat we find him
preaching in the same spirit to peasants in his native area.
However, because of the superior strength of the armies of
the princes, the fate of these peasants was soon sealed as
well. Thereafter Hut belonged to the fugitives whom the
lords sought to hunt down with the aid of special agents.
Crowded Nuremberg probably provided the opportunity
for Hut to disappear temporarily.

However, the person and message of Müntzer remained decisive for Hut's destiny even after the defeat. Like Müntzer he became convinced that God had destroyed the peasants because they had not been the pure, unselfish champions of God's honor for which he had taken them. Since the bodies of Müntzer and his student, Heinrich Pfeiffer, had not been buried but put on spikes, it was possible for Hut to identify them with the two witnesses of Revelation 11:3, whose bodies, according to Revelation 11:9, were to lie unburied for three and a half days. By combining other scriptural texts and popular prophecies with his interpretation of the days as years, Hut came to the conclusion that Müntzer had erred in dating the end. It was now to be expected for Pentecost 1528. Then the judgment on the ungodly parsons and lords would begin. Hut found his expectations illustrated in the psalms of vengeance and in the prophetic passages of the Old Testament. The Turks supported by the godly were to serve as God's instrument of punishment. But who would fill the role of the godly?

Hut found the answer to this question when he made the acquaintance of some Anabaptists—probably during the spring of 1526. For on Pentecost of that same year he was baptized by Denck. At that time Hut did not experience a "conversion" to a nonresistant, peaceful Anabaptism. Rather, he found in the Anabaptists the truly godly, who the peasants had failed to be. According to Revelation 7:2 he understood the baptism received from Denck as the sign of the sealed who were to be spared in the approaching judgment; indeed, they would help to administer it. From that time on Hut saw himself as the man of Daniel 12:6 and Ezekiel 9:2-5 whose duty in the short time remaining it was to mark as many as possible of the 144,000 elect with the sign of the cross on the forehead.

A restless, secretive activity ensued. Hut began his mission in remote mills, villages, and little towns among former leaders or participants of the Peasants' War. They longed for the day of vengeance and for the kingdom of Christ, which was expected to bring equality of person and property. Hut provided a rationale for the distress and suffering of the present as well. Suffering, after all, had to be endured for some time yet. According to his "Gospel of all creatures"—proclaimed by all creatures—the entire creation was appointed to serve man (Genesis 1:27ff.). Creation cannot do that in its "natural" state. It can do so only in a processed condition. Through his labor, man causes the creatures to suffer, bringing them at the same time to their appointed end—to serve him. Similarly man can come to his appointed end—service of God—only after God has freed him from the servitude to this world by means of suffering. With reference to the various occupations of peasants and artisans to whom he primarily addressed himself, Hut knew how to make such ideas intelligible, continuing a cruder version of Müntzer's basic assumptions. However, by contrasting the patient suffering of the present with violent future change he separated again what for Müntzer, during the course of his life, had grown into a necessary unity. In other respects Hut did not require his followers to follow any particular norms. He admonished them to keep the commandments of God and to initiate among them the practice of brotherliness which was to be the distinguishing feature of the world after its judgment.

Hut found his first followers in Northern Franconia, in the villages around Coburg and Bamberg and in the valley of the Regnitz around Erlangen. The authorities were soon aware of them. They intervened with the severest penalties even though Hut's followers and sympathizers did not constitute a serious threat to the existing order, simply because of their small numbers. In the expectations of judgment for 1528 the authorities could only see preparations for a new peasant rebellion. Thus the discovery of Hutian Anabaptists became the occasion for a general persecution.

The nature of the movement seemed to warrant proceedings by Protestant authorities as well, who otherwise showed no interest in persecuting anyone for matters of faith.

The persecution in Franconia that began during the spring of 1527 prevented Hut's return to the area after a brief stay in Augsburg. Possibly because Balthasar Hubmaier, the preacher who fled from Waldshut, had been successful in establishing an Anabaptist reformation in Nicolsburg, Hut now moved down the Danube to Moravia. However, the theologically trained Hubmaier wanted no part of Hut's end-time fantasies. He feared that such expectations would arouse the magistracy against the Anabaptists and lead to the demise of his own work. As it turned out, the "Nicolsburg Articles" were to play a significant role in anti-Anabaptist polemics. They were a tendentious selection of the teachings of Hut which Hubmaier identified as false plus statements by Hut's followers, as well as additional anti-Catholic articles. Hut was imprisoned in Nicolsburg following a public discussion of these articles with Hubmaier. Only by flight was Hut able to escape a threatened extradition. During the journey which followed through Lower and Upper Austria, Hut was able to establish small conventicles in Vienna, Steyr, Linz, Freistadt, Salzburg, and Passau. However, the authorities destroyed them quickly with fire and sword. Late in the summer of 1527 the most important disciples of Hut gathered for the so-called "martyrs' synod" at Augsburg. Here, too, disagreements surfaced between the Upper German and the Hutian form of Anabaptism. To be sure, the confrontation was not as pronounced as in Nicolsburg. Here the diverging branches of Anabaptism had been living side by side for some time. At these meetings Hut rejected outright the "Sermon on the Mount ethic" of the Swiss Brethren that had pervaded the "Schleitheim Articles." For his part he promised to reserve the end-time expectations for those who expressedly wished to hear them. It was not very difficult for Hut to make this concession since he had treated these expectations from the beginning as secret doctrines reserved for an initiated few.

A few weeks later Hut was arrested in Augsburg. The trial that followed lasted several months. By torture, and

Hans Hut

through information communicated from outside of Augsburg, Hut's connection to Müntzer and the peasants, as well as his expectations of judgment on the present order, were brought to light. The verdict was a foregone conclusion. It called for Hut's execution and the burning of his body. The sentence was completed in spite of Hut's escape by premature death.

The mystical-apocalyptical Anabaptism founded by Hut disintegrated quickly, for because of the expected imminent end, Hut had done little to provide it with a stabilizing order aimed at permanency. Vigorous persecution by the authorities did its share. However, since Hut had kept the end-time expectations, the heart of his proclamation, secret, many of his followers were able to associate with other groups within Anabaptism. Only the thoroughgoing community of goods which continued to distinguish the Anabaptists of Moravia still reminded of Hut. Others turned their backs on Anabaptism in disappointment after the deadline set by Hut had passed. Only a few carried his apocalyptic expectations further by postponing the deadline for the judgment and the coming of Christ's kingdom once more. Only in some isolated cases, such as in Thuringia, were preparations made for violent action. All this helps to explain why it was left to historical research to make the voice of the man with light brown hair and pale little beard heard again, the questioning voice of one who refused to separate personal salvation from earthly existence and from the salvation of society as a whole. In the face of resistance by force against his conception of Christian society, Hut could conceive of its realization only in terms of the miraculous intervention of force, not in terms of the miracle of love.

For further reading:

W. O. Packull, *Mysticism and the Early South German-Austrian Anabaptist Movement 1525-1531*, Scottdale and Kitchener, 1977.

S. E. Ozment, *Mysticism and Dissent*, New Haven and London, 1973, 98-115.

G. Rupp, *Patterns of Reformation*, London, 1969, 325-353.

L. Müller, *Glaubenszeugnisse oberdeutscher Taufgesinnter*, Leipzig, 1938.

G. Bauer, *Anfänge täuferischer Gemeindebildungen in Franken*, Nürnberg, 1966.

H. D. Schmid, "Das Hutsche Täufertum. Ein Beitrag zur Charakterisierung einer täuferischen Richtung aus der Frühzeit der Täuferbewegung," *Historisches Jahrbuch,* 91, 1971, 327-344.

—————————, *Täufertum und Obrigkeit in Nürnberg,* Nürnberg, 1972.

G. Seebass, "Bauernkrieg und Täufertum in Franken," *Zeitschrift für Kirchengeschichte,* 85, 1974, 284-300.

—————————, "Müntzers Erbe. Werk, Leben und Theologie des Hans Hut." Theologische Habilitationsschrift, Erlangen, 1972 (unpubl.)

Terkel Hansen, "Reformation, Revolution und Täufertum-Eine Einführung," *Mühlhäuser Beiträge zu Geschichte und Kulturgeschichte,* Heft 3, 1980, 3-20.

4. Hans Denck

Fugitive from Dogmatism

On one hand Hans Denck seems to fit into all of the ideal types constructed by historians and theologians, and on the other, he fits into none of them. He has been variously classified as a radical evangelical Reformer, contemplative Anabaptist, individualistic Spiritualist, and mystical humanist; a forerunner of eighteenth-century rationalists or pietists and nineteenth-century theological liberals; a representative of the German *Volksgeist;* a pioneer of unitarianism; and a champion of an undogmatic, ethical, action-oriented Christianity. He obviously remains one of the most fascinating yet elusive personalities of the first generation of Reformation radicals.

Little is known of his background. Born around 1500 in Upper Bavaria, he attended the University of Ingolstadt from 1517-1520. His reaction to the momentous events unleashed by Luther during that period must have been positive. For when he arrived in Basel in 1522 he associated himself with the reform efforts initiated by John Oecolampadius. Denck's philological skills (he knew Latin, Greek, and Hebrew) suggest a good literary education and humanistic commitments. These commitments were reinforced by exposure to humanistic and mystical texts which he proofread while working for printers at Basel.

Denck's career as a dissenter began in Nuremberg, where upon Oecolampadius's recommendation he accepted responsibility for the St. Sebald School in 1523. Soon the city council found it necessary to reprimand the young teacher for forbidding his students to assist in Catholic Church ceremonials. Denck was associating with a group of radicals for whom the program of reform taken by the established authorities was too conservative. Apart from a Swiss humanist or Reformed influence the radicals appear to have found the ideas of Andreas Karlstadt and Thomas Müntzer particularly congenial with their aspirations. Both Karlstadt and Müntzer had broken with Luther, distinguishing themselves by more overtly anti-clerical reform programs.

The Wittenberger's close association of the Word of God with Scripture was singled out for particular criticism. Such a view undermined Luther's earlier pronouncements regarding the priesthood of all believers. It tended to reestablish a privileged position for the literate clergy. Denck himself became implicated in the trial of the "godless painters," students of Albrecht Dürer, who scandalized Nuremberg's elite by propagating these and other irreverent blasphemies. Out of this context came Denck's own confrontation with an emerging Lutheran confessionalism. His ideas were closely scrutinized for their orthodoxy by a pastoral inquisition presided over by Andreas Osiander. When Denck's reply to the systematic questionnaire did not meet the confessional Lutheran standards, he was deprived of his position and exiled. Henceforth he was to be a marked fugitive.

Denck's movements after expulsion from Nuremberg in January 1525 remain problematic. So does his attitude toward the revolting peasants. From a contemporary source we know that he had been invited to Mühlhausen by Müntzer and Heinrich Pfeiffer, and it is possible that he was an eyewitness to events in that city. He surfaced shortly after the collapse of the rebellion in the canton of Schwyz, where he was promptly imprisoned for negative views on pedobaptism. Upon release he contacted Anabaptists in St. Gall. It would be simplistic to infer from this sequence that Denck had been converted to a sectarian pacifist form of evangelical Anabaptism. Even Swiss Anabaptism was still in a phase of ferment. Anabaptists around St. Gall expressed determination to defend themselves and their leader Hans Krüsi with the sword. Whether Denck's later pacifist position had already crystallized is not clear. His personal circumstances, as well as his intellectual disposition, must have favorably inclined him towards solidarity with the Anabaptists. However, what drew the ire of the local Reformers of St. Gall on Denck was not his espousal of Anabaptism but a new spiritual egalitarianism in the form of universalism— the teaching that all men would eventually be saved.

Sometime in September 1525 Denck arrived in Augsburg. Here he hoped quietly to earn his daily bread by tutoring in Latin and Greek. These hopes were shattered by his inability to keep his personal convictions private. He had become a practicing Anabaptist. Among others he met Balthasar Hubmaier, and in the spring of 1526 he baptized Hans Hut. Rumors of his radical activity and unorthodox teachings led to a confrontation with Urbanus Rhegius and the other Lutheran ministers. He withdrew before a proposed public debate could take place. When he arrived in Strassburg late in 1526 he found that his heterodox reputation had preceded him. Relations to other Anabaptists, particularly Sattler, appear to have been strained, and confrontation with the established Reformers proved unavoidable. A debate with Martin Bucer followed the predictable pattern. Denck's defense was considered sly and sinister. He was expelled from Strassburg. Even in a town reputed to be a haven of refuge for the persecuted he was now considered a liability.

From Strassburg Denck turned toward Worms. His journey was punctuated by a public disputation regarding baptism with Johann Bader at Landau. At Worms Denck joined with Ludwig Hätzer in translating the Old Testa-

ment prophets, apparently drawing upon the advice of
Jewish scholars. Although the task must have absorbed his
energies, he inevitably made contact with the radical fac-
tion of the city whose spokesman was Jakob Kautz.
Denck's influence is discernible in the "seven theses"
publicly defended by Kautz. These were critical of both Lutheran and Catholic teachings. Understandably, they provoked a response in kind from both sides. The suppression
of the radical movement in Worms followed. Denck moved
back up the Rhine.

In August 1527 he appeared at some of the meetings of
the "Martyrs' Synod" in Augsburg. His own role was
modest. The center of attraction was Hans Hut, whose apocalyptical teachings provoked lively discussion. Two months
later Denck contacted Oecolampadius to ask for permission
to settle in Basel. He was in the process of reexamining his
career and beliefs when he fell victim to the plague.

Denck's last effort was posthumously published as a recantation. But a recantation of what? A whole system of
thought or his involvement with Anabaptism? The document does not read like a blanket self-indictment. As a
confession it serves as an excellent introduction to Denck's
thought world. Implicitly it constitutes an indictment of
the "climate of opinion" created by the Reformation. Denck
confessed that he lacked the disposition for dogmatic controversy. To be at odds with brothers who worshiped the
same God was painful. Hence he asked those whom he had
unintentionally offended to forgive him as he forgave those
who had wronged him. He was willing to reexamine and
moderate his own position on Scripture, the suffering of
Christ, on faith, on free will, on good works, sects, ceremonies, baptism, the Lord's Supper, and oaths. The Scriptures were the most precious treasure entrusted to men,
but he could not equate them with the unfettered, eternal,
living, and powerful Word of God, which alone was capable
of reaching those unable to hear or read. The redemptive

merit of Christ's work was sufficient for all men, but its appropriation should produce evidence of a sanctified life. Faith was inseparable from moral obligations and a disposition of humility and long-suffering. The controversy regarding free will and good works appeared to him one of words rather than substance. He could not separate accountability and responsibility from freedom of choice.

With regard to divisions, ceremonies, and sects, he reaffirmed his mystical and humanistic conviction that inner piety was of greater importance than external conformity. The gospel could not be chained to temporal elements. Separation and sectarianism were not wholesome manifestations, but every individual should be free to seek his soul's salvation without obstruction. Denck said that he separated himself from others not because of a superior moral attitude but out of weakness—fear of persecution, fear of being coerced into beliefs against his conscience. Ceremonies and rites were harmful or helpful to the extent that they properly directed or misdirected the believer's trust from externals to true worship. Infant baptism was not ordained by Christ but of human origin, as such the Christian community had the freedom to use or reject it. Teaching discipleship was more important than baptizing. He himself was willing to stop baptizing altogether rather than give offense. He warned the zealous that no one ought to appropriate to himself the authority to introduce a different mode of baptism unless specifically commissioned by God. The Lord's Supper in turn was given a spiritual interpretation as the believer's union with Christ. As to the swearing of oaths, which had given Anabaptists pangs of conscience, Denck argued that Scripture did not forbid them, but that one ought not to swear, promise, or confirm anything which he could not keep with a good conscience.

When these last statements of Denck are placed in the context of his embattled career, it becomes clear that he "recanted" only his Anabaptist practice. (The changed cir-

cumstances made early Anabaptist social expectations un-
realistic.) The growing divisions within the movement
which accompanied its metamorphosis into a (more purely
religious) sectarian mold with its own peculiar dogmatism
may have contributed to his disillusionment, as did his personal desire for respite. In essence, however, Denck
remained committed to the individualistic spirituality
expressed in his earlier writings. An analysis of these reveal a sensitive independent mind. There was in this
Reformation radical a good measure of Christlike identification with the poor and despised of the world. "Let no one
look to the mighty in this world, be it for their strength, art
or riches. He whose heart is set on the kingdom of heaven,
let him turn to the despised and lowly. . . . " The anticlerical
echoes in his writings carried an implicit social critique.

His consistent gravitation toward radical local causes
lends itself to a similar interpretation. Denck reserved his
harshest words for the servants of institutionalized Christianity—scribes, false preachers, and pompous ecclesiastical representatives who sought their own material
advantage under the cloak of religious practices. Through
their hypocritical and unreflective ways the Christian faith
had been reduced to externals: belief in systemized,
abstract deductions about the nature of God and mankind;
practice had degenerated to mechanical observance of
inherited superstitious rites. The Reformation he
envisaged would correct these abuses and redirect religious
observance to following Christ's example, and understanding the true spiritual meaning of his teachings. This meaning was accessible through the direct revelation of the "inner Word," and Denck encouraged the illiterate to turn
"with full confidence" to this pristine source of spiritual
truth "within them." Such an appeal to a universal revelation had to be at cross purposes with those "importing
God's word in books from across the sea."

Nevertheless, there is in these statements—unless they

are subjected to a modernizing and ahistorical demytholo-
gizing—little that would permit the classification of Denck
as a socio-political radical. He did not consciously perceive
himself as a spokesman for a particular social group. And
no compelling historical reason exists to see his anti-insti-
tutional statements as the mere means of communicating
other "objective" or "real" materialist interests. However,
it would be equally unwarranted to conclude that the differences between Denck and his antagonists were the
result of mere personality clashes, personal frustrations,
or misunderstandings. Ultimately these antagonists
derived from a different theological consciousness of the
relationship between God, creation, and mankind. Denck
approached the problems raised by the Reformation from
humanistic and mystic presuppositions. His mystical
tendency to internalize religious experience provided the
basis for his individualistic egalitarian and ecumenical
view of divine revelation, while complementing his humanistic insistence on Christlike conduct as a measure of true
faith.

Central to Denck's religious perception was the axiom of
divine immanence. God's sustaining presence in all creation and in man provided the basis for the possibility of
human redemption and regeneration. "The light which is
the invisible Word of God shines into the hearts of all
men.... It is in our very hearts not idle, but [active] to do
the will of the Father." This *logos* theology, which confirmed the transhistorical Word as the enabling grace in all
men, provided the undercarriage for an anthropology that
rejected Luther's holistic view of human sinfulness. Man
partook of both a material and a spiritual reality. Even
though his lower nature remained absorbed in physical,
transient things, his inner divine connection made it possible for him to participate in the spiritual realm. The focus
on the pre-incarnate Word carried also Christological implications. The human Jesus became the great example and

teacher. The difference between the believer and Christ, because of the emphasis on the human Jesus, became one of degree. Real contact between mankind and God had never been lost, only ignored. The fullness of God's presence had revealed itself in Christ. Christ's true followers were called upon to live in the light of the divine presence within them. Denck's humanistic appreciation of his fellowmen was thus a derivation of his belief that every person carried within oneself God's image and revelation.

But the "inner Word" was both individual and universal. Because of its unity, it did not lead to individualistic anarchy but spiritual consensus. As such it was in harmony with the record of historical revelation. Christ's true followers were expected to practice his teachings. Teaching thus replaced the sacraments as the means through which Christ's presence was brought to the people. Christ had taught that God was love and love was the fulfillment of the law. Love of God and one's neighbor were the only appropriate relationships within the divine economy. From this perspective the soteriologically significant distinction between law and gospel, as well as the vicarious nature of Christ's suffering as understood by Lutherans, was deprived of its meaning. Denck's alleged universalism also becomes explicable. A God of love could not punish the sinner vindictively and eternally. His love would find a way to overcome evil by correctives that would not coerce the individual's free will.

This perception of God found expression in Denck's quest for truth, which he was willing to pursue in "lowly or high" places. Concerned with the increasing divisiveness and dogmatism of theological disputes, he pleaded for an impartial hearing of all views. Because accessibility to the "inner Word" was universal as well as individual, no single party held a monopoly on truth. Differences seemed to be the result of an externalist-literalist appeal to isolated parts of Scripture. In his introduction to his collection of scriptural paradoxes, he sought to show that seemingly irreconcilable texts were compatible in a larger spiritual context. At any rate, even when persuasion failed, it was more Christian to leave others in error than to compel them against their conscience.

Thus through his life and thought Denck became an advocate of toleration, not because of indifference to religious truth or social justice, but because of his concern for them. He bequeathed the legacy—that the kingdom of God derives its life from and through the hearts of people and not from institutions reformed or otherwise. In his own person he combined a radical commitment to reform with a rare sensitivity toward the personal dignity of each human being. In this sense he became a spokesman of freedom of conscience for all other individualist dissenters. (By this emphasis he contributed to and was part of what recent social historians have referred to as the "legitimation of rebellion.") On the other hand, he personified the involution of a chastened Anabaptist movement into a quietistic, socially pacific sect. Henceforth the meek were to inherit, if not the earth, then at least the Anabaptist movement.

For further reading:

G. Baring and W. Fellmann, *Hans Denck, Schriften,* 3 Vols., Gütersloh, 1959-1960.
Selected Writings of Hans Denck, transl. and ed. by E. J. Furcha, Pittsburgh, 1976.
S. E. Ozment, *Mysticism and Dissent,* New Haven and London, 1973, 116-136.
R. M. Jones, *Spiritual Reformers in the 16th and 17th Centuries,* London, 1914, 17-30.
J. Kiwiet, "The Life of Hans Denck," *Mennonite Quarterly Review,* 31, 1957, 227-259.
—————————, "The Theology of Hans Denck," *Mennonite Quarterly Review,* 32, 1958, 3-27.
G. Baring, "Hans Denck und Thomas Müntzer in Nürnberg 1524," *Archiv für Reformationsgeschichte,* 50, 1959, 145-182.
G. Goldbach, *Hans Denck und Thomas Müntzer—ein Vergleich*

ihrer wesentlichen theologischen Auffassungen. Eine Untersuchung zur Morphologie der Randströmung der Reformation. Theol. Diss. Hamburg, 1969.

D. Steinmetz, *Reformers in the Wings,* Philadelphia, 1971, 209-218.

W. O. Packull, *Mysticism and the Early South German-Austrian Anabaptist Movement 1525-1531,* Scottdale, Pa., 1976.

G. Seebass, "Hans Denck," *Fränkische Lebensbilder,* Vol. VI, 1976, 107-129.

5. Sebastian Lotzer

An Educated Layman in the Struggle
for Divine Justice

Sebastian Lotzer welcomed the beginning of reform as a great privilege of his generation because the Scriptures were rescued from the monopolistic control of the clergy and faith had once again become a responsibility of all believers. After 1,500 years the Christian faith, given new youth through Luther's rejection of unbiblical traditions, seemed again to be godfather to the beginning of a new epoch. The rotting edifice of the internationally powerful church with its pope and pomp, sacerdotal hierarchy, and means of salvation available for money began to totter. A movement hostile to Rome which penetrated every stratum of the population, hoping for the reform of the church in head and members long since called for, quickly adopted the rebellious accents of the Augustinian monk. Artisans and peasants demanded to be heard as the true interpretation of the Christian faith was undertaken. The recently awakened hunger for education of these people was fed by a flood of pamphlets which were directed at a broad reading public, and which blended the avant-garde religious ideas with pressing social problems.

The furrier's apprentice Lotzer, who, according to the deprecating conventions of the time referred to himself as a "simple judicious layman," took to the pen with enthusiasm for the new teaching. He wanted to help spread the gospel and strongly urged its practical application in the congregation. It quickly became clear that the good news functioned not only as a watchword for the inner liberation of the Christian, but that idea and cause could be combined in ways other than the reformer-elector alliance at Wittenberg. During the tempest of the Reformation, the year in which the common man took the field with scythe and flail against the bastions of feudal society, Lotzer joined the rebellious peasants. The biblically literate urbanite composed their most important manifesto, the Twelve Articles.

The name of this man is joined to the history of Memmingen in the agitated second decade of the sixteenth century. Only for the interlude of his sojourn there does he emerge from the obscurity which otherwise surrounds his life. The few known facts of his young life are quickly told. Horb, in the territory of Hohenberg, was Lotzer's birthplace. There he was born about 1490 and raised in an educated home. Sebastian Lotzer, senior, matriculated at the University of Tübingen in 1485. A son named Johannes became personal physician of the bishop of Strassburg after academic training. The young Sebastian, however, did not follow his academic relatives, although his father would presumably have been pleased for him to become a theologian. He learned the trade of the furrier and as journeyman passed through several cities until he finally settled in Memmingen. In this imperial city he took the daughter of the shopkeeper Weigelin for his wife, lived in the city quarter Behind the School and achieved citizenship. The tax list of the year 1521 reveals that as taxpayer of the city he paid one pound. He was not indigent but certainly did not belong to the rich or even to the well-to-do bourgeoisie.

The beginnings of a reform movement appeared in Memmingen in 1522 and Lotzer was one of the first to join. Luther's writings had in the meantime become a preferred commodity and the publication of the Edict of Worms had not been able to change that. The priest Megerich, who was pastor at the Church of Our Lady, was already complaining peevishly about the loss of income due to the sudden drop in pious foundations and anniversaries.

His opponent was Christoph Schappeler, for nine years preacher at the church of St. Martin and advocate of the new religious views. A licentiate in theology from St. Gall, he had frequently adopted a critical stance on social issues in his earlier sermons. A year before he had protested the disadvantages of the poor in the judicial process. There were good reasons for his social concern. The sixteenth century had brought the mercantile city economic difficulties and a shift in property ownership. The number of the propertyless had grown by 50 percent. These were the people that suffered most under the burden of scarcity, taxes, plagues, and the distress of war. Like the members of the guilds, they had no choice about their lack of political power.

Because of the crisis people saw more clearly the church's dereliction of duty. Too obviously the clergy combined neglect of their obligations with a proneness to high living. The increasing yearning for salvation of the people seemed to be satisfied less and less by traditional institutional Christianity. When, in the second half of 1522, Schappeler energetically attacked the priests' manner of life, the position of the pope, the mass, and canon law, he provoked those in the old faith who were secure either among the clergy or the high society of the patricians to opposition. In the guilds and in the poorer quarters of the city his support increased steadily. Before long the sympathy for reform grew also in the Council which had thus far been satisfied to play the role of mediator. In June 1523 the proposal of a Councillor of the old faith to prohibit public sale of Lutheran tracts was rejected by the majority.

At this point Lotzer entered the public disputation concerning the Reformation with his first written work "A salutary Admonition to the Residents of Horb." It was written in the spirit of Schappeler whose close friend he had been for some time. This letter to the residents of his home city was a call to hold firmly to the new evangelical faith in spite of the local government, and if need be, to accept suffering for this faith following the example of the imprisoned lay preacher "Karsthans."* In the vehement anticlerical spirit of those years he examined the traditional church practices one by one, all of them of immediate practical concern in the life of the Christian of the day. Fasts, holy days, indulgences, intercession of saints, pilgrimages, monastic piety, and religious fraternities turned out to be human invention and abuse when measured by the Scripture principle of the Reformation. Lotzer's criticism of the church became social criticism. The clergy impose fasts on "the working people who can scarcely get soup three times a day" under threat of the ban, while they themselves are "as full as ticks."

Primarily, however, he challenged the traditional claim of the clergy to be sole interpreters of Scripture as Luther had done in his book to the nobility. He believed that the clergy had forfeited their divine mandate through self-seeking and false teaching. The common people were again the best managers of the divine Word as in the time of Christ. The words with which Lotzer sought to persuade those with evangelical sympathies to take charge of their own instruction could have been written by Müntzer: "Whoever has two coats, let him sell one and buy a New Testament. Then you can learn the living words of God yourselves and will understand wherever they try to mislead you." The biblically literate layman was to take the place of the priests and the educated professors. The egalitarian thinking of the layman clearly emerges here as well as in the conviction that the equality of baptized Christians

---

*This is a colloquial expression, literally translated John Hoe; Karst=hoe. Transl.

before God has nothing to do with the hierarchical structure of the church of Rome. For Lotzer, the church was
nothing more than the gathering of all the believers.

As evangelical ideas advanced, an independent group of
lay people met regularly to discuss Christian faith. The
members of this conventicle, to which Lotzer also belonged,
came from the lower ranks of the bourgeoisie with one or
two exceptions. The pastoral letter of the bishop of
Augsburg, Christoph von Stadion, dated July 19, took offense at heretical expressions of "several unlettered
laymen." But the course of events overtook the diplomatic
acquiescence of the Council in a spectacular street scene. A
provocative document was handed to parson Megerich in
public view. He had distinguished himself by especially in-
sulting tirades against Schappeler and his supporters. The
document contained a clear confession of adherence to
Luther's teaching which agreed with the divine law, as well
as an attack upon the unbecoming manner of living of the
parson and all the clergy. The conventicle was responsible
for the document. It was composed by the teacher of Latin,
Paul Hoepp. Eleven citizens had signed it, including Sebastian Lotzer. Four days later the writer and the signatories
of the protest document were summoned to appear before
the Council upon the urging of the clergy. The stern warning they received on this occasion to hold no gatherings in
the future revealed a lively suspicion of the lay movement.

In the late summer of 1523 Lotzer's "Christian Letter"
was published. It strengthened the basic affirmations of
his first tract and was designed to provide the movement
with a foundation. It defended the priesthood of all believers from which followed the right of the laity to speak,
teach, and write about the Word of God. His demand to
begin the proscribed religious discussions with Jews
enlarged the Reformation practice of the public, dialogic
determination of the truth with lay participation, to include non-Christians. When he emphasized the maturity of

church members and charged them to represent matters of faith before others in a knowledgeable way, and not to delegate their responsibility for personal choice to popes and councils, he fairly represented the popular efforts made in the circle of Schappeler's activity. For some time Schappeler had advocated the liberation of the laity from clerical tutelage.

Besides Schappeler it was primarily Lotzer who was suspected by the conservative authorities as the spiritual source of the dissension. He was heard to debate questions of faith in the streets, and it was known that he lectured on the new teachings to a small group. Finally he challenged a representative of the old faith to answer questions about a sermon in the presence of the congregation. This lively activity led to a new clash with the city government. On September 2 he was sternly reprimanded along with his supporter, the weaver Ambrosius Baesch. Now that Lotzer was prohibited from taking the controversy concerning the gospel onto the street he disappeared from public view for a while. His name was missing from the Council minutes of the following months. At the same time several new publications appeared under his name during the next year.

In February 1524, the ecclesiastical ban was proclaimed against the obstinate preacher of St. Martins. It did nothing to lessen his popularity with the city residents or the peasants in the surrounding villages, and even the Council was ready to risk intervention by the Swabian League rather than to support the bishop. Several months later Lotzer pointedly dedicated a work to his excommunicated friend Schappeler in which, as a layman, he had attempted an exposition of a chapter from the Gospel of Matthew.

In the second half of 1524 there were new successes in the reform movement in Memmingen. Since laymen had demonstrated their concern over Christian equality the religious barriers between spiritual and secular had been breached. Now, however, official action was taken against the legal and social privileges of the clergy. In addition, Schappeler introduced a new liturgy for the Lord's supper

Title page of the Twelve Articles (1525)

and baptism in his church without serious opposition from the Council. On December 7 the Cup, the liturgical symbol of equality in the church, was passed around the first time among the believers. Excitement began to spread when the congregation of the parish of Our Lady also exerted pressure to introduce the evangelical rite. As expected, they encountered the embittered opposition of Megerich. He was able to extricate himself from a tumultuous church meeting near Christmas only by agreeing to a public debate with Schappeler.

Sebastian Lotzer was also among the priests, monks, and lay preachers who, along with elected representatives of the guilds and a few doctors, had been invited to the debate in the city hall at the beginning of the new year. The chronicler Schorer entered his name as "Beste Wergelin," the family name of Lotzer's wife which was better known in Memmingen. Judged by the conditions of the debate agreed upon in advance, the sole authority of the Bible and the right of decision by the laity, the decision of the five-day verbal battle clearly went to Schappeler. Several of the concerns which Schappeler discussed such as the sacrifice of the mass, aural confession, veneration of saints, the Lord's supper, and the priesthood of all believers, Lotzer had discussed in a book published the previous year. This largest work of Lotzer, entitled "A very salutary comforting Christian irrefutable book of refuge in thirty-one articles," was written not simply for edification and instruction, but to provide laymen with a systematic arrangement of scriptural proofs for the various dogmatic issues in order to arm them against the persecutors of God's Word. The outcome of the disputation cleared the way for a fundamental reordering of church affairs and ultimately for the victory of the Reformation in Memmingen.

The turbulent church service in the Church of Our Lady at Christmas became the pretext for Lotzer's apology which appeared in the first weeks of 1525 entitled "Justification of the godly Christian congregation in Memmingen and of its bishop and true messenger of the Lord Christoph Schappeler the preacher." With his version of the controversial events Lotzer was concerned to rescue the honor of the city which was now regarded as the citadel of re-

bellion in the whole region. In his discussion of the claim of
government on the believer he connects with a motif found
in his earlier writings. He emphasizes the necessity of
obedience in all matters relating to physical life, but the secular power may not act contrary to the Word of God. All
human authority is delegated by God and subject to his
law. Thus the only legitimate government is a Christian
one. The spiritual shepherds had provoked the legitimate
resistance of true Christians, when, like Megerich himself,
at first they resisted the gospel. Similarly, the secular arm
cannot count on obedience when it issues orders contrary
to biblical law and becomes tyrannical. Luther, too, had
allowed that God was to be obeyed before man if a believer
thought his personal salvation was endangered. At the
same time he had urgently warned the authorities about
the common man who seemed to him to have become
clever.

Although Lotzer began with Luther's teaching on
government, the accent shifted in his work to favor the
interests of the subjects. His assessment of the results of
the evangelical movement thus far indicated that his
understanding of the Christian mandate in the world included the possibility of social radicalism. "Alas, we don't
do many evangelical works as yet. There is much talk, but
the heart will not follow, nor peace. No Christian order is
being established to help the poor." Only the outlines of
such a Christian order are visible. Lotzer regarded the race
for power and wealth as incompatible with the spirit of the
gospel. The apostolic community of goods, a peaceful communal life based on neighborly love rather than on selfishness, appeared to him to be an ideal worth striving for in
his time as long as it was voluntary.

Thoroughgoing changes were in the offing when the
Peasants' War reached the gates of Memmingen in the
spring. From that time forward the literate furrier
combined his commitment to the Reformation with the

cause of the insurgents. The peasants between the Danube, Lake Constance, and the Lech had followed those from the Black Forest into insurrection in February 1525, to throw off the yoke of feudal oppressors and priests. Since the middle of the month several villages belonging to Memmingen had taken their grievances concerning local conditions to the Council. On February 24 representatives from all the villages gathered in Memmingen. They made no concrete demands at this time. However, they called upon the Council to grant the Word of God to all subjects as a fundamental right, and to recognize it as the basis of subsequent rights and obligations. It was Lotzer who formulated this request, firm in its essence, but moderate in tone.

The struggle over the tithe in July 1524 had already revealed that, in their opposition to ecclesiastical and secular tithes, the artisans of the urban guilds and the surrounding peasants were beginning to grant validity to the Scripture principle also in secular matters. The Council now granted the request of the peasants and in its decision finally accepted the divine law as a binding norm in social conflict.

Soon thereafter the confidant of the Memmingen tenants became the military secretary of the largest of the Swabian peasant armies. On February 27 Ulrich Schmid, the commander of the Baltringer company, had come into the city among other things to have the grievances of the peasants of Ried systemized, following their unanimous decision to make the Word of God arbiter of their affairs. Lotzer was recommended to him as "a man well versed in Scripture and all these things." Upon the request of the peasant leader he accepted the post as military secretary somewhat reluctantly because he did not have the normal training required for it.

While he was working at the Memmingen Articles for the local villages, Lotzer wrote his most significant work between February 28 and March 3. With the cooperation of

Schappeler and in the context of the grievance submissions
of the Baltringers he wrote "The fundamental and chief
articles of all the peasants and subjects of spiritual and
temporal authorities by which they believe themselves to
be oppressed."

This document quickly became known as the Twelve
Articles in the remotest villages and beyond the imperial
borders, and had very strong influence on the programs of
nearly all the insurgent areas. The articles demanded the
elimination of the small tithe, parish administration of the
great tithe, abolition of serfdom and the death duty. They
called for the restoration of earlier communal benefits of
meadow, forest, and stream, a reduction in and payment
for compulsory services, reexamination of feudal dues and
a just fixing of legal fines. In case confirmed rights were in-
jured, the parish would settle peacefully with the lord. All
the demands were now based exclusively on Scripture
passages according to the principle of divine justice.

The Twelve Articles broke the dams between the evangelical and the social movement. It was not an accident
that the introduction defended the smoldering revolt as
just counterforce to the violent suppression of the gospel.
The first article called for the right of the parish to elect
and depose the pastor by design. The chain of demands was
concluded quite deliberately with the reservation that they
would be valid only if they agreed with Scripture. The older
norms based simply on custom and human law for the
most part no longer had any validity. The Word of God now
became the constitution for the ordering of society which
was still understood in terms of the medieval corpus christianum, a unified sacral institution under the umbrella of
Christianity radicalized by the scriptural principle.

The Twelve Articles did not follow Luther's fracturing of
the unity of life into spiritual and secular kingdoms. They
paved the way for the rigorous application of the yardstick
of their own constitutional claims based on the gospel to

the existing constitutional arrangements. This explanation which committed itself to obedience to authority and peaceful resolution of conflict nevertheless had revolutionary explosive power, first of all through the coherence of the apologetic for their position, but also through individual demands such as the articles concerning choice of pastor, tithe, and serfdom, which struck at the supporting pillars of feudal society. The rulers and chroniclers of the time never doubted the seditious nature of the Twelve Articles. They agreed with the Wittenberg Reformers that a danger for the existing order could arise precisely out of the link between social demands and the gospel. That explains why Luther attacked the manifesto as the work of a "rebellious prophet," and why Melanchthon suspected that the devil himself had a hand in it. That the articles belonged to the moderate stream in the peasant war was established only later.

Before long the leaders of the Baltringers were making efforts to bring about a union of all the upper Swabian peasants for the defense and protection of the gospel. On March 6 the leaders of the three large armies met in the hall of the shopkeepers' guild in Memmingen in a peasant parliament. The discussion of a draft constitution, which bore Lotzer's signature because of concern for the primacy of the divine Word, nearly destroyed the fledgling idea of union. According to the account of Kessler, Lotzer and Schmid reacted with "great sorrow and weeping eyes" to the stance of the peasants from Lake Constance who preferred the sword to the Word.

The traces of the last-minute compromise were visible in the draft of the instrument of union agreed upon the following day. It rested on the Bible as the norm for the obligations of the newly founded Christian union, suspended the payment of all dues to the feudal lords until an agreement could be reached, settled some questions of military organization, and made decisions regarding

internal order and the general peace. The evangelical
character of the Union, however, was somewhat
diminished. Lotzer's proposal for centralization of political
power and demand for centralized taxation were missing.
On the other hand, there was an article concerning the
destruction of the castles which was clearly out of
harmony with the protestations of peaceful intention. The
nature of Lotzer's contribution to the "general constitution," a combination of the constitution of the Union and
military procedure, which was discussed shortly
thereafter, remains uncertain.

The attitude of the Memmingen peasants stood in striking contrast to the great success of unification in the
villages and the majority of the cities in the second half of
March. They joined none of the armies which were camp-
ing in the vicinity of the imperial city because they de-
pended upon an eventual agreement with the Council. The
Council had already given their word to most of the articles
prepared by Lotzer with relative generosity.

The strategy of nonviolent settlement proposed by
Lotzer and Schmidt nevertheless proved to be fateful in
view of the fact that the Swabian League, which was play-
ing the game of negotiation, was at the same time arming
for the destruction of the rebels. Barely twenty days after
the founding of the peasant Union the six peasant negotia-
tors were prepared to again surrender all the decisions of
the meeting in Memmingen in return for the vague
assurance of a court settlement. On the other hand, a majority of the insurgents was less and less ready to make the
carrying out of their demands dependent upon the goodwill
of their opponents. The next day, March 26, 1525, they can-
celed out the compromises of their representatives at the
Ulm negotiations by burning the first castle. Even while
Ulrich Schmid was still negotiating after the bloody defeat
of Leipheim, the League's general Jörg Truchsess decided
to fight rather than talk. In mid-April the Baltringer army

suffered annihilating defeat. The Agreement of Wein-
garten of April 17, 1525, sealed the fate of the whole upper
Swabian peasant movement.

The degree to which the military secretary Sebastian
Lotzer participated in the defeat of the peasants is not
historically verifiable. When the Swabian League urgently
summoned the Council of Memmingen in a letter of April
21 to arrest citizen Lotzer since he had "been an adherent
of the wicked feud of the peasants," he was no longer in the
city. In all likelihood he sought asylum in Switzerland in
the days of the defeat of the Baltringer army. Later in St.
Gall he met Schappeler who on June 9 had barely escaped
when the League's forces entered Memmingen. Months
later the minutes of the Council mention his name twice
with reference to property he left in Memmingen. After
that his tracks disappear.

The democratization of sacral knowledge in the twenties
of the sixteenth century was an important precondition for
Lotzer's spoken and written Reformation activity. The
German Bible became the most important weapon in the
liberation struggle of the laity against the clergy. The
literary image of the biblically literate common man,
presented by so many authors of popular dialogues in the
symbolic figure of Karsthans as the opponent to the
scholastic wisdom of the masters and doctors, became a
reality in a man like Lotzer. The furrier had not enjoyed
the traditional theological training of the universities and
did not know the intellectual language of the time.
Nevertheless, he managed to acquire an astonishing
knowledge of Scripture. In addition, he had contact with
contemporary literature beginning with Eberlin von
Günzburg to Luther and Vadian, and finally to the popular
tract "The New Karsthans." As many in his time, he did
not read much, but what he had he read again and again.

Lotzer sought to win his readers for intensive Bible
study. Knowing about the gospel was, in any event, the

first step on the path of the simple man out of an im-
maturity for which he was not accountable. To claim
precedence for the divine law in the Scriptures over the
purely human law, ecclesiastical as well as secular,
represented a concrete beginning toward the abolition of
ancient churchly error and the binding social privileges of
the clergy. It also meant to subject the societal order of
human life to the authority of the gospel. Since the Scriptures as the revelation of God could apparently alone
guarantee the truth, and since Lotzer sought to make this
truth supreme, he assumed that it might be necessary to
defend it at the cost of life and property and eventually
also against the government. His apology for the community of Memmingen left no doubt that he also included
active resistance. He left open the choice of means and personally certainly preferred nonviolence.

It represented no discontinuity in Lotzer's development
when he gave spiritual firearms to the peasants. He expected answers from the Bible not only for religious life,
but equally for secular social life which had to be harmonized with the divine Word. That the divine law became
the watchword for inclusive efforts at emancipation which
were directed not only at ecclesiastical authority claims
can in considerable measure be credited to Lotzer. At the
beginning the Scriptures were enlisted for the partisan
aims of the peasants, and used decisively as an instrument
of criticism and of legitimation for peasant demands. In
the course of the conflict, however, the naive confidence in
the Word's power to convict, and the obligation of the
moderate assistants around Lotzer and Schmid to observe
the Christian virtues to love of neighbor, humility, and
nonviolence became the nemesis of the movement. Sebastian Lotzer belonged to those who counseled peace even
after war had begun because they believed that the Word
of God could bridge the chasm of conflicting interests.

For further reading:

A. Goetze (ed.), *Sebastian Lotzer: Schriften*, Leipzig, 1902.

G. Franz (ed.), *Quellen zur Geschichte des Bauernkrieges*, Darmstadt, 1972 (contains the Text of the Twelve Articles).

W. Vogt, "Zwei oberschwäbische Laienprediger," *Zeitschrift für kirchliche Wissenschaft und kirchliches Leben*, 6. Jg., 1885, 413-525.

G. Bossert, *Sebastian Lotzer und seine Schriften.* Reprint from *Blätter für württembergische Kirchengeschichte.* Beilage zum Evangelischen Kirchen-und Schulblatt für Württemberg, 2. Jg., Nr. 4ff. (1887), Memmingen 1906.

W. Schlenck, *Die Reichsstadt Memmingen und die Reformation.* Phil. Diss. printed in *Memminger Geschichtsblätter*, 1968.

M. Brecht, "Der theologische Hintergrund der Zwölf Artikel der Bauernschaft in Schwaben von 1525: Christoph Schappelers und Sebastian Lotzers Beitrag zum Bauernkrieg," *Zeitschrift für Kirchengeschichte*, 85, 1974, Heft 2, 30-64.

P. Blickle, *Die Revolution von 1525*, München und Wien, 1975.

R. G. Cole, "The Dynamics of Printing in the Sixteenth Century," in L. P. Buck and J. W. Zophy (eds.), *The Social History of the Reformation*, Columbus, Ohio, 1972, 93-105.

H. J. Hillerbrand, "The German Reformation and the Peasants' War," in L. P. Buck and J. W. Zophy (eds.), *The Social History of the Reformation*, Columbus, Ohio, 1972, 106-136.

Ph. L. Kintner, "Memmingens 'Ausgetretene.' Eine vergessene Nachwirkung des Bauernkrieges 1525-1527," *Memminger Geschichtsblätter*, Jg. 1969 (Memmingen, 1971), 5-40.

6. Michael Gaismair

An Early Proponent of Social Justice

On May 14, 1528, two men on horseback arrived at an inn in St. Niclaus in the Engadine. The farmers gathered there over a glass of wine are curious about the travelers who are obviously from Italy. The strangers are cautious, but the wine gradually eases the tension. Conversation develops. Suddenly a farmer asks: "Where is Michael Gaismair?" After some hesitation the taller of the two says: "I am Gaismair. I do not hide myself where people know me or ask about me, since I am neither a brigand nor a murderer. I am a pious, honest man and have no cause to deny my name. I am forced to avoid my fatherland for the sake of the gospel."

That statement, reported to King Ferdinand of Austria by a spy, reveals the man's estimate of himself. It stands in complete contrast to the judgment of the royal council in Innsbruck, which referred to Gaismair as "the chief agitator, ringleader, and commander in the recent peasant rebellion against His Roman and Royal Majesty . . . a public enemy of his own fatherland. . . . By this he committed the major crime of lèse majestle."

Such divergent judgments were common in the tumultuous 1520s. Today, after 450 years, we are better able to establish the truth about Michael Gaismair.

He was born about 1485 in the village of Tschöfs above Sterzing, Tyrol. His grandfather had been a farmer. His father had expanded the ancestral farm and had in addition become a mining entrepreneur. His parents were therefore able to send young Michael to school and to prepare him for the profession of secretary. Beyond that we know nothing of his early life. He married about 1507 and likely entered upon his professional career about that time. In 1523 he was state secretary in the offices of Leonhard von Völs the vice-regent of Tyrol. In May 1525, we find Gaismair in Brixen as secretary of prince-bishop Sebastian Sprentz.

On May 9, 1525, the peasant revolt erupted in Brixen, the climax of a long process of repression and resistance. The episcopal administrators were driven out and the bishop himself fled. Church property, especially the monastery Neustift, was plundered, but the bishop's palace was saved from destruction by his secretary Michael Gaismair, who refused the angry peasants entry. The marks of their pikes may be seen on the steel-covered door to this day. The next day, May 13, the peasants elected that same man, Michael Gaismair, as their leader.

What could have led to so unlikely an event? We can only surmise. Gaismair's sympathies for the cause of the peasants must have been known among them. Indeed, there must have been extensive contacts between them before this date, for only thus could the necessary confidence have developed in a man whose profession was a byword for arrogance. Equally enigmatic is Gaismair's acceptance of the leadership. One can only assume that by some process Gaismair was transformed from an ambitious civil servant to a fiery social reformer. It was probably a combination of observing the frequent oppressions of his employers and the influence of the Bible with its clear call for social justice. References by Gaismair in the margin of court proceedings suggest such a process. German Bibles were available at the annual fairs in Bozen, a city near the castle of the vice-regent at Völs. His preoccupation with divine justice further supports this hypothesis. What is significant is that when Gaismair steps into the light of history he is possessed by a passionate sense of justice.

But the peasants must also have known about his abilities as an organizational and military leader. In some way he must have proved himself, perhaps by creating a

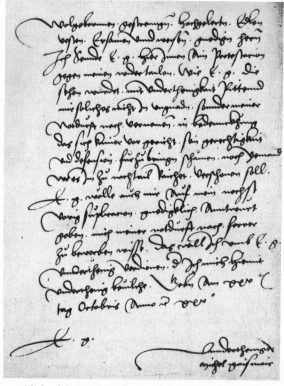

Michael Gaismair to the Royal Council in Innsbruck

network of dissident groups for eventual action. He was a strong and determined leader. As soon as he had assumed control of the movement the excesses stopped, a new government was established, and new religious leaders were brought in to reform the church.

The purpose of the revolt was to deprive the church and the nobility of their power and to turn the land over directly to the king. With few exceptions, the peasants had total confidence in the goodwill and justice of Ferdinand. Lists of grievances were prepared which, for the most part, were very similar to lists of peasant grievances in Germany. Among them were the demands for the right to appoint their own pastors, for unobstructed preaching of the clear Word of God, and the return to common law as the law of the land. From their base of power in Brixen combined with their trust in the king, the peasants attempted to negotiate with Ferdinand at the Diet in Innsbruck in June and July, 1525. But Ferdinand proved a capable negotiator, skillfully exploiting peasant differences for his own end which was the suppression of the revolt. It was eventually decided to restore control of the prince-bishopric to Ferdinand, who agreed to secularize it and thus deprive the church of its worldly power. Subsequent events prove that Ferdinand never intended to carry out the secularization. Some peasants suspected this and many others developed second thoughts about Ferdinand's goodwill. Thus the agreed-upon transfer of power was made very reluctantly at the end of July. It was now clear that popular unrest had not been allayed. Gaismair himself had lost confidence in Ferdinand's integrity and at one point threatened to assassinate him.

All of this prompted the royal council to lure Gaismair to Innsbruck under the pretense of further discussion. On his arrival he was quickly imprisoned. When he had not been brought to trial within the stipulated seven weeks he escaped and fled to Zürich. With the support of Huldreich Zwingli, the Zürich reformer, he now made plans for invading Tyrol and wresting it from the Habsburgs. Two letters from this time to the royal council clearly reveal his sense of betrayal and his determination to become the liberator of Tyrol. In the meantime Ferdinand sent an army of mercenaries through the countryside to punish the peasants and to insure that there would be no reoccurrence of a popular uprising.

Gaismair began by gathering an army of fugitive peasants from various areas many of whom had taken refuge in the Swiss Confederacy. Then, in February 1526, he wrote his famous *Landesordnung*, a revolutionary program for his army. It describes in broad strokes the main features of a new Tyrol. Gaismair envisages a Christian order from which the godless exploiters, mainly the clergy but also the nobility as well as the sovereign will be excluded. Justice and equality will be its foundation. Legislators and judges will be elected by the people. All special privilege is to be abolished and justice is to be equal and prompt. Church property will be converted to the common good for administrative offices, hospitals, and homes for the aged and orphans. The commercial enterprise will be taken over by the government with regulation of production and distribution and control of prices. Standard weights and measures and stable currency are to be established. The mining enterprise will be wrested from the hands of European bankers and administered for the benefit of the people. A university is to be established at which only the Word of God will be taught for it alone reveals what divine justice is. The whole is to be an order established for the glory of God and the common good.

This document has no parallel among the numerous peasant statements and plans for reform of the time. Unlike all the others it called for the complete abolition of feudal society. It is the product of an independent mind and is clearly an important early modern state utopia.

Gaismair's first plan to invade Tyrol from the west was betrayed and had to be abandoned. Undeterred, he took his army safely through the heart of Tyrol to Salzburg, where a revolt was in progress, and then, when that too failed, attempted an invasion of Tyrol from the east. He crossed the Hohe Tauern in the shadow of the Grossglockner and marched up the Puster valley toward Brixen hoping the peasants would rally to him. But the brutal pacification inflicted on them by Ferdinand the previous autumn prevented it. Gaismair was also aware of the League of Cognac, just then formed. He assumed with some justification that his attack from the east might encourage the allies to launch an attack against Habsburg in the south of Tyrol. But that too proved to be a vain hope. Threatened by the Swabian League, Gaismair took his army to the Republic of Venice.

Gaismair's march through Tyrol with an army of 2000 men without any losses was a major achievement. Traversing about 180 km. of high mountain terrain in three days is a tribute to his skill as a leader. The records show further that the decision to go to Venice was made by the army and not by Gaismair alone. He knew how to retain the loyalty of his followers.

With the support of Venice, a traditional enemy of Habsburg in the south, Zürich in the west, and France keeping the emperor occupied elsewhere, Gaismair now hoped to launch a successful invasion of Tyrol from Venice and establish his Alpine republic. By becoming a mercenary captain in Venetian service he hoped to obligate the Venetians to support him. Unfortunately for Gaismair, all these "allies" were prepared to use his services to further their own policies, but not to aid him in his plans. Zürich withdrew support several times at critical points; neither Venice nor France was inclined to aid the establishment of the radical social experiment which Gaismair intended. He made frequent journeys to Switzerland to gather mercenaries for Venetian service and his own revolutionary plans, but the long delays and the end of hostilities between France and the empire with the dissolution of the

League of Cognac in 1529 eroded the vision, and his revolutionary army gradually dwindled away.

During the whole of Gaismair's exile Ferdinand and his council made no fewer than one hundred attempts to destroy him mainly by hired assassins. An enormous price was put on his head. They finally succeeded in striking him down in April 1532 on his estate in Padua. Because he was reputed to be a heretic the local clergy refused him a church burial. Whether the anguished letter of his faithful wife to the *Signoria* requesting their intervention was successful, we do not know.

Gaismair's life as a leader of disaffected peasants was filled with action; he obviously had little time for writing. Hence we have from his hand only three letters and the *Landesordnung*. The letters to prince-bishop Sprentz and to the royal council in Innsbruck were statements of self-defense. Still, an examination of these few documents reveals a good deal about the man and his convictions. Basic to everything was the insistent and urgent call for social justice for the poor and the powerless. He believed fervently in God who had revealed the nature of true justice in the Bible. He believed that retribution for wrong done and reward for righteousness were inevitable. For him true faith in God had little to do with personal justification by faith alone. Godliness was equivalent to commitment to social justice. Godlessness was not some separation from God through unbelief or sacramental exclusion. Rather, Gaismair saw it simply as social unrighteousness and the perversion of justice. For him even a sacramentally ordained priest was godless if he oppressed the poor. These things were for Gaismair the sum of the gospel, even though his understandings were based primarily on the Old Testament. Not once does he mention Jesus or the central affirmations of Christian faith regarding redemption so important to Catholic, Protestant, and Anabaptist alike.

Perhaps Gaismair's ready assumption of the leadership in May 1525, was even then based on the sense of being chosen by God to avenge injustice which is later expressed in his letter to Bishop Sprentz and other words attributed to him. It is clear that he regarded himself as a Moses leading the dispossessed peasants into their promised land. The *Landesordnung* can be understood as a conscious parallel to the law given on Mount Sinai.

He seems particularly concerned to base himself in all things on the Bible, especially the Old Testament. Virtually all of the provisions of the Landesordnung can be documented with references from Deuteronomy. From it he also justifies his consuming hatred of the clergy whom he identifies especially as the godless. The destruction of idolatrous shrines and the killing of the priests as described in 2 Kings 23 may well have been Gaismair's model for the total abolition of the old church with its shrines, clergy, and power. In Zürich he saw a functioning model of a total religious-political community which evidently impressed and influenced him. Zwingli gave him a theological justification for revolt including tyrannicide. From Zwingli, as well as perhaps from older writings such as Marsilio of Padua's *Defensor pacis*, he learned that political power rests with the people and that they have the right to make and unmake rulers.

While Gaismair was clearly influenced by Zwingli, the main source for shaping his ideas and convictions were the Old Testament Scriptures which he must have read and absorbed long before he became a peasant leader. He may also have been influenced by the social justice tradition of the Catholic Middle Ages expressed in works like Dante's *De monarchia* and the *Reformatio Sigismundi*. This older tradition was then strengthened by the social justice concerns of Zwingli. Of Lutheran influence there appears to be none in Gaismair's thought.

Correspondence concerning Gaismair which passed

between the city government and the Signoria in Venice in 1530 suggests that Gaismair had regular contacts with religious dissidents and that he was in possession of heretical books. The refusal of the clergy to give him canonical burial has already been referred to. What the nature of his views at that time was cannot be ascertained. It is certain that he had rejected the old church, but he seems not to have committed himself to any variety of Protestantism or Anabaptism, even though he had personal contact with both. He appears thus to have been another of the fraternity of unattached spirits during the Reformation era who had the strength and the imagination to go their own way in spite of the relentless pressures to conform.

For further reading:

Walter Klaassen, *Michael Gaismair: Revolutionary and Reformer*, Leiden, 1978. (Contains Gaismair's letters and his Constitution of 1526 in translation.)

G. Franz, *Quellen zur Geschichte des Bauernkrieges*, Darmstadt, 1972.

K. Schadelbauer, "Drei Schreiben über Michael Gaismair im Staatsarchiv zu Zürich," *Tiroler Heimat*, N.F. 3, 1930.

A. Hollaender, "Michael Gaismairs Landesordnung 1526," *Der Schlern* 13, 1932, 425-429.

O. Vasella, "Ulrich Zwingli und Michael Gaismair, der Tiroler Bauernführer, *Zeitschrift für schweizerische Geschichte*, 24, 1944, 388-413.

E. Auckenthaler, "Michael Gaismairs Heimat und Sippe," *Der Schlern* 21, 1947.

J. Macek, *Der Tiroler Bauernkrieg und Michael Gaismair*, Berlin, 1965.

J. Bücking, *M. Gaismair. Reformer, Sozialrebell, Revolutionär. Seine Rolle im Tiroler "Bauernkrieg" (1525/32)*, Stuttgart, 1978.

Ferdinand Seibt

7. Johannes Hergot

The Reformation of the Poor Man

The Nuremberg printer and book peddler belonged to the marginal figures of the revolutionary process. After a long crisis, it had come to ferment in Germany in the twenties of the sixteenth century when the religious justification for the right of resistance threatened to destroy the social structure but issued in the end in the victory of the highest estate, the nobility. The little work, "Concerning the New Changes in Christian Life," was more a symptom than a participant in these events. But it was a revealing symptom, since it takes us into the thought world of extreme polemic among the "common people."

We know little regarding the fate of Hergot; even his authorship of the little book, for which he had to go to the block in Leipzig on May 20, 1527, is not secure against all doubt. Research concerning Hergot and his book happened in two stages. It began in 1878 when A. Kirchoff identified the "unknown socialist agitator of Reformation times." He returned to him repeatedly and his work created a modest echo. In 1953 the work and its presumed author aroused new attention when an edition of the work "Concerning the New Changes in Christian Life" was published as one of the *Flugschriften* of the Reformation period. Now followed the work of Marxist authors who felt obligated to interpret this "untimely precursor" of modern socialism with more or less insight as the "literary-political expression of the concerns of the preproletariat." Gerhard Zschäbitz was the most thorough of these authors even though his interpretations were marred by faulty understanding.

Meanwhile Hergot has found a place in the history of early printing. It was in this connection that his authorship of the "New Changes" was doubted and the work was attributed to the Nuremberg preacher Wolfgang Vogel, who had been executed in Nuremberg about the same time. Against that conclusion stands the contemporary testimony of Peter Sylvius who said about Hergot that he "had attempted to accomplish with his vision" what Luther had tried with his writing and Pfeiffer and Müntzer with their rebellion. Besides, neither the structure nor the manner of expression of the small pamphlet would allow the conclusion that the author was a preacher, since preachers were usually somewhat trained in Latin, in spite of the low level of clerical education in these times.

It is, of course, also possible that Hergot did not regard the utopian project in the framework of his whole work as his own invention, but that he was simply repeating what was in the air in the humanist circles of those years. Thomas More had made his elegant story of the "Fortunate Island of Utopia" into a best seller. Oecolampadius, Hugwald, and Karlstadt each in his own way idealized a simple peasant communism. Perhaps this is what Müntzer meant when, under torture, he intimated his ideal of society with the concise words: ". . . quod omnia sint communia" (. . . that they may all be one community).

No matter. Fate and his profession entwined the colporteur Hergot in a stream of communication in which what was his was mixed with that of others made permanent by the medium of the pamphlet. His small Nuremberg printery had handled sensational pamphlets for several years before he took to the road with his dangerous agitation literature. The most important item was *The Explicit Disclosure of the False Faith.*

This work, soon confiscated by the Nuremberg Council, was alleged to have been printed in Hergot's establishment without his knowledge. The liberal Nurembergers sentenced only one of Hergot's apprentices to three days in prison, but it may be that the printer himself left town for this reason. We don't know his whereabouts following his

Title page of The New Changes by Hans Hergot

departure or where he spent the exciting turning of the
years 1524/1525, nor what his attitude was toward the
unheard of although brief thunderstorm of the peasant
uprising, which was by no means a revolution as is sometimes said, but could easily have produced one. In
December of 1526 his wife completed a financial transac-
tion in Nuremberg by herself, and a year later she married
a printer from her husband's workshop.

Hergot's own tragedy had taken place meanwhile. He
was arrested with two students in Zwickau in Saxony
while he was selling the pamphlet "New Changes."
Zwickau had been a conspiratorial center in the preceding
years, perhaps because its indigent weavers were not far
from the Bohemian center Saaz which had become the
heart and training center for German Hussites a hundred
years earlier and apparently continued to be so for a long
time. Four years before Thomas Müntzer had passed
through Zwickau on his way to Saaz and Prague.

The sale of the book itself does not really explain the
death sentence passed on Johannes Hergot. The two
students were released without trial after a detention of
several months. Rather, the death sentence constituted evidence that the government of Saxony accused him not only
of purveying highly dangerous propaganda, but regarded
him as the author of the anonymous book which alleged
that it was not fomenting insurrection but that it identified
those "who sit in wickedness."

That takes us into the problems of the little book, since
this indication of purpose, the immediate quarrel, relates
only to the second part of the text, that half in which the
author addresses his book and its purpose three times. By
contrast, the first part is devoted to a sketch of a completely finished utopia in its main features. This was
recognized in the older literature but never carefully investigated. In fact the "New Changes" conceals the curiosity of
a complete, functional utopia, comparable in its declara-

tions with the great classical models of More and Campanella, although without the brilliance of style. In its political intentions it was one of those extreme handbooks accompanying the radical wing of each of the great European revolutions, in this case one that could not be consummated. Despite its modest style this program must be evaluated in its total context, in the vertical tradition of the European utopia as well as in the horizontal political situation following the collapse of the peasant revolt and the formation of Anabaptist congregations.

Hergot's vision, or the one "he knows as a simple poor man" following an unknown author, rests on an agrarian-communist state organization including the whole world. Agrarian-communist foundations for utopian plans were advocated into the nineteenth century. Urban utopias with emphasis on manufacture originated at the beginning of the seventeenth with Johann Valentin Andreae. Thomas More, the godfather and humanist exponent of utopian modeling, provided for a two-year alternation between urban and rural residence for all citizens of his ideal state.

Hergot's projection dissolved the territories but not the towns. The focus of attention is agricultural land which in general is to be organized into "Flurgemeinden"* along the lines of the existing parishes. The population will be equalized and will all participate in agrarian production as well as in the necessary crafts, the whole under the leadership of the "Common Provider." "No one will say 'that is mine'.... It will be futile for anyone to think that he can remain in his estate."

The organization of the world state is simple but not unconvincing, seen under the premise of a utopian conception. Countries will be preserved as they are according to Hergot. They will be ruled by an official elected for life,

---

*This is not a geographical but a social designation meaning that all land will be like the medieval "common." Transl.

chosen by the Common Providers. Twelve countries together constitute a "Quarter" in the new division of the world; four Quarters will constitute the area of Latin Christendom, itself a "Tongue" or language alongside similarly organized Greek and Hebrew "Tongues." The three "tongues," or the three biblical languages, formed the framework for something like a predetermined division of the world, as it may have reflected the horizon of simple education. There is a total of 144 countries in Hergot's political world. The Quarters and the Tongues are each reigned over by an elected ruler who has nothing in common either by descent or rank with the higher nobility of Hergot's time. There are thus no rulers, kings, nor emperor in Hergot's world, but rather "Quartermasters" who are such by virtue of their economic and theological knowledge. Since a unitary government for each of the three tongues is missing, there is a "Worldmaster" who is required to know all three languages. There are no taxes in this new political order, but certain services are rendered, among them militia service. A militia seemed inevitable to Hergot, evidently for defense and to deal with rebellions.

The economic order is not quite so clear, even if we recognize in the unassuming arguments of this vision a fundamental misunderstanding for economic complexities which it shares with the most sophisticated utopias to the present day. A "certain economic backwardness" is characteristic of European utopias. Horizontal comparison would reveal the same flaw in contemporary humanist circles. German humanism in particular was preoccupied with the ideal of the peasant. It was practiced by Hugwald and Karlstadt, propagated, for example, by the clandestine printer Hans Sporer in his panegyric on peasants entitled "About the First Nobleman," and as the reform movements of the fourteenth century had already articulated it. Luther's motto "Expand agriculture and restrict commerce" expressed a widespread resentment in words.

Hergot therefore proposed extensive autonomy for the individual "Commons," and communism of production according to which "all things" should be put to "common use." Contrary to Zschäbitz, he did not exclude trade. True, this trade is primarily distributive. As in Gaismair's peasant republic, the state will determine need and surplus at annual conferences of the "Commons Providers" and the rulers. In the smallest communities there will be barter "for other wares," a point not quite consistent with the basic communistic vision. At the higher levels the state makes purchases and uses money. This is obviously where the coinage, which is parallel to the political order, relates to the whole. The coin of the Worldmaster is worth 144 times the coin of the rulers of the countries. This explains the somewhat striking interest of the communist program in a universally valid currency system, a point not too well integrated into the progression of the work.

Care for the sick and aged in Hergot's program of a universal state agrees with the basic form of the classical utopia as also does his emphasis on penal education of criminals. The analogy between the defects of the body and those of the soul which we encounter here is as important for the subject as the comparatively modest structure of thought. Remarkable for this untutored author from a Nuremberg workshop, although not for a utopian plan, is the provision for education. In its details it is superior to what the highly educated Thomas More said on the subject. Children are to be turned over to child training centers at about the third or fourth year in a solemn ritual, after which the parents commit them to the community and the hands of the Commons Provider. Henceforth boys and girls are to be trained separately and educated according to their abilities. Every twelfth young man is appointed to become a priest. Advanced education, too, is assimilated to the political hierarchy and organized according to Countries and Quarters. It is to provide the two most important social-political abilities which will in future guide the community, theology and economics. The graduates will therefore be "Scripture-wise" and "Commons-wise."

The classical European utopia had been born only ten years before in the famous book of Thomas More. It may therefore be somewhat startling to find in Hergot its basic pattern, applied in such an obviously independent manner. Upon closer examination it must be placed into a conception of that time. In no case was it "the literary-political expression of the concerns of the preproletariat" in contrast to the "communism of the urban humanists." Rather, it was the extensive consonance between intellectual projections of a total revolution and the yearning of the "little people," the poor and the underprivileged, for a totally new world which appeared in those turbulent years. The events correspond to the propaganda of Hussite chiliasm spread by lay preachers and people from the lower rungs of the university one hundred years before. To be sure, a rationally optimistic utopianism had emerged from the biblical chiliasm, not independently, but under humanist influence.

In 1960 Zschäbitz made connections between the socially critical second part of Hergot's work and Anabaptist ideas. That is correct and then again it is not, for "Anabaptist" cannot be simply defined as unitary. It was a complex collection of anxieties and yearnings of that time following the terrible example of the peasant uprising and its collapse. Frequently it is nothing more than the resignation of the "little people." On the other hand there are some striking similarities. Partly they aim at the deification of self and the world, a common, appealing constituent of popular heresy in the late Middle Ages, expressed in Hergot, for example, in the Joachimite expectation of the third age of the Spirit. In part they are filled with resentment against higher education. In the world of the "little people" this precisely disciplined knowledge is replaced by directly received complements to revealed truth in the form of visions, dreams, and revelations. These, however, often extend beyond some Anabaptist circles into the broader context of late medieval lay movements. Taken as a whole, the concept Anabaptism easily puts one in danger of missing the true intention of this revolutionary thinking about a middle state, not veiled by but filled with religious concern. "Three tables were seen in the world. . . ." With these words Hergot concludes his work, and explains in this parable that the first table "overflowed with far too much on it." The second was "medium and comfortably sufficient," and the third much too spare. Then the people at the rich table became aggressive against "those at the poor table and that is the source of the struggle." Now it is God's cause to overturn the "overflowing" table as well as the table of the poor. The middle table will be confirmed by him.

For further reading:

A. Götze und L. E. Schmitt, eds., *Johann Hergot. Von der newen wandlung eynes Christlichen lebens. Flugschriften aus der Reformationszeit*, Bd. 20, Halle, 1953, 53-64.

M. Steinmetz, ed., *Hans Hergot und die Flugschrift von der newen Wandlung eynes Christlichen Lebens.* Facsimile reprint with transcription, Leipzig, 1977.

A. Kirchhoff, "Johann Hergott, Buchführer in Nürnberg und sein tragisches Ende," *Archiv für Geschichte des Deutschen Buchhandels*, 1, 1878, 15-36.

R. Weissbach, "Bemerkungen zum ältesten gedruckten christlichkommunistischen Werk in deutscher Sprache. Über Johann Hergots, 'Von der neuen Wandlung eines christlichen Lebens,'" *Weimarer Beiträge. Zeitschrift für Literaturwissenschaft*, 15, 1969, 167-178.

G. Zschäbitz, " 'Von der newen wandlung eynes Christlichen lebens'—eine oft missgedeutete Schrift aus der Zeit nach dem Grossen Deutschen Bauernkrieg," *Zeitschrift für Geschichtswissenschaft*, 8, 1960, 908-918.

F. Seibt, *Utopica. Modelle totaler Sozialplannung*, Düsseldorf, 1972.

S. Hoyer, "Die gesellschaftlichen Hintergründe der Hinrichtung
    Hans Hergots (1527)," *Zeitschrift für Geschichtswissens-
    chaft*, 27, no. 2, 1979.
W. O. Packull, *Mysticism and the Early South German-Austrian
    Anabaptists*, Scottdale and Kitchener, 1977. (Note bib-
    liography.)

James M. Stayer

8. *Wilhelm Reublin*

A Picaresque Journey Through Early Anabaptism

Wilhelm Reublin successfully avoided martyrdom, he left behind no important writings, and he was not steadfast until the end in his Anabaptist faith. His biography is not especially edifying; thus it has not been written. The comment of the Strassburg Reformer Wolfgang Capito, that Reublin had the air of an honorable and pious man, but that he was in reality not a paragon of reliability, may serve as his epitaph. Reublin was one of the large band of university-educated priests who flocked to the Reformation full of aspirations, both to renew the gospel and to assume personal leadership. Unlike most, but like many of them, he found a third-rank status in the new establishment unacceptable and identified himself with the explosive social and religious discontent of the 1520s.

Driven by what appears 450 years later to have been a mixture of radical conviction and personal ambition, his career is the picaresque tale of a would-be leader wandering through the world of diverse social elements and religious experiences that constituted early Swiss, South German, and Moravian Anabaptism. Reublin's was a wavering compass: his Anabaptism lacked the distinctness of the faiths of Conrad Grebel, Michael Sattler, Hans Denck, Pilgram Marpeck, or Jacob Hutter, although he knew and mingled with them all. Hence his career gives a better insight into the underlying social forces, the successive phases, and the fundamental plurality of early Anabaptism than any of theirs.

Born an approximate contemporary of Luther and Zwingli in Rottenberg on the Neckar, Reublin was about forty years of age when he began to figure in the events of the Reformation. A Swabian priest who had spent some years at the universities in Freiburg and Tübingen, he was one of the first to challenge the old faith in Basel. For a few months in 1521 and 1522 his following of thousands of guildsmen excited the awe of the council. Reublin instead of Oecolampadius might have become the Reformer of Basel, but he pressed his attack on the veneration of the saints and sacrament harder and faster than the cautious city fathers were willing to tolerate. Banished from Basel, the obvious hospitable refuge for Reublin was nearby Zürich, where politically astute initiatives of the leading priest, Ulrich Zwingli, were undermining the traditional religious practices.

It was fateful that no urban preachership was available to Reublin, but that instead he found refuge in the rural community of Witikon up a mountain southward from Zürich. The religious care of this region was absentmindedly attended to by the chapter of canons of the Grossmünster, the leading Zürich church and the one where Zwingli preached. The canons of the Grossmünster, who enjoyed the incomes from the tithes paid in these rural territories, were members of Zürich's patrician families. Behind them in an increasingly prominent supervisory role stood the government of Zürich, which had exploited the corporate rights of bodies like the Grossmünster chapter to cement the beginnings of a territorial church and a territorial state among the 50,000 rural subjects of the relatively small late medieval commune of 5,000.

In the early Reformation, when it was impossible to distinguish an Erasmian from a Lutheran and when the fine points of Luther's theology were hardly understood in Wittenberg University itself, the religious renewal was understood as an attack based on the gospel against the sacrilegious usurpations of the clergy. No slogan of the early Reformation caught on so fast and well as Luther's that everyone was a priest and a bishop. Reublin and Zwingli were at one in their debunking of externalized religion, veneration of the saints, fast regulations, and clerical celibacy. Reublin was, however, a bit brasher than Zwingli, he was the first of the Zürich clerics to marry openly, at a time when Zwingli still kept his marriage a secret. (This was to avoid offense to those with weak faith, as Zwingli later explained.)

Reublin's radical identification with his rural neighbors

Peasants pelt the authorities with stones

in Witikon was sealed when on Christmas Day of the year he fled Basel they appointed him their pastor. As they undertook to support him, they began with his encouragement to refuse to send their tithe money to the Grossmünster chapter in Zürich. Reublin traveled about the neighboring villages encouraging the peasants to cease paying for the "useless and frivolous" lifestyle of the aristocratic canons in Zürich. At the same time he advised priests, monks, and nuns to marry, as he had done, and entertained the anticlerical prurience of his congregations by telling stories about masturbating nuns. In these same sermons he disabused the "pious peasants" of their false reverence for "stinking" patricians, burgomasters, and bailiffs.

For Zwingli, who had built a common interest with the ruling elite in Zürich, even while gradually purging it of his enemies, such attacks as Reublin's threatened the Zürich Reformation. This rural onslaught on the religious, social, and political prerogatives of the Zürich ruling class, which reached a peak in the summer of 1523, brought the first hint of a split in the Zürich Reformation. The clergy of the city of Zürich sided with Zwingli *en bloc*, but siding with Reublin were not only radical rural priests like Simon Stumpf and Johannes Brötli but also urban laymen like Conrad Grebel and Felix Mantz. In their view Zwingli was misled by unsavory communal political considerations, opposing the root and branch Reformation of church and society, which Reublin had begun.

Wilhelm Reublin was the first to persuade parents to refuse to submit their babies for baptism, early in 1524 in his rural sphere of influence south and east of Zürich. For him it was but another blow against the false, external religion of the pope; for the Zürich Council it was another attack upon its authority. In the decisive January 1525 debate over infant baptism, Reublin, Grebel, and Mantz led the attack against Zwingli and the urban clergy. The result was the Zürich government's banishment of Reublin from his rural parish and an order of silence against Grebel and Mantz. Zwingli's opponents responded with the introduction of the baptism of adult believers on the fateful January 21, 1525, thus creating an irreparable breach in the Swiss Reformed movement.

The exiled Reublin and his friends, however, did not immediately accept their relegation into a minority dissenting church. They tried to maintain their more radical alternatives as a pattern for that general Reformation of Christendom about which Reformers of all theological and social stripes still felt confident in the early 1520s. The year 1525 was a particularly auspicious time to broaden the appeal to the peasants which Reublin had exercised in the two previous years. Galvanized by the Reformation, which made all hierarchies totter, the peasants of Southern Germany and neighboring Switzerland raised the cry that they should be accorded the "divine justice."

Reublin and his comrade, Johannes Brötli, went directly to the storm center of peasant insurrection in Northeastern Switzerland, the village of Hallau. A community with a vigorous sense of local autonomy and an imposing collection of ecclesiastical, political, and economic grievances, it seemed an excellent base for a baptist Reformation of Northeastern Switzerland and neighboring Southwestern Germany. Hallau was situated between Schaffhausen, which held a precarious and resented political authority over it, and the Habsburg town of Waldshut. Sebastian Hofmeister, the leading priest in Schaffhausen, and Balthasar Hubmaier, the priest of Waldshut, were both leaning toward a radical Reformation which included the abolition of infant baptism. Peasant armies were springing up everywhere and had already established themselves as indispensable allies of Waldshut, while in Schaffhausen the large guild of vineyard laborers sympathized with the peasants' cause and championed the pastors' call for radical reform of the church. To Reublin and Brötli the common man and the gospel seemed joined in the same cause against all religious and political "big shots."

In Hallau almost the whole community, person for person, received baptism; and they protected the Anabaptist priests from arrest when the Schaffhausen council sent an armed band to capture them "dead or

alive." While Brötli tended to stay in Hallau, Reublin
worked for the conversion of Waldshut, where he succeeded, and of Schaffhausen, where it was such a close
thing that the ruling elite had to suppress the radical opposition by force. Ultimately this territorial form of
Anabaptism was viable only so long as the general
peasants' insurrection prospered. The successive crushing
military defeats of the German peasant armies in the late
spring gave rise to a widespread religious and social reaction. In December Waldshut submitted to the Habsburgs
and Hallau to Schaffhausen. Their radical priests took to
the road as homeless refugees. It was evident that,
whatever the Reformation meant, it did not mean a
genuinely radical transformation of Christendom. Where
these aspirations persisted, as they did for Wilhelm Reublin, they now had to assume a different form.

In early 1526, together with many other refugees of the
Peasants' War and Anabaptism, Reublin found himself in
the free, imperial city of Strassburg. Here everything still
seemed fluid; the pastors were in intimate contact with
Zwingli, but Strassburg was not Zürich. The pastors' relation to the government was tense and indefinite. They had
not made up their minds about many matters of religious
form, including infant baptism, and just as there was no
established church, so among the radicals there were no
dissenting sects, only kaleidoscopic patterns of contact and
influence. Here the most open-minded of the pastors,
Capito, dispensed hospitality and had long conversations
with men who would later become Anabaptist sect leaders.
His opinion of Reublin we have already noted. A dissident
refugee to whom he gave higher marks for constancy was
Michael Sattler. Sattler and Reublin may have known each
other previously as co-workers in the radical movement in
Zürich, but their Strassburg contact was the decisive one.
Reublin led Sattler from Strassburg to the Neckar valley,
to his birthplace, a region still under rigid Habsburg au-

thority, as the next Anabaptist mission ground.

Sattler, the former prior, was rethinking the radical Christian experience in terms of the separation of a gathered people from the temptations and wickedness of the world, thus in conceptions reminiscent of his monastic vocation. Reublin and he met with other Anabaptists from Switzerland and the empire in February 1527 at the border village of Schleitheim near Hallau, a place where Reublin had almost certainly preached in 1525. Their object was to define a radical Christian brotherhood, separated from established Reformed churches like the one at Zürich, but also from the doctrine and practice of various "false brethren" who taught the baptism of believing adults. The seven articles of Schleitheim, which decreed that genuine Christians could have no commerce with the world, with its civic oaths, its magistracy, its false worship services, implicitly repudiated the anarchic Anabaptist mass movement which Reublin led in 1525. They also severed the linkage between radical reform and the material and social concerns of the common man in the world, a theme which had preoccupied him ever since he arrived in Witikon in the fall of 1522. Now the Christian brothers could begin to think that the very creation of Christendom, a false Christendom, by the conversion of the Emperor Constantine, had marked the fall of the church.

On the way back from Schleitheim to the Neckar mission territories the traveling Anabaptists were pounced upon by Habsburg constables. Sattler and others, including Reublin's wife, were arrested, but Reublin escaped. Sattler endured a terrible and heroic martyrdom at the hands of barbarous Habsburg officials. Reublin's wife saved herself by recantation and eventually was returned to him, and Reublin wrote a pious report of the martyrdom. For the next year he stayed in the safer, Protestant jurisdictions of the Swabian imperial cities, making his headquarters at Esslingen, the home of a sizable Anabaptist congregation.

In this milieu he was exposed to new varieties of Anabaptism, to the mystical ideas of Hans Denck and, above all, to the millennial hopes of the followers of Hans Hut. Sattler, too, in his last writings had shown himself caught up in apocalyptic hope for the end of the world. The ideas of Hut's disciples that the transformation of the world was indeed before the door, that the second coming of Christ and the vengeance of the saints were to be expected in 1528, stirred the government of Esslingen to action. Again Reublin was lucky, he was ceremoniously whipped out of the city while others lost their lives.

In Esslingen and then in Strassburg, where he returned for a second stay, Reublin exercised great authority as a leader of an organized Anabaptist congregation. Imprisoned in Strassburg, he delivered the classic sectarian stricture against established Protestantism:

> Your preachers are like bad carpenters. They were able to break the pope's congregation down, but not to construct a new congregation according to Christian order.

In 1530, lame from imprisonment, banished successively from Basel, Zürich, Esslingen, and Strassburg, after repeated narrow escapes from death, Reublin, his family, and a handful of followers arrived at the ultimate Anabaptist refuge, Moravia. Here at Austerlitz a growing number of Anabaptists from all parts of Central Europe had committed themselves to a peaceful, communitarian life. Welcomed by the Moravian nobility, which profited from the industry of diligent immigrants and which cherished traditions of religious diversity dating back to the Hussite wars of more than a century earlier, these Anabaptists would seem to have offered an answer to Reublin's quest for a world transformed. Saddened by the failure of the social and religious program of 1525 and by the disappointment of the apocalyptic hopes of 1528, he must have seen Moravia as a gathering place for his

separated people. If the world could not be overcome, or
ended, at least here was a spot of territory where the new
world of Christ's kingdom might grow up in the womb of
the old, until God in his good time would transform the not
yet into the eternal now.

Alas, Austerlitz turned out to be a disappointing realization of the kingdom. Reublin explained in a letter to Pilgram Marpeck, whom he had met in his second stay in
Strassburg, that the leading elder, One-eyed Jakob
Wiedemann, had established a corrupt personal dictator-
ship there. Although possessions were supposed to be held
in common, special houses and privileges had been granted
to the rich. The government had been paid off by the submission of a tax to subsidize its war against the Turks, thus
implicating the peaceful, separated people of God in the
wars of the world. Worst of all, only persons confirmed by
One-Eyed Jakob and his elders were permitted to preach,
not people like him who had received the call of the Spirit.
Under these circumstances Reublin had no choice but to
separate the pure from the impure and to lead 250
followers in the bitterly cold January of 1531 to establish a
new community at Auspitz. (Marpeck appears to have been
unpersuaded, since he maintained fellowship with the
Anabaptists at Austerlitz.)

Reublin's leadership of "the Christian Church at
Auspitz," as he called it, was short-lived. He turned out as
dictatorial and hostile to newcomers as Wiedemann had
been. He had assembled his flock by insisting on the most
rigorous communalism, but, like the biblical Ananias, he
had withheld some of his own wealth from the common
treasure. During an illness twenty-four gold pieces were
found in his possession, and after a sober investigation
presided over by Jakob Hutter, newly arrived from the
Tyrol, he was banned and made to leave the community.
He confessed that the judgment against him was just, or so
we are told in the *Hutterite Chronicle's* humorless and un-

compassionate dismissal of all Moravian Anabaptist leaders who preceded Jakob Hutter.

The discredited leader appears to have made a last effort to gather a following in his Swabian homeland, but the deadly persecution of the Habsburg-directed Swabian League made this impossible. He returned to Moravia, where he was safe from his persecutors, but from the beginning of the 1530s his connection with Anabaptism was over. Reublin's meteoric career as a radical religious leader was the episode of one decade of his long life, his forties. He lived to almost eighty. His last three decades were spent like Voltaire's Candide, another picaresque hero, tending his own garden. Matters of business, claims to his inheritance, brought him into strange contacts with old enemies. He carried messages for Zwingli's successor as Reformer of Zürich, Heinrich Bullinger, who well remembered Reublin's role in the debate over baptism of January 1525 and included it in his history of the Swiss Reformation. He successfully petitioned to be allowed to receive his inheritance to King Ferdinand, under whose authority Michael Sattler, Balthasar Hubmaier, Jakob Hutter, and so many others, had died in the flames.

Wilhelm Reublin entered onto the Anabaptist way when it was broad and occupied by masses of people with complicated mixtures of social and religious goals. He followed it as it narrowed, but eventually it became too narrow for him, and he too impure for it. His picaresque journey through early Anabaptism was concluded, although his life continued.

For further reading:

E. Egli, *Actensammlung zur Geschichte der Zürcher Reformation in den Jahren 1519-1533*, Zürich, 1879.

L. v. Muralt and W. Schmidt, *Quellen zur Geschichte der Täufer, Bd. I, Zürich*, Zürich, 1952.

H. Fast, *Quellen zur Geschichte der Täufer, Bd. 2: Ostschweiz,* Zürich, 1973.

G. Bossert, "Die Täuferbewegung in der Herrschaft Hohenberg," *Blätter für württembergische Kirchengeschichte,* 4, 1889, and 5, 1890.

H. Fast, "Neues zum Leben Wilhelm Reublins," *Theologische Zeitschrift,* 11, 1955, 420-425.

J. F. G. Goeters, "Die Vorgeschichte des Täufertums in Zürich," in L. Abramowski and J. F. G. Goeters, *Studien zur Geschichte und Theologie der Reformation. Festschrift für Ernst Bizer,* Neukirchen-Vluyn 1969, 239-281.

M. Haas, "Der Weg der Täufer in die Absonderung. Zur Interdependenz von Theologie und sozialem Verhalten," in *Umstrittenes Täufertum,* 50-78.

J. M. Stayer, "Reublin and Brötli: The Revolutionary Beginnings of Swiss Anabaptism," in M. Lienhard, *The Origins and Characteristics of Anabaptism/Les débuts et les caractéristiques de l'anabaptisme,* Den Haag 1977, 83-102.

9. Conrad Grebel

The Covenant on the Cross

As one walks through medieval Zürich one can see an inscription on the stately mansion at number 5 in the Neumarkt: "This was the residence of Conrad Grebel, who together with Felix Mantz founded Anabaptism." The inscription, put there on the occasion of the Mennonite World Conference in 1952, epitomizes that view of the beginnings of Anabaptism which was to emerge from the work of historians on the basis of new source discoveries and from the controversy with the polemical confessionalism of earlier centuries, namely that the Anabaptist movement of the sixteenth century did not have its beginnings in Thomas Müntzer nor its climax in the Anabaptist kingdom of Münster. Its origins were in Zürich; it developed in the womb of the Zwinglian Reformation, received its character, clearly distinguished from Spiritualists and enthusiasts from Zwingli's disciples Conrad Grebel and Felix Mantz, and became a third option, the first Protestant "free church," alongside of the two great Protestant churches.

In fact, already during the Reformation, down to about 1550, Grebel and Mantz were regarded as the founders of Anabaptism by theologians and historians in Switzerland. Grebel occupied a unique position insofar as he was known as "the first Anabaptist." He had, after all, rebaptized the priest Jörg Blaurock on January 21, 1525, and thus launched Anabaptism. Zwingli called him Coryphaeus, the ringleader of the Anabaptists. But Felix Mantz, too, uniquely impressed his contemporaries. He was the first Anabaptist to suffer a martyr's death in Zürich. By putting them at the head of the Anabaptist movement, historical inquiry of our century established the main theological supports of Anabaptism, believers' baptism and the readiness to suffer. Central articles of faith were the congregational principle and discipleship. Grebel and Mantz, the cofounders of the movement, thus exemplified the content of Anabaptist faith.

Since then research has taken the next step in developing a more differentiated picture of the Anabaptist movement. Not only are the non-Zürich factors in the development of the several variants of Anabaptism given attention again, but the development in Zürich itself has become visible in the variety of persons involved as well as in the unfolding of its energy on several levels succeeding each other. Men like Simon Stumpf, Wilhelm Reublin, Jörg Blaurock, Johannes Brötli, and others have gained in importance alongside of Grebel and Mantz. Their goals and the style of their participation were significantly different from one another.

The beginning of "the new baptism" was indeed marked by the first rebaptism on January 21, 1525. The expectations associated with it, however, ran along widely separated paths. Besides, it was likely not Grebel but Jörg Blaurock who started the ball rolling that night when he was the first to request baptism, and then himself baptized the others. Still, he received baptism from Grebel, and that fact underscored the latter's prominence in the company of the first Anabaptists. However, this prominence can only be described with appropriate care if one does not begin with the finished portrait of a church founder.

The role of Grebel in the storm of the Reformation in Zürich began with several spectacular scenes in the summer of 1522. On these occasions he did not hesitate to browbeat the recusant clergy or to put pressure on the still hesitating government, all for the sake of the gospel. He attended the preaching of monks with three supporters and interrupted the sermons whenever they defended the veneration of saints. When he was thereupon summoned before the Small Council and called a devil by recusant council members, he flung the epithet back at them, and warned the Council not to frustrate the advance of the gospel. He banged the door as he left the Council Chamber. Soon after others who were of his mind gathered in a house owned by Grebel's father outside the city called Oberhof to organize a one-day rally with drink and food in one of the guildhouses or on the Lindenhof. It was planned that all who listened to Zwingli and the gospel with favor should meet for "a meal with one another in pleasant brotherly love." By this means they anticipated the conversion of those who were not yet fully committed to the gospel. When the rumor spread that about 500 persons from city and country were expected, the Council intervened and vetoed the plans.

In these actions Grebel proved himself to be an unconditional adherent of Zwingli. Five years earlier, when he was still a student in Vienna, Zwingli had made contact with him by letter. Closer relations between the two had developed when Grebel again lived in Zürich after mid-1520 following his abortive two years as a student in Paris. At that time he studied Greek language and literature with a group under Zwingli's guidance, but then his interests still had a purely humanist cast. Not until the spring of 1522 did he experience the decisive turn toward the gospel which Zwingli preached. It was a personal conversion which turned his life in a new direction. Until now this promising son of a Zürich patrician had had to put up with bitter disappointments in his search for education and material security; now his eyes were fixed on a clear goal. He committed himself to it with his whole life and with no consideration for the reputation of his name and family. At the age of only 24 years he became a dedicated partisan of Zwingli in the work of the Reformation in Zürich.

Grebel, however, was only one of several who clearly declared themselves as they fought against the old procedures and conceptions and fought for Zwingli's

The Grossmünster in Zürich
(sixteenth century)

Reformation. His collaborators, who with him had been made responsible for the sermon interruptions, were the shoemaker Klaus Hottinger and the two bakers Heinrich Aberli and Bartlime Pur. All three had participated in the meat-eating episode in Lent 1522, an event that had caused a public sensation because it was seen as a protest. Others mentioned at this early stage were the weaver Lorenz Hochrütiner, the carpenter Wolfgang Ininger, and the tailor Hans Ockenfuss. It was a group of Zürich artisans who had been persuaded by Zwingli's preaching and who, like Grebel, indeed preceding him, had given it their total support at considerable personal risk. Grebel played a special role among them because he had received a better education as son of a patrician. That is likely why Grebel did not participate, when in the spring of 1523 these artisans met for regular Bible study under the leadership of Andreas Castelberger, studying the letters of Paul, and discussing matters of Christian teaching. However, in autumn 1523 he was there. "In this group, a lay movement gathered around the New Testament ... we may see the cradle of Anabaptism among the Anabaptists of Zürich" (J. F. G. Goeters).

Indeed, the challenging actions of the radical disciples of Zwingli contributed to the decision of the First Zürich Disputation of January 1523 that the gospel and the Scriptures were to be the basis for preaching and church management. During 1523 the concern was to carry out this decision. The debate between Zwingli and this group of his disciples erupted around three issues: the questions of the tithe, images, and the sacrifice of the mass. Tensions developed in public dispute and finally into a schism. The letters of Grebel to his brother-in-law Vadian in St. Gall, and his personal appearance at the Second Zürich Disputation in October 1523, document the fatal development step by step.

At the beginning there was agreement about the necessity, basis, and content of reform, as well as about the method of execution. It was expected that the renewal would obviously be carried through by the city government. Consequently, the aim was to win the government for the implementation of the reforms. Zwingli and his supporters, including Grebel, agreed on this. Most likely they also agreed that there would be some resistance from the government; they had after all already had considerable experience of that, but it had also been overcome. The unanimity broke down over the question of the point at which the resistance or hesitation of the government would become intolerable. Zwingli had more patience on this issue than Grebel and his friends. During the six months from June to December 1523 the limit of tolerance was reached in the eyes of Grebel and his partisans on all three issues under discussion. The working partnership broke down, and the Reformation in Zürich was ruptured.

Diverging explanations of the break were offered by both sides. From Grebel's point of view Zwingli had betrayed the gospel he had preached so convincingly. He had made harmful compromises, and had surrendered the truth to a government that was an enemy of the gospel. Zwingli's view of the meaning of the break was that his confidence in the power of the divine Word, his faith and his hope, had been put in doubt by his closest friends. When the break had become obvious at the end of the Second Zürich Disputation, Zwingli could not hold back tears. Today's historians tend to explain the difference psychologically and we will present the legitimate arguments for this position below. But it should be considered that, if divergent decisions about concrete action flowed from the same theological presuppositions, this may be rooted in the difficulty of the theological problems of this process of perception and decision.

The break with Zwingli was the occasion for examination of their own position by Grebel and his companions. The result appeared nine months later in September and October 1524 in the letter of Grebel to Thomas Müntzer. It testifies to continuing extensive dependence on Zwingli, but nevertheless reveals a totally different pattern. These laymen had themselves set about to study the Scriptures. They were certain about what the learned had neglected to say or had taught perversely. As before, the issue was still the fearless preaching of God's Word and the execution of the new order based on the Word alone. They were confident that Holy Scripture "has more than enough of wisdom and counsel" "how all estates and all people shall be taught, governed, guided and made into believers." As with Zwingli, the gospel had universal application. But it was no longer "bound to rulers." Believers were called upon to be obedient to the Word of God and to build a Christian congregation independent of government. This was to happen without coercion, alone through the Word of God and the measures compatible with it. Whoever is contrary "is not to be killed, but is to be regarded as a pagan and tax-gatherer and allowed to remain such." Christians are not to suppress such pagans but to be with them without protection. For "the Gospel and those who accept it are not to be protected with the sword and they themselves are also not to do it." "True believing Christians are sheep among the wolves," and "must be baptized in anxiety and distress, tribulation, persecution, suffering and death." Nor can it be otherwise, for, beyond his own physical suffering, Christ must "suffer still more in his members."

The totally different direction of this thinking was not derived from the attending new views on baptism. Rather, it was a consequence of replacing the hope for reformation by means of the government, which Grebel had until now shared with Zwingli, with the hope of a reformation from below carried by the "poor in spirit" whose strength is the suffering of Christ. "In the course of time we will also see persecution coming on us from them [i.e., the preachers]."

It was thus only a small group. "We are not twenty who believe the Word of God." However, "it is much better that a few be taught by the Word of God, truly believe and live by the virtues and (primitive Christian) order, than that many believe through false teaching and hypocritically." These are the constituents of a different view of the church, illustrated by the descriptions of the Lord's Supper, baptism, payment of preachers, and church disciplines. These prescriptions were not propagated for their own sake but because they were integral to the "calling and being" of the brethren of Christ in the world. It would in fact be possible to call this free church congregationalism, provided that the conception of a free church is understood in terms of the "master and head" whose "covenant on the Cross," according to Grebel, obligates all members of the body of Christ to undertake discipleship, free from all self-assertion by means of worldly power. This understanding, however, appeared at that time to be the view of Grebel and his most intimate companions rather than of all who attacked infant baptism.

And that is precisely the reason why the first "rebaptism" by Grebel on January 21, 1525, was not identical with the founding of an Anabaptist free church. Certainly the Anabaptist movement began at that point. But the sign of baptism still represented quite different interests and understandings.

The Anabaptist movement became the haven after January 21, 1525, not only for the little groups around Grebel, Mantz, and Castelberger, which was disappointed in Zwingli, and pushed to one side by him.

Important in the formation of the Anabaptist movement alongside these Zürich Anabaptists were a group of priests who were working in parishes near Zürich as radical disciples of Zwingli. They were Simon Stumpf in Höngg, Wilhelm Reublin in Witikon, and Johannes Brötli in Zollikon. Not only had they joined in the propagation and realization of individual reforms such as the question of the tithe, clerical benefices, marriage of priests, the sacrifice of the mass, and images, regardless of consequences, and with signal success. They had also been able to win their parishes as a whole for the Reformation long before Zwingli was able to gain the full support of the Council in Zürich. In their agitation for reform they had taken advantage of the catastrophic economic plight of the peasants and their dissatisfaction with political conditions which was soon to lead to the peasant revolt. The opposition to the Reformation did not come from the village parishes themselves, but from outside, namely, from the ecclesiastical and political governing bodies.

The first refusals to baptize infants occurred in these parishes in early summer 1524. There was as yet no thought of changing to a "believers' church," but only of rejecting the unbiblical form of the sacrament. Actually, the Reformation happened as Grebel had hoped it would in Zürich and as Zwingli still expected it—that is, that it would be carried out not by a minority but by the whole civic community.

When the first rebaptism took place in Zürich, the Reformation split into three parts. Not only were Zwingli and the Anabaptists now opposed to each other. Within the Anabaptist movement itself the two goals were present, the "free church" and the reformed parish church, nonresistance and the readiness to use the sword. The letters of Grebel continued to express the consciousness of proceeding along a path marked by the cross of Christ. At the same time Anabaptist civic churches came into being in Hallau and Schaffhausen under the leadership of Reublin and Brötli, in Tablat near St. Gall under Krüsi, and in Waldshut under Hubmaier. In these instances whole parishes or towns adopted Anabaptism, but they were prepared to attempt defense of this Anabaptist Reformation with force in the spirit of Zwingli. This is what the historian James M. Stayer has in mind when he writes about the "beginnings of Anabaptism in a reformed congregationalism." This, too, was reform beginning at the grass roots. However, it assumed that the Christian congregation has the right and the competence to maintain itself by means of secular power.

The common opposition to Zwingli in the struggle over the true baptism did not allow the difference between the two Anabaptist alternatives to become visible. They were not aware of the contradiction in their own camp. Individual Anabaptists appear on one side, then on the other. It is often impossible for the historian to identify them clearly with one of the alternatives. He is working with a movement which had to clarify its identity both internally and externally during the first year of its history. This took place, on the one hand through the consistent failure of Anabaptist attempts to maintain themselves by means of secular power. The theology of self-maintenance failed. On the other hand, those Anabaptists who were ready to suffer lost the possibility of working publicly after the third public disputation with Zwingli in October 1525, and had to go underground. They understood this as confirmation of the rightness of their way. A martyr theology is proved by martyrdom, and this was precisely what Grebel had predicted for himself and those with him.

The importance of Grebel in the context of this development therefore is that he developed a conception of Christian faith after his break with Zwingli which realistically calculated the consequences of independence from political power. It was for him Christ's "covenant on the Cross." During the short time which remained to him between the first baptism and his arrest on October 8, 1525, he bore this out in tireless activity. He sold his books, risked complete separation from his wife, children, and parents, and became a traveling evangelist in Schaffhausen, Waldshut, St. Gall, and the Zürich Oberland. The imprisonment in Grüningen and then in Zürich of Grebel and the other Anabaptists must have seemed to Grebel as the climax of his life, for the authorities had determined to simply "let them die in the tower" if they would not recant. When on March 21, 1526, they were able to escape through the negligence of the prison guard, they hesitated because they wanted to "die in the tower." In fact, their freedom no longer proved to be of any use. Grebel died soon after, presumably in May or June 1526 in Maienfeld in the Grisons of the plague.

Quite another way of interpreting the life of Grebel which can be documented from the sources is the psychological explanation. A characteristic of Grebel that has often been noticed was his impetuous manner, his biting criticism of others, his legalism, and his overrating of the importance of secondary issues. It is not by accident that these character traits have been connected to his almost continuously tense relationship with his father. In the eyes of his son, Grebel senior was totally arbitrary and full of selfishness and dishonesty, and thus, particularly because of his position on the Small Council, a master without authority. The letters from Conrad Grebel's student days in Paris 1518-1520 clearly reveal the weaknesses caused by obvious repressions. We read about sexual license, drunkenness, and partly self-inflicted poverty. With other Swiss students he belonged to a group who killed two Frenchmen in nationalistic fervor. He had a violent quarrel with his humanist teacher, Glarean, whose acquaintance he had made earlier during his first years in Basel, and whom he held in high honor. Afflicted by a number of illnesses, those he experienced at this time he considered extremely ill-starred. Thus, when he returned to Zürich, he experienced his conversion to the gospel as Zwingli preached it, against that background as rescue from a shipwreck, as salvation from a sinful life, and as an obligation to a rigorous ethic.

The same thing, however, that clouded his relationship to Glarean, now repeated itself in his relationship to

Zwingli. He could assert himself over against this father figure only by surpassing it. Since the personal conditions made that impossible, it could happen only as a rupture. This also happened soon after to his relationship to his teacher and brother-in-law Vadian in St. Gall. The most bewildering aspect of the continuity of this fundamental psychological structure is Conrad Grebel's death instinct. In the face of the plague and the miserable conditions in Paris he wrote in 1520: "Even if I don't actually call for death, I am not terrified if he approaches the one prepared to meet Christ. So much ... has befallen him, that I could not wish for a longer life from the gods for any return whatever." In view of the unhappy relationship to his father and other friends he said: "I surrender myself to the torture of fate and the gods until their raging against me ceases once I am dead." In the same year he saw his current situation captured by a proverb: "I clutch the wolf by the ears while I stand between the victim and the knife." About his future he writes: "I will have the feelings and habits of an actor in an average tragedy." These expressions correspond to others five years later when he announced his readiness to suffer as a Christian, for example, his threat against Vadian: "If you give in, I will give my life for you. If you do not give in, I will give it for these brothers.... I will make a witness through imprisonment, exile, and death...." When Grebel was arrested for fomenting unrest in the Zürich Oberland on October 8, 1525, Zwingli stated succinctly: "Supplied with plenty of evil omens he always pursued tragedy; now he has it."

Can it be that Grebel's theology of martyrdom, his passion for the gospel, his break with Zwingli, and his defense of a church according to the New Testament model were merely the working out of a given psychological dynamic? One cannot answer that question without making a judgment about Grebel's understanding of Christian faith, which everyone will have to decide personally in theory and practice. Acceptance of Grebel's view of Christian faith does not, however, require the rejection of the psychological and therefore thoroughly human substructure of the man. He felt an obligation for the "poor in spirit," and personally experienced that the treasure of the gospel is contained "in earthen vessels."

Grebel's influence can be seen on several levels and varies in its extent. As the first "baptizer" he has his place at the beginning of the extensive Mennonite and Baptist movement. As advocate of the separation of church and state he is the forerunner of a worldwide family of free churches which, to be sure, having largely discarded the theology of suffering, lives in favorably adapted relationships with the secular authorities. Grebel's concept of the church was restated in Michael Sattler's Schleitheim Articles of 1527 without modification, and gave to the Anabaptist group called the Swiss Brethren their ecclesiological foundation. Grebel's duality of church and world, however, was overlaid in the Articles with a fundamental dualism which permanently fixed the separation into which the congregations were now forced. Finally, "the covenant on the Cross," adopted by Grebel with such intense seriousness, enrolls him in that cloud of witnesses, whose importance does not consist in creation of confessional groups and borders, but rather in their participation in the ways of Jesus Christ.

For further reading:

E. Egli, *Aktensammlung zur Geschichte der Zürcher Reformation in den Jahren 1519-1533*, Zürich, 1879, reprint 1973.

L. von Muralt and W. Schmidt, *Quellen zur Geschichte der Täufer*: Bd. I: Zürich, Zürich, 1952.

H. Fast, *Quellen zur Geschichte der Täufer, Bd. II: Ostschweiz*, Zürich, 1973.

Harold S.Bender, *Conrad Grebel*, Scottdale, 1950, second printing 1971.

John Ruth, *Conrad Grebel: Son of Zürich*, Scottdale, 1975.

Leland Harder, *Grebeliana*, Scottdale, 1983.

Fritz Blanke, *Brothers in Christ*, Scottdale, 1961; second printing 1975.

James M. Stayer, "The Swiss Brethren: An Exercise in Historical Reflection," *Church History* 47(1978), 174-195.

James M. Stayer, "Reublin and Brötli: the Revolutionary Beginnings of Swiss Anabaptism," in Marc Lienhard, ed., *The Origins and Characteristics of Anabaptism*, The Hague, 1977.

L. v. Muralt, "Konrad Grebel als Student in Paris." *Zürcher Taschenbuch auf das Jahr 1937*, 57. Jg., 1936, 113-136.

H. Fast, "Hans Krüsis Büchlein über Glaube und Taufe. Ein Täuferdruck von 1525," *Zwingliana*, 11, 1962, 456-475.

P. Klassen, "Zwingli and the Zürich Anabaptists," in M. Geiger, *Gottesreich und Menschenreich, E. Staehelin zum 80. Geburtstag*, Basel und Stuttgart 1969, 197-210.

J. F. G. Goeters, "Die Vorgeschichte des Täufertums in Zürich" in L. Abramowski and J. F. G. Goeters, *Studien zur Geschichte und Theologie der Reformation. Festschrift für Ernst Bizer*, Neukirchen, 1969.

J. M. Stayer, "Die Anfänge des schweizerischen Täufertums im reformierten Kongregationalismus," in *Umstrittenes Täufertum*, 19-49.

H. Fast, "Reformation durch Provokation. Predigstörungen in den ersten Jahren der Reformation in der Schweiz," in *Umstrittenes Täufertum*, 79-110.

R. C. Walton, *Zwingli's Theocracy*, Toronto, 1967.

10. Michael Sattler

On the Way to Anabaptist Separation

Michael Sattler is one of the figures of the Reformation era who is difficult to characterize biographically. We are well informed only through extant theological writings of his later years. These include, in the main, the Schleitheim Confession and his farewell letter to the Strassburg theologians, along with his letter to the congregation at Horb. They witness to a surprising theological maturity, and have become of fundamental significance for later Anabaptism. Otherwise, our bits of knowledge are surprisingly meager, including those found in the public record.

Sattler, who came from the town of Staufen in Breisgau (Baden), entered Saint Peter's Monastery in the Black Forest, where a promising career obviously awaited him. He advanced to the office of prior. However, the Reformation affected him powerfully, and he left the order and married. For reasons which elude us, he then made his way to Zürich. It may be that he was attracted by Wilhelm Reublin. Reublin had for several years been a zealous Reformer in Witikon.

It is as good as certain that Sattler joined the young Anabaptist movement as early as February or March 1525. On March 25, along with other nonresident Anabaptists, a "Brother Michael with the white coat" was expelled from the town by the Council of Zürich. A short time before, a disputation had been held with a large group of prisoners, to induce them to renounce their Anabaptist faith. This first large Anabaptist congregation had emerged in the village of Zollikon, beyond the city gates of Zürich. At that time Michael Sattler renounced his Anabaptist faith and left the canton. Soon thereafter, however, he changed his mind and returned to his Zürich brethren. In any case, by November he was again in the custody of the Town Council, and was forced to take part in a new disputation. Obviously his contacts with Grebel, Mantz, and Blaurock had impressed him too deeply for him to have been able to disavow his original Anabaptist convictions.

The congregation which had to defend itself before the magistracy in November had temporarily established itself in the Zürich Oberland, primarily in the jurisdiction of Grüningen. There it had grown into a veritable mass movement, which Michael Sattler too had joined.

After this Anabaptist center of activity was also eliminated through governmental measures, the movement shifted to the Zürich Unterland. Bülach and environs became a new major center, with outreach extending as far as the jurisdiction of Baden. Sattler, upon his release from prison, also became active in this geographic area. In addition to Mantz and Blaurock, who were soon imprisoned, the leaders were Pfistermeyer, Muntprat of Constance, Konrad of Wassberg, Karl Brennwald, and Michael Sattler. It will be noted below that those cell groups in the Zürich Unterland contrasted markedly with earlier congregational formations.

Sattler, who possessed a good theological education, was not content to circulate only among the simple peasants here; he turned to his peers and attempted to convert them. Thus he appeared suddenly in Strassburg, where he established contact with Capito and Bucer. Yet the Strassburg Reformers continued to hold to their previous position, and so toward the end of 1526 or early 1527 Sattler decided to leave town.

At that time Sattler went either to South Germany or back to the Zürich Unterland, ultimately appearing at the

Anabaptist meeting in Schleitheim am Randen as a central figure, where on February 24, 1527, he apparently drafted the Schleitheim Confession. Since he also had connections with the Anabaptists in Rottenburg and Horb, he turned again to South Germany, where he shared leadership responsibilities with Wilhelm Reublin. Soon, however, Sattler and his wife were apprehended, along with many other congregational brethren. Court proceedings were brought against the group, resulting in execution on May 20, 1527.

The task of incorporating these facts into the backdrop of the early Anabaptist movement now lies before us. The history of early Swiss Anabaptism can be sketched here only with a few broad strokes which suggest certain essential characteristics.

One such stroke is the striving toward universality. Following the first adult baptism in Zürich on January 21, 1525, it became apparent that the Town Council and Zwingli were taking vigorous steps, seeking to quell the movement. But the Anabaptist leaders were not intimidated and refused to be coerced into becoming a small opposition group. Since they were for the most part educated men, they intended to mobilize a comparable following open to their ideas outside of Zürich.

Grebel and Reublin turned immediately to Schaffhausen, attempting to win over the local theological doctors Meier and Hofmeister. Later, Grebel also went to St. Gall, to influence Vadian. Reublin found his way to Waldshut, where he baptized Hubmaier. The latter set his sights on Basel, in order to find adherents there. Michael Sattler too may have thought along this line when he later turned to the theologians in Strassburg.

These attempts, however, were not crowned with much success, because Zwingli decided at once to oppose the Anabaptist movement via a vigorous publishing program, and sent his writings to all authoritative quarters of the confederacy. In addition the Zürich Council left no doubt that it would not tolerate the new Anabaptist movement. It persecuted Anabaptist adherents, and encouraged governmental colleagues in other surrounding towns to persecute them also.

When Mantz and Grebel were finally forced to transfer their activities to the Zürich Oberland, they already had alienated themselves from the major centers of political power. Even with the support of the peasants, the most that could now be hoped for was to establish an opposition movement. This, however, had not been the original Anabaptist intent.

**Brüderliche vereyni=
gung etzlicher kinder Gottes/
siben Artickel betreffend.**

**Item/Eyn sendtbrieff Michel sat=
laß/an eyn gemeyn Gottes/sampt kurtz
em/doch warhafftigem anzeyg/wie
er seine leer zu Rottenburg am
Necker/mitt seinem blut
bezeuget hat.**

M. D. XXvij.

Title page of the Schleitheim Articles (1527)

Another essential characteristic was the mass movement. Whereas the group in Zollikon was still operating in

a locally confined geographic area, in the region of Schaffhausen and in the environs of St. Gall and Appenzell,
Anabaptism developed into far broader, scattered movements.

To be sure, adult baptism there remained as only one of
several characterizing features. Other streams emerged
which determined the life of these Anabaptist groupings.
The principle one was anticlericalism. The Anabaptists demanded that the minister be chosen by the congregation,
and abstain from collecting all fixed land revenues. The
basis of his existence was to be the trade in which he was
engaged, along with voluntary contributions from the congregation. The education of the minister on the other hand
was of lesser import.

In this manner Anabaptism came close to evolving into a
mass movement—the Peasants' War. In fact the unlettered
lay person found it difficult to differentiate between
Anabaptist concerns and general ferment vis-à-vis the
clerical class. In this way the situation developed into
resistance movements, operating simultaneously on
several levels, which grouped themselves around Anabaptism, and in which the Anabaptist leaders also participated. The use of armed force in this way harmonized in
every way with the everyday life of the Anabaptists.

After the magistracy had with utmost determination
quelled such attempts of resistance and was again able to
establish law and order, the great majority of the rebels ac-
quiesced, and submitted to the demands of power. Only
those remained loyal to the movement who were confident
in their own theological views, who recognized dogmatic
differences with Zwingli, and who refused to be moved by
outward circumstances.

Along with these changed conditions, essential characteristics within Anabaptism which had earlier been at
most only intimated now became dominant. They had been
developed by Grebel and Mantz earlier, but had disap-

peared in the whirlpool of the mass movement. These new characteristics branded Anabaptism increasingly as a minority group; they outlined the road to separation, which now was consciously chosen.

Prohibition of the oath is foremost among these characteristics. In the letter of the Grebel circle to Müntzer there was as yet nothing on this theme, and there is little trace of this as an Anabaptist postulate during the beginning months of the movement. When the first Anabaptists of Zollikon were imprisoned and cross-examined, they were ready and willing to swear an oath, that in the future they would no longer baptize. Michael Sattler also was of this view. Yet even at that time, a few held to another view. Mantz, in particular, refused to swear. And in the further developments, the broader the dissemination of the refusal to render an oath (and it was promoted by the work of Grebel, Mantz, and Blaurock), the closer the whole movement tended toward political separatism, for the oath was the form which reinforced the whole of the political and legal fabric.

The use of the sword also underwent a transformation. Whereas there was initially a general tendency toward violence, the demand for an emphasis on pacifism was now increasingly stressed. To be sure, it took some time until this direction became programmatic in Anabaptism. For example, Hubmaier held firmly to the use of the sword, and the Schleitheim Confession speaks of the need to separate from those groups which affirmed the use of the sword. From this point on, the view could more easily be espoused that a Christian had no place in magisterial structures. Earlier in Waldshut, and also in St. Gall, there had been Anabaptists who participated in the town council, and who could reconcile such participation completely with their faith. But now, since the movement in general had already taken the form of an opposition group, this question was no longer of practical importance for Anabaptism. For

its adherents it was clear that they could never work their
way into a magisterial function.

Changes of view in the area of tithes and interest also
held a significant place on the path to Anabaptist separation. Even in the summer of 1525 in Grüningen (earlier,
also, in Hallau and in East Switzerland) many peasants of
Anabaptist persuasion placed unusual weight upon refus-
ing to pay tithes, and saw therein the essential attraction
of the movement. Meanwhile, the pace-setting Anabaptist
leaders themselves attempted to disassociate themselves
from this segment. Blaurock stated this pointedly in
Grüningen: Those who refused to pay tithes were not
Anabaptists; those who were, paid them. It fit exactly into
the pattern of nonresistance, of suffering in relation to the
world, and of separation from the unchristian magistracy,
to separate from those in whose sincerity they could not
believe. The principals of the events in the domain of
Grüningen were incarcerated in the autumn of 1525 and
taken to Zürich. Michael Sattler was among them, and so it
is obvious that he experienced at firsthand the transformation of the Anabaptist congregation.

One of the characteristics of the Anabaptists was the attempt to make the Anabaptist church visible for its
adherents—tangible, so to speak, with outward signs of
solidarity. The Anabaptists, for example, avoided costly
clothing, preferred coarse cloth, and wore broad felt hats.
They disdained expensive food and drink, and in general
their ways suggested humility. They carried neither sword
nor dagger, at the most a broken-off bread knife. These
signs may be taken as the expression of a minority group
that wanted to continue to exist, persecution notwithstanding. In addition, these signs were to promote the consciousness of fellowship and brotherhood. The parameters of
such norms were given in the Bible.

In order to demonstrate that Anabaptists no longer had
anything to do with the world, they no longer greeted any

outsider they would meet. Of course, this also meant no common living quarters, and no common meals with people of the world.

The most important way to make the fellowship conscious and visible to the members, and the obvious basis for separation from the world, was the collective church discipline. Originally, few differences had existed between them and Zwingli in this area. Meanwhile, however, Zürich had introduced its divorce-court laws which gave rise to Anabaptist criticism on two counts. First of all, the organization of the divorce courts completely aligned itself with the magisterial powers, especially after the second mandate of 1526. The functionaries ruled, and the common people at the bottom were excluded. Second, mandates affecting social norms were introduced in 1526, insofar as they went beyond the traditional forms at hand before the Reformation. In keeping with the low levels of participation of the populace, the short-term effects upon the quality of life remained insignificant.

Parallel to this, Anabaptist efforts concentrated on a better church discipline within their own ranks. Few sources grant insights into the introduction of the ban within the Anabaptist church. The determination henceforth to organize a church discipline among themselves surfaced in Zollikon in March 1525. Jakob Hottinger stated to the whole congregation that whoever submitted to baptism and thereafter fell into wickedness would from that point on be punished with the ban in accordance with Scripture. Mantz and Grebel had this in mind in November when at a cross-examination they also demanded that misers, usurers, gamblers, adulterers, and others who were listed in the Bible were not to be tolerated in the congregation. That at that time the ban was actually administered is substantiated in *Kessler's Chronicle*. The zeal with which this disciplinary measure was applied led without doubt to a rapid cleansing of the group. It also sharpened the distance from the world around them which they perceived as being wicked.

In the course of this tendency toward separation, attitudes also changed toward the worship services of the established church. Within the earliest Anabaptist era, church services were interrupted with a view to winning over the whole congregation. Blaurock's acts of interrupting the preachers are examples of this. Then came the counter-movement. As early as March 1525 an Anabaptist in Zollikon decided not to attend the service, because nothing had actually changed in the church. This view spread. By March 1526 the Anabaptists had clarified their position. The fellowship determined not to attend public services anymore, for it was afraid of being led astray by false teachers. With this step, however, the movement came full circle. In order to maintain their own convictions unwaveringly, they remained to themselves. When an Anabaptist suggested that the local minister be invited for discussions within their group, he was excommunicated by means of the ban. Anabaptists also refused to attend the formal communion service, for all the sinners partook of it without the punishment of the ban, and without demonstrating repentance or remorse. Yet known sinners had no right to the table of the Lord. It would not have been possible to drink the common cup with them.

These broadly sketched characteristics will need to suffice. The conclusion is that this church had not completed its development in Zollikon, nor in the domain of Grüningen, nor in the area of Schaffhausen, nor in the region of St. Gall/Appenzell.

The first Anabaptist church, in which all of these essential characteristics were present, was located in the Zürich Unterland. Indeed, it was there that Michael Sattler was directly involved as one of their teachers. Mantz, and also for a short time Blaurock, were active there with him, but especially Konrad of Wassberg and Muntprat of Constance. Mantz was, however, soon apprehended, and executed in early 1527. In accordance with his level of education, it fell to Sattler at this point to become the spiritual head of the church, and to formulate definitively its theological foundations.

Against this background it becomes clear exactly how significant a place Michael Sattler held as a theologian of Anabaptism: after the first leaders had all been expelled or executed, he formulated anew the basis of faith of the movement, according to the way this faith had gradually developed in practice. In this way the Schleitheim Confession, which gathered together all of these new aspects of Anabaptism, became the real point of its crystalization. The document formulated for the first time those elements which later, within the whole of the Anabaptist movement, would define the essence of the Swiss Brethren.

In keeping with the historical transformations within Anabaptism, certain emphases in the Schleitheim Confession differ from the earlier writings of Grebel and Mantz. Whereas there was little change in the views on baptism, the ban, and congregational structures, a long new segment was now composed on separation where, in one new turn of expression after another, the idea was impressed upon the congregations that children of light had nothing to do with the dead works of darkness. There was to be no fellowship with those on the outside, for Christ and Belial could have nothing in common with one another.

The idea of "separation from the world," which is so clearly established in the Schleitheim Confession, is also to be found in other extant writings of Sattler. The epistle that he sent to the Strassburg Reformers addressed itself in its theological theses for the most part with the theme of separation from the world. The devil is a prince of the world; Christ, a prince of the spirit. The devil seeks to destroy; Christ, to save. In this way the conflict between flesh and spirit becomes a fight between evil and good, between the world and the believer, between light and darkness, between Christ and Belial.

The idea of separation from evil is expressed with unusually strong emphasis in the epistle to the congregation at Horb. It is a warning to beware of unbelievers on the outside, of worthless servants, of those whose hearts are thoroughly lazy and indolent. In addition there is a clearly defined expectation of the end times. The small flock of believers will experience death, cross, suffering, prison, and self-abnegation. The nearness of the end times is outspokenly affirmed: "For the time of threshing is close at hand. The abomination of desolation is evident among you. God's chosen servants and maids will be marked on their foreheads with the name of their Father. The world is being provoked against those who are being saved from their errors. The Gospel will be proclaimed throughout the whole world. After that it will be urgent that the Day of the Lord no longer tarry."

Without doubt, the whole endeavor of separating from the world and of persevering as a faithful remnant until the Day has come, is to be seen from the perspective of this apocalyptic expectation of the imminent coming of the end. Despite all the biblicism inherent essentially in the basic characteristics of Sattler's theology, ecstatic elements can also be seen in his congregation, such as during a baptismal service, when a believer, in recognition of his human weakness, beat his head bloody, began to weep, and finally requested the symbol of baptism. Ecstasy and apocalyptic visions waned within later Swiss Anabaptism; the idea of separation, however, had been defined by Sattler so conclusively that it continued to set the direction of the Swiss Brethren through the centuries.

For further reading:

B. Jenny, *Das Schleitheimer Täuferbekenntnis 1527*, Thayngen, 1951.

J. H. Yoder, ed., *The Legacy of Michael Sattler*, Scottdale, Pa., 1973.

_____, "Der Kristallisationspunkt des Täufertums," *Mennonitische Geschichstblätter*, 24, 1972, 35-47.

K. Deppermann, "Die Strassburger Reformatoren und die Krise des oberdeutschen Täufertums im Jahre 1527," ibid., 25, 1973, 24-41.

M. Hass, "Der Weg der Täufer in die Absonderung. Zur Interdependenz von Theologie und sozialem Verhalten," in *Umstrittenes Täufertum*, 50-78.

C. Arnold Snyder, "Rottenburg Revisited: New Evidence Concerning the Trial of Michael Sattler," *Mennonite Quarterly Review* 54, 1980, 208-228.

_____, "The Life of Michael Sattler Reconsidered," *Mennonite Quarterly Review* 52, 1978, 328-332.

_____, "Revolution and the Swiss Brethren: The Case of Michael Sattler," *Church History* 50 (1981), 276-287.

Christof Windhorst

11. *Balthasar Hubmaier*

Professor, Preacher, Politician

In the struggle for the truth of Christian faith and for the renewal of the church, one man with special talent and abilities stood out in the compass of the Southern German Reformation to whom the growing Anabaptist movement was indebted; this movement was decisively influenced by him and bore his stamp, above all, in the evolution of its doctrine.

Hostile contemporaries saw in him the "patron and first beginner," the "head and the most important of the Anabaptist sects." They classed him among the first leaders and bishops of the Anabaptists, and they vouched for his scholarship, obviously misled, and for his eloquence which led astray. The Council of Trent listed him beside Luther, Zwingli, Calvin, and Schwenckfeld: Hubmaier belonged to the "heresiarchs" whose writings were forbidden. Early Lutheranism, not surprisingly, ranked him among the "fanatics," standing with monastic orders and sects near the papacy. Its authorities persecuted him as an agitator. Aware of his great importance, they all deemed him to be a heretic, and identified him as far as possible with the opposite party.

From Anabaptism came at least one positive voice in the "Oldest Chronicle of the Hutterites," although not without some reservations. His education as well as his writings on baptism and communion receive high praise, but the treatise "On the Sword" is omitted. The Hutterites could not accept his favorable attitude toward worldly authorities. He was said to have withdrawn this position in a letter. That is, however, very unlikely.

Presumably the chronicler was trying to vindicate the clever theologian and "brother Balthasar Hubmaier" and, thereby, his writings on baptism and communion that were so indispensable for early Anabaptism. Thus, Hubmaier found only conditional sympathy among the Anabaptists, even though he and they both wanted to reestablish Christian truth by means of a "radical reformation."

Balthasar Hubmaier was born between 1480 and 1485 in Friedberg. In nearby Augsburg he received the foundation for his education at the cathedral school. Provided with minor holy orders he was enrolled at the University of Freiburg in the Breisgau. After taking the basic courses, he turned to theology. Johann Eck, one of the keenest polemicists among Catholic theologians during the Reformation, became his teacher and promoter. In 1510 Eck accepted a call to teach at the university in Ingolstadt. Hubmaier, now ordained as a priest, followed him in early 1512 and went on as his student to get the doctorate in theology. From a eulogy by his teacher, it is clear that he already had the reputation of giving highly learned lectures to students, as well as useful sermons to the people.

In Ingolstadt he was active as a preacher at the Church of St. Mary and as a professor of theology. He likely taught in the spirit of nominalism, which had formed his thinking while he was a student. Later on, he himself said that he was well acquainted with Thomas, Bonaventura, Scotus, Occam, and Biel. He found the concepts and structures of his own theological thinking and speaking in their works. At the peak of his career, when as prorector he was the director of the university, he suddenly left Ingolstadt in January of 1516 to become preacher in the cathedral at Regensburg. Regarding his motives, there is only conjecture, ranging from irregularities in the prorector's office up to a better endowed position in Regensburg.

Here Hubmaier appeared in the role of the religious leader of the people for the first time when he got involved in the decades-old struggle of the city against the Jews. With unyielding severity he denounced their practice of taking interest and their excessive profiteering, which was forbidden according to church doctrine. Moreover, he saw that exploitation by the Jews was also ruining the economic base of the city. In his sermons he used the traditional theme claiming the Jews were blasphemers and mockers of Mary, and thus stirred up the hostile mood of the citizens. Since the Regensburg Jews enjoyed imperial protection, the cathedral preacher was accused of preaching sedition and had to justify his actions before Maximilian I at the Diet held at Augsburg in 1518. Nonetheless, shortly after the emperor's death the Jews were driven out of Regensburg. The synagogue was torn down and in its place a chapel to "Beautiful Mary" was built. With two miracle-working images of Mary, it soon became the center of one of the greatest pilgrimages of that time. Hubmaier came to be leader of this downright epidemic movement. Here he could fully unfold his gift for preaching. People fell into ecstasy and there were miracles. All this made him famous far and wide.

As he did in Ingolstadt, Hubmaier here, too, suddenly departed from the scene at its high point in 1520. Again the motives are unclear. Doubts about the cult of Mary which he had ignited, first contacts with Lutheran thought, and difficulties dealing with his church salary might have caused the successful preacher to assume the preaching position at the Church of St. Mary in the provincial town of Waldshut in the Austrian lands of Southwestern Germany. To begin with, he performed the priestly duties of the office loyally and especially promoted piety regarding the sacraments. At the same time, however, a radical change in his thinking was in the making.

Contacts with the reform-minded humanists took place

frequently. He began to study in the letters of Paul. Writings of Erasmus, Melanchthon, and Luther were changing his mind away from the old church and its theology. Above all, Luther's criticism of the sacraments made a deep impression on him. Here he learned that what mattered was preaching God's Word, which was heard in faith and realized in love. In 1522 Regensburg once again called him to be the pilgrimage preacher, but he could no longer fulfill what was expected of him as "Christ was starting to sprout in me." There he encountered a circle of craftsmen who were spending time with Luther's writings and who were adherents of the "new" faith. At this point the decision was made for the Reformation.

Early in 1523 the bishop of Constance, Hugo von Landenberg, observed with deep concern the evolution of his Waldshut priest who was denouncing the clerics "who preach monks' dreams and hold back the Gospel." On a trip to St. Gall, he was hailed as an evangelical preacher. In Zürich he talked with Zwingli particularly about infant baptism, which, at that time, both rejected. A little later Hubmaier took part in the October Disputation of 1523 on images and mass in Zürich. He demanded that the mass be eliminated and be replaced, along the lines of Zwingli's ideas, by a plain ceremony in memory of Christ's death. His thorough study of Luther's writings shows that Hubmaier wished to have the sacramental words understood as words of proclamation.

Back in Waldshut, Hubmaier prepared the reform of the mass. While ecclesiastical and civil authorities were demanding his extradition, the Waldshut council stood behind its pastor and his reformation work. For a disputation on religion in Waldshut (April 1524), Hubmaier drew up the "Eighteen Theses." They contained a clear reformation program: only personal faith as the acknowledgement of God's mercy makes a man just before God, and this expresses itself necessarily in "every work of brotherly love." All human doctrines and customs of the old church become superfluous. The Catholic party in Waldshut could not accept this program. Their priests had to leave town. Meanwhile, Archduke Ferdinand of Austria threatened to bring his disobedient subjects into line by force. In this grave situation Hubmaier went to Schaffhausen in order to provide some political leverage for his troubled town.

Hubmaier wrote a series of theses here against Johann Eck which documents the break with the old church. The pamphlet "On Heretics and Those Who Burn Them" originated at about the same time. It was a fiery defense against any kind of inquisitional and violent "conversion" to the "right faith of the church"—an early expression of the concept of toleration: The mixing of secular and ecclesiastical arguments and jurisdictions should cease for the sake of the gospel, and there should be more patience in striving for the truth of the faith. Faith under attack is not heresy for Hubmaier but rather a station on the way to truth which in the end will prevail. It is, therefore, a matter of holding to the idea that "truth cannot be killed." He affixed this motto to almost every one of his writings.

Upon returning to Waldshut in October 1524, he was received enthusiastically. Mass was celebrated in the German language; images and holy objects were taken out of the churches. The political situation was getting worse. A small troop of volunteers came from Zürich to protect the town. Among them were followers of the Grebel circle. At this same time, during the peasant uprisings in Southern Germany, Waldshut was allied with insurgent groups to whom it was offering help and protection. Hubmaier quite consciously promoted this policy against the background of the "Twelve Articles of the Peasantry in Swabia." The Habsburgs, however, were tied down in the war against France, and could not be concerned with Waldshut.

In the meantime, Hubmaier kept working theologically.

He read pamphlets by Karlstadt and Müntzer and probably met the latter in Waldshut in 1524. In their writings, infant baptism was questioned, as it also was by the Grebel circle. He corresponded about this problem with Oecolampadius, with whom he found far-reaching agreement. He still took his time, however, even when Reublin started

BALTHASAR HVBMOR DOCTOR VON FRIDBERG.

Balthasar Hubmaier

to baptize in Waldshut in early 1525. The political situation was not conducive to radical church reforms. Besides, Hubmaier was more interested in agreement with Zwingli than in the separatist activity of the Zürich Anabaptists. Finally, he wanted to prepare the congregation as well as possible by instruction and the sermon.

The crucial step came at Easter in 1525. The uprising of the peasants reached its climax, with their troops and those of Waldshut being victorious. The occasion was favorable. On Easter Sunday Hubmaier, along with sixty other citizens, received baptism from Reublin and then he himself bestowed it on some three hundred people and on the majority of the Council. Immediately afterward, they celebrated mass as a plain memorial service. In Waldshut under Hubmaier's leadership a "territorial Anabaptism" had arisen. The Reformation had thus taken a radical turn here which was like what Grebel first had in mind for Zürich, but which was stopped there by Zwingli and the Council. Despite this diverse development, Hubmaier still kept endeavoring to come to terms with Zwingli, but without success. Instead, a literary battle between the two Reformers flared up. Zwingli had already written a book in May against the "deniers of baptism" and defended infant baptism. Hubmaier answered in July with a precise refutation without, however, naming Zwingli, prompting the latter to counter with an even sharper reply, which Hubmaier naturally did not leave unanswered. All told, Hubmaier wrote seven pamphlets on the question of baptism.

His baptismal book "On the Christian Baptism of Believers," which appeared in July 1525, was one of the best arguments for believers' baptism of that time. The real order of Christian living consists in the succession of the Word, faith, baptism, and deed. The beginnings consist of the sermon, repentance, and faith in forgiveness. He calls this process the "baptism of the Spirit" and describes it as a rebirth which the Holy Ghost brings about through the sermon. This is followed by the double confession of sin and faith, as well as the double obligation to the "new life according to Christ's rule" and subjection to brotherly admonition and the ban. All this is bound together in the act of water baptism. It is a public confession and admits a person into the church. Thus baptism outwardly becomes a visible sign of a newly acquired inner quality, which is then expressed in external behavior. Consequently, the Christian stands in contrast to the world which has "its own ordinances and rules." In this struggle between Christ and the world, the believing person will come to experience suffering and persecution.

Baptism, the "sign of faith's obligation corresponds to the "supper of Christ," the sign of love's obligation. In this and three other pamphlets, Hubmaier portrays the Lord's supper as being a communal and memorial meal. It leads Christians into the obligation to love. Remembrance of Christ's passion evokes in people's hearts an intense inner incitement which in turn sets Christians in motion: they become "doing Christians." This animation of the heart produces new behavior which does not shrink from suffering or dying for others. While a fundamentally medieval passion piety persists here, Hubmaier, in other respects, reworked, on his own, the thinking of Luther, Zwingli, and Karlstadt and developed a doctrine on the Lord's supper close to the Reformed type.

Baptism and the Lord's supper draw the Christian to the obligation of faith and love in order to make the world "devout and just." It becomes an area for mission and at the same an area for social activity. In his last printed work "On the Sword" (1527) his theme was the determination to take responsibility for the world. Christians must use the spiritual sword of the Word of God, but they are especially equipped and challenged to use the material sword, which must be distinguished from the former, "for the protection of the devout and the fear of the wicked." Thus, not only is the cooperation of Christians in government worth striving for, but even Christian government is to be desired, for it possesses the true ethical prerequisites for the functioning of human community. This theology, developed out of criticism of the sacraments, evolves into a code of ethics for the Christian, who does not live apart from the world, but who faces it as a member of his congregation, while also living in responsibility for it as a Christian and a citizen. Hubmaier tried to demonstrate this with his own being and with his reforms in Waldshut and later in Nicolsburg.

In the autumn of 1525 Waldshut's situation worsened. The troops of the town and the peasants were defeated. The result of the "radical reformation" was that former partisans, like Zwingli and Oecolampadius, turned against Hubmaier. Seriously ill, he could no longer delay the surrender of Waldshut. In December 1525 he fled to Zürich with his wife Elsbeth Hügline, to whom he had been married since the beginning of the year, while Habsburg troops occupied Waldshut and restored the Catholic faith. Hubmaier later described the period in Zürich as the most difficult of his life. After staying a short while with Anabaptist friends, he was held in mild confinement and forced to recant. Instead, however, he made a speech in favor of believer's baptism. Severe imprisonment and torture, however, forced him into submission. Amid profound inner struggles he publicly recanted his faith and at the end of April 1526 left the city.

He moved with his wife through Constance and Augsburg to Nicolsburg in Moravia, where a certain amount of freedom in religious matters existed and where the Reformation in the Zwinglian sense was far advanced. Before long Hübmaier was able to establish Anabaptism in the city. Again the government gave him support, the ruling Prince Leonhard von Liechtenstein himself receiving baptism. Once again Hubmaier became the center of a large popular movement. Because of the great numbers some abuses developed, manifesting themselves especially in the lack of good Christian living. To combat this condition, Hubmaier produced a series of fine writings. In his catechism "A Christian Instruction," he again summarized his whole doctrine. In "Concerning Brotherly Discipline" and "Concerning the Christian Ban," he dealt with the biblical basis and practical application of church discipline. With the "Forms" for baptism and the Lord's supper derived from his theology and practice, he provided the congregation with orders for worship. In the two works on free will, fundamental aspects of his Anabaptist theology become apparent.

In his teaching on baptism he utilized the traditional theological motif of the threefold baptism of spirit, water, and blood. He interpreted it in a completely new way: it was a process moving on through the whole Christian life, from rebirth in spiritual baptism, to joining the church through water baptism, and, finally, to blood baptism, which as the suffering of discipleship and daily repentance, describes and forms Christian life. Hubmaier stressed more than ever that believers are "Christians of the Cross," and that, in suffering, they take the surest path to salvation. This is what his own experience had taught him. It inveighed against an effortless habitual Christianity which threatened to creep in and which routinized believer's baptism. Hubmaier attempted to meet this problem energetically with his emphasis on the freedom of the will. Here assumptions and structures of his thinking that helped form his Anabaptist theology and provided the framework for its characteristics become evident.

The starting point was traditional classical anthropology, which held that man consisted of body, soul, and spirit. When the Word was preached, the soul was given the ability to distinguish between good and evil, as well as free will to decide for the flesh or the spirit, evil or God. This capability of consciously distinguishing and deciding was the prerequisite for receiving baptism based on faith. Since it was lacking in children, infant baptism had to be abolished. Thus the explosives for the radical reform of the church were rooted firmly in its own traditions of thought. It merely had to be carried out systematically, starting from the spark of biblical-reformation understanding that the Word of God summoned men to believe and conferred salvation upon each person individually. While preaching was heavily stressed, this process remained a gift of the Spirit who wanted and needed to make itself known to the spirit in man. No outside element, neither the Word nor the sacraments could mediate the Spirit of God and so bring about salvation.

This "spiritualistic" thinking corresponded thoroughly to Neoplatonic medieval ontology, along the lines of which Hubmaier, with most of his contemporaries, thought and argued. It forced him to take leave of Catholic sacramentalism, since, for him, the Holy Spirit brought about salvation only following the preaching of the Word of God. That was God's manifest, preached will. He firmly committed himself to this idea. "We should drop" all talk about the hidden, almighty will of God. The nominalistic distinction between God's absolute power, and his power regulated and bound by itself, turned out to be one of the most profound and consoling impulses of his Anabaptist theology, for by it he saw both a merciful God and the order for the congregation revealed in the New Testament. Again, therefore, the impulse for his reforming action lies in traditional thought.

Toward the end of his activity in Nicolsburg, there was a clash and also a debate with the famous Anabaptist missionary, Hans Hut, on the basis of theological differences. The apocalyptic preaching of Hut, about the world's imminent end, as well as about "peaceful" refusal of service to government and payment of war taxes, were both judged by Hubmaier to be seditious. Even before the Nicolsburg Disputation Hubmaier had expressed sharp disagreement with the teachings of Hut in a series of "theses against Hut," and had taken strong steps against his adherents. For the disputation he compiled the "Nicolsburg Articles," a collection of theses based on Hut's writings. These were debated in the church and in the castle at Nicolsburg, resulting in Hut's hasty departure from the city. Leonhard von Liechtenstein favored Hubmaier's cause. He was interested in an agreement between the two contending parties. This fight, however, bore within it the seeds of disintegration for Hubmaier's established Anabaptist church, especially since Hut was able to win over many followers. His pamphlet "On the Sword" was meant to clarify the question of governmental authority. Very likely it was also an answer to the Schleitheim Articles, that bound the Christian to absolute defenselessness.

Meanwhile, King Ferdinand, who had become ruler of Moravia, had initiated investigations against him. In July 1527 he was arrested for fomenting rebellion. He was put into prison and interrogated at Kreuzenstein Castle near Vienna. In "Account of Faith," addressed to Ferdinand, he attempted to defend himself and his teaching. But he could not stave off his fate in this way, since Ferdinand had ordered the popular preacher arrested primarily on account of the "great deal of mischief, opposition, tumult, and rebellion" that had arisen because of him.

On March 10, 1528, Hubmaier was burned at the stake in Vienna as a rebel and heretic. His wife was drowned in the Danube three days later. The fighter for immortal truth became the best witness for the earnestness and strength of his theology and faith through his martyrdom. His teaching on baptism and the Lord's supper lived on in Anabaptism. Thus the truth that he knew could not be executed with him.

It is certainly regrettable that his concept of a Christianity which suffered at the hands of the world, but which was nevertheless responsible for that world, so carefully worked out in theory and practice, found no acceptance in separatist Anabaptism. Not until recently have the Baptists thought of this outstanding theologian and practitioner as being among their Reformation fathers, a man who, as a scholar and preacher, was successful and was, in the places where he worked, able to accomplish reforms that radically changed the worn-out fabric of church and society in the sixteenth century. He was, therefore, doomed to run into the decisive opposition of the guardians of the old ways and, in the end, to fail as a politician in the face of the superiority of the ruling powers. The peculiar charm of his personality most likely does not lie only in the outward dramatic course of his life, but rather much more in his theology, which determined and formed his life from the inside. In many ways this theology has continuity with late medieval thought. It picked up impulses from all the various Reformation theologies. With the help of these it consistently took inherited thought further and so developed a thoroughly independent Reformation and Anabaptist theology. The result is that he cannot be assigned clearly to any camp of the Reformation period. The sum of his theology, faith, and life was the irrevocable insight that all of this had to be seen and verified in a Christianity that was active and world-changing.

For further reading:

B. Hubmaier, *Schriften,* ed. by G. Westin und T. Bergsten, Gütersloh, 1962.

The Writings of Balthasar Hubmaier, vols. 1-3, collected and photographed by W. O. Lewis; transl. by G. D. Davidson, 1939. Microfilm at Conrad Grebel College, Waterloo, Ont.

J. Loserth, *Doctor Balthasar Hubmaier und die Anfänge der Wiedertaufe in Mähren,* Brünn, 1893.

C. Sachsse, *D. Balthasar Hubmaier als Theologe,* Berlin, 1914. (Reprint: Aalen, 1973.)

W. Wiswedel, *Balthasar Hubmaier, der Vorkämpfer für Glaubens- und Gewissensfreiheit,* Kassel, 1939.

T. Bergsten, *Balthasar Hubmaier: Seine Stellung zu Reformation und Täufertum 1521-1528,* Kassel, 1961.

T. Bergsten, *Balthasar Hubmaier: Anabaptist Theologian and Martyr,* ed., W. R. Estep, Valley Forge, 1978.

D. C. Steinmetz, "Balthasar Hubmaier (1484?-1528). Free Will

and Covenant," in *Reformers in the Wings*, Philadelphia, 1971, 197-208.
J. K. Zeman, *The Anabaptists and the Czech Brethren in Moravia 1526-1628: A Study of Origins and Contacts*, The Hague-Paris, 1969.
W. R. Estep, ed., *Anabaptist Beginnings (1523-1533): A Source Book*, Nieuwkoop, 1976.
Ch. Windhorst, *Täuferisches Taufverständnis. Balthasar Hubmaiers Lehre zwischen traditioneller und reformatorischer Theologie*, Leiden, 1976.

12. Jakob Hutter

A Christian Communist

The story of Jakob Hutter is inextricably tied to the story of his people, the Hutterian Brethren. Although this people had come into being before Hutter came on the scene, Hutter so directly influenced and molded the movement that his name has been attached to the brotherhood from the first decade of its existence.

The story of Jakob Hutter is consequently the story of a people, and provides the milieu within which can be seen the import of one man who himself was but one brother among many, in a brotherhood movement where the community defined and determined ultimate truth. Hutter did not determine the theology of the movement. During the first five years in Moravia, 1528 to 1533, his influence was felt only from a distance. For during these years Hutter was an Austrian Anabaptist leader who had seen the futility of attempting to maintain a religious movement in a land where fierce persecution was killing many of its adherents. Hutter therefore organized an emigration of hundreds of Tyrolean and other Austrian Anabaptists to Moravia, for in Moravia lay promise of toleration and the potential of establishing a place where God's people could gather and grow into a brotherhood.

Hutterian chroniclers, writing from the perspective of the mid-sixteenth century, interpreted the historical emergence of their movement as follows: God intended to reestablish his own people, separate from all other peoples, in the last age of the world. To be sure, Erasmus of Rotterdam, Martin Luther, and Ulrich Zwingli had begun the renewal of Christian life, but they had not succeeded in crowning the Reformation with a renewal of the people. Consequently, it was left to God to reestablish his people upon the earth through other means. The events leading up to the birth of this new reality had occurred in Switzerland. Conrad Grebel, Felix Mantz and Jörg Blaurock, along with Balthasar Hubmaier, were the leading figures. The official Hutterite chronicler of the 1560s, Kaspar Braitmichel, then went on to establish a direct succession between the events of 1525 and Hutterian beginnings. Blaurock and Wilhelm Reublin were the connecting links.

This does not deny the likelihood that pre-Reformation brotherhoods had existed for decades in Tyrol and surrounding areas such as Salzburg, where oral tradition tells us that already in the fifteenth century towns such as Zell am Ziller and Zell am See had their beginnings as locations for cell groups centering in the study of newly translated, unpublished fragments of the Bible, groups led by learned monks and friars who took seriously the "reform of the church in head and members." Whether adult baptism within any of these cell groups predates 1525 is a question that still needs to be investigated. But it is of the highest significance that the Hutterite chronicler interprets the Hutterian heritage as derived from Blaurock and Hubmaier.

The first major link in the story leading to the birth of Hutterianism was Balthasar Hubmaier and the short-lived urban Anabaptism which he developed in 1526 at Nicolsburg, Moravia. As many as twelve thousand Anabaptists are said to have been drawn to South Moravia, with Nicolsburg as the center for the larger religious community. The form of Anabaptism which Hubmaier established has sometimes been called "magisterial Anabaptism." Indeed, the lord of the area, Leonhard von Liechtenstein, himself submitted to (re)baptism. One of the tenets of Hubmaier's creed was the acceptance of defensive warfare, an element which the Zürich Anabaptists had rejected from the outset.

By 1528 a small group of dissenting Anabaptists had begun to meet separately from the main community of Nikolsburg Anabaptists. This group did not believe in any form of warfare and were known as the "Stäbler" (staff carriers) because they held to nonviolence and rejected war taxes, in contrast to the "Schwertler" (sword carriers), who followed Hubmaier. The leader of the Stäbler group was Jakob Wiedemann, "the Jacob with one eye." The group, numbering some two hundred adults with their children, lived and worshiped just outside the walled city of Nicolsburg, in the village of Bergen.

In the spring of 1528 the Stäbler felt compelled to leave the Nikolsburg area. Already accustomed to a close sharing process in spiritual and material things, the group decided to pool its resources. The account in the Hutterian Chronicle reads:

> At that time these men laid a coat on the ground, and each person put what he had on it willingly and without coercion for the support of the needy. This was done according to the teaching of the prophets and apostles.

The Stäbler brotherhood settled at Austerlitz, assured by Lord Ulrich von Kaunitz and his brothers that they would be exempt from payment of war taxes and from military service for a period of six years. The following year another Anabaptist communal group was established at Auspitz, and in 1530 still another community was founded there by Jörg Zaunring and Wilhelm Reublin.

During these years neighboring groups also formed. Although there were some tensions, amicable relationships prevailed. The communal idea was taking form and substance; the Stäbler tradition was setting the doctrinal tone; and Reublin, despite his personal troubles and later disavowal of Anabaptism, assured the historical continuity with Zürich Anabaptism. After his expulsion from Zürich,

A nocturnal Anabaptist meeting taken by surprise

Jörg Blaurock ultimately fled to Tyrol in the spring of 1529. He related closely to the Anabaptists already there, who had been won through the efforts of earlier leaders such as Hans Hut, Leonhard Schiemer, and Hans Schlaffer. For four months Blaurock served throughout much of South Tyrol; he was apprehended and put to death in September 1529. The brevity of his ministry notwithstanding, his presence in Tyrol is another strand of historical continuity between the Swiss Brethren and the developing movement later known as Hutterianism.

In the same year that Blaurock was martyred, the name of Jakob Hutter appears for the first time in Hutterian chronicles, the man who was to become the acknowledged leader within Tyrolean and Moravian (communal) Anabaptism.

Jakob Hutter, born around 1500, was a native of the hamlet of Moos, not far from Bruneck in the Puster Valley of Tyrol. After only a short period of formal education in Bruneck, he learned the hatter's trade in nearby Prags. Hutter traveled widely, plying his trade, and probably was introduced to Anabaptism in Kärnten. The exact date of his conversion is not known. The Hutterian Chronicle simply says: "He accepted the covenant of grace, which is a good conscience, in Christian baptism with true surrender, and to live in a godly manner."

In 1529 Hutter succeeded Blaurock as the major Anabaptist leader in Tyrol. He at once established contact with the Moravian communal groups, visited the area, and reached an agreement with them, which led to the emigration of hundreds of Tyrolean Anabaptists over the next few years.

By 1531 the Anabaptist brotherhoods in the Auspitz and Rossitz region of Moravia had formed a loose confederation through the mediating efforts of Hutter. Hutter had undertaken three journeys to Moravia to coordinate the Tyrolean refugee work. Unfortunately, disunity gained the upper hand, and by 1533 conditions in Auspitz had deteriorated to such a degree that Hutter, convinced of his apostolic mission and backed by his Tyrolean flock, decided to act. Through strict disciplinary measures he "cleaned house" and effectively reorganized the small brotherhood which had originally been led to Auspitz by Jörg Zaunring and Wilhelm Reublin. Two other communal brotherhoods, the Gabrielites and the Philippites, continued to be plagued by discord and within the next few years many of their members joined the Hutterites.

The beginning years were difficult for the Hutterian brotherhood. The Münster debacle of 1534/35 affected the Moravian as it did the other Anabaptist groups, and persecution dislodged the Hutterites. Ferdinand, archduke of Austria, succeeded in forcing the hand of even the tolerant Moravian lords to expel the Anabaptists. Month after month, forest and cave provided primitive shelter. Jakob Hutter wrote a letter of protest to the Moravian lord, Johann Kuna von Kunstadt, but returned once again to Tyrol. His activities there were cut short by his arrest and martyrdom at Innsbruck in 1536.

Although Jakob Hutter was not the first to entertain the idea which later came to be known as Hutterianism, it was he who brought unity and stability to the brotherhood. During a span of two years, from 1533 to 1535, Hutter led the communal movement at Auspitz with a strong sense of divine calling and implemented an order, which has carried the brotherhood through 450 years.

But Hutter was also an activist who dared to protest against injustices meted out by civil and ecclesiastical authorities. This note carried throughout sixteenth-century Hutterian history, and is an important clue to the tenacity of the movement. Later Hutterian missioners such as Paul Glock exemplified this spirit of resistance, with his emphasis on obedience to God, and its sometimes necessary corollary, a defiant and conscious opposition to the world.

Hans Arbeiter, Leonard Dax, and many other missioners followed this example of obedience and the defiance which defines the relationship of the Christian to the kingdom of God and the kingdoms and powers of the world. This spirit, given to the movement by Hutter, created a healthy self-affirmation which is still evident in twentieth-century Hutterianism.

When the violent persecution set in throughout Moravia in 1535 the movement seemed doomed, for the communities were forcibly broken up and the brethren dispersed. It is significant that the movement did not die. That it held on was due in part to the determined spirit of Jakob Hutter, who encouraged others to cling to their convictions. It was also due in part to another aspect of their faith in God's kingdom: the "tending of the gardens." For the Hutterian concern to care for God's creation, the earth, made the brethren economically useful. Hence the nobles soon not only tolerated them again, but welcomed them back. Keeping the garden helped the Hutterites through many threatening times in their long history.

During the early years of Hutterian consolidation amid social and political ferment, brotherhood order developed as a fundamental part of the idea of communal life. And although many Anabaptists stemmed from the spiritualistically inclined mission of Hans Hut and Hans Denck and their followers, they soon exchanged their quasi-individualistic views of Christianity for the stronger Anabaptist pattern of brotherhood unity and consensus. This transformation is most strikingly evident in the life and writings of another Hutterite leader, Peter Riedemann. In his Gmünden ("Confession") (ca. 1529), Riedemann expresses the typical early spiritualistic interpretations of God's kingdom, the key to which is the Spirit of God working within the individual. This interpretation indicates a loosely organized Anabaptism, the only form possible in the face of the ruthlessness of the im-

perial policy of persecution. In fact a fuller development of
God's kingdom on earth, as Hutter understood it, would
have been impossible to achieve throughout much of
Europe. Consequently Riedemann's early views of Anabaptism
lack the strong, social vehicle necessary to carry a
brotherhood movement.

But Hutter did not build upon the spiritualistic idea of
Austrian Anabaptism. In Moravia another option became
viable, namely, the establishment of God's kingdom in the
present world. This conviction stems from the Anabaptist
conference at Schleitheim in 1527, and from the first
Zürich Anabaptists, Conrad Grebel and Felix Mantz, who
as early as 1524 recognized the historical realization of
such a kingdom of God among the early Christians—a visible
brotherhood of peace and love, a gathered church, conscious
of the opposing reality of the world. Hutter must
have caught something of this brotherhood vision in his
Tyrolean days through the work of Jörg Blaurock, and then
again at Auspitz, where he found in embryonic form the
Schleitheim concept of peace and nonconformist living.

Hutter died too soon to develop fully his views about
God's kingdom on earth, but it is evident in his careful attention
to establishing a firm brotherhood structure.
Indeed, all the points of a kingdom-of-God Christianity, as
developed at Schleitheim, were integral to Hutterianism
from its inception.

How do we evaluate the life of Jakob Hutter? Most significant
is the strong leadership that he provided during
the six years he related to the brotherhood movement. He
worked as actual leader of the community only two years.
Hutter felt a strong inner calling to lead out in organization,
and to some degree forced the hand of several other
leaders within the brotherhood. Yet his assumption of
leadership must have been the will of the majority, for
from that time on stability prevailed over disorder, and the
movement grew measurably over the ensuing months.

Hutter must have been given the nod of the brotherhood, otherwise his strong-willed actions which led to "cleaning house" would ultimately have failed. Hutter walked the fine line between setting and maintaining the needed structure of the movement, with the consent of the members, and autocratic, unilateral pronouncements "from above" which would have placed him apart from the brotherhood process itself. But this fine line Hutter seems not to have violated. For although he moved in as a leader of action, seemingly self-proclaimed, in reality the majority of the brotherhood backed his leadership—indeed, desired such a firm hand. The clue may lie in the fact that Hutter did not proclaim a new theology; in matters of establishing truth, he was more than content to yield to the common convictions of the community, derived by group process. In thus submitting to the group spirit in matters of faith, he could genuinely act in the name of the total brotherhood in his mandate of leadership, even when circumstance called for decisive action. He was able to reconcile his charismatic style of leadership with the principle of fraternal decision-making.

Perhaps the deepest concern and vision of Jakob Hutter was the realization and fulfillment of close community, on the basis of apostolic patterns of communal sharing (Acts 2 to 5). In 1533 he transformed the existing loosely constructed policy of communal sharing of goods into a full-fledged communal pattern of complete economic sharing. It is this Hutterian resolve to maintain community which is the central clue to the tenacity and longevity of the communitarian idea, an idea as strong for the 20,000 Hutterites living today as it was 450 years earlier. The Hutterites fulfilled historically what many Renaissance intellectuals only dreamed of—a utopian idea became a reality.

Yet the intriguing question still remains: What special quality has kept the Hutterian spirit alive these four centuries, when all other communal groups enjoyed but a short-lived, fleeting moment in the annals of history? The Hutterites, eluding a "scientific" response to this question, would attribute their endurance in no small measure to their fearless obedience as a people of God to the norms and example of Christ and the apostolic church.

There are few Christian groups that have taken faith in the reality of God's kingdom seriously on this level, and only few of these have realized the biblical concept to such a degree as did the Hutterites. The Swiss Brethren soon gave up in their mission to the world in this respect. The Dutch and North German groups joined with the world in many areas of life. For decades the Hutterites avoided both options. They remained instead a powerful Christian nucleus, opening themselves to world mission and mutual sharing to any and all—whether ragged and penniless, or moneyed-newcomers who would simply affirm an openness to this new way of life.

For further reading:

J. Beck, *Die Geschichts-Bücher der Wiedertäufer in Oesterreich-Ungarn, 1526-1785,* Wien, 1883.

A. J. F. Zieglschmid, *Die älteste Chronik der Hutterischen Brüder,* Ithaca, 1943.

R. Wolkan, *Geschicht-Buch der Hutterischen Brüder,* Wien, 1923.

Jacob Hutter, *Brotherly Faithfulness: Epistles from a Time of Persecution,* Rifton, N.Y., 1979.

R. Wolkan, *Die Hutterer. Oesterreichische Wiedertäufer und Kommunisten in Amerika,* Wien, 1918.

H. Fischer, *Jakob Hutter. Leben, Frömmigkeit, Briefe.* Newton, Kans., 1956.

R. Friedmann, *Hutterite Studies,* Goshen, Ind., 1961.

J. A. Hostetler, *Hutterite Society,* Baltimore, Md., and London, 1974.

Leonard Gross, *The Golden Years of the Hutterites,* Scottdale, Pa., 1980.

William Klassen

13. Pilgram Marpeck

Liberty Without Coercion

The most extensive and most vivid literary legacy of all Anabaptist writers was left by Pilgram Marpeck. The strength of his mind, the range of issues he dealt with, and the power of perception he displayed mark him out as the most competent of all sixteenth-century Anabaptist leaders. Nevertheless, he is virtually unknown even among those who consider themselves children of the Anabaptists. He founded no group which continues to the present time and most of the theological developments among the children of the Anabaptists between the 16th century and the present are antithetical to Marpeck's position. However, the fact that the apostle Paul was misunderstood or neglected by the later church fathers does not mean that we should do the same. Nor does Marpeck's importance relate to his immediate success as a founder of a group. With respect to Marpeck it is generally acknowledged today that, although he stands as an independent Anabaptist, he is worthy of serious study by those who would understand the radical Christian traditions which were born and established in the 16th century.

Around the year 1490 Pilgram Marpeck was born in the vicinity of Rattenberg in the Inn Valley of the Tyrol. He came from a family which remained faithful to the calling of Jesus Christ even as he served his city as a loyal public servant. He played a leading role in the civic and cultural affairs of that region, and as such, undoubtedly received a thorough education. He enrolled with his wife, Anna, in the

Brotherhood of Mining Workers of Rattenberg on February 26, 1520. He participated actively in the civic affairs of the city, first as a member of the Lower Council after February 24, 1523, then as a member of the Upper Council after June 11, 1525.

As a measure of the esteem in which he was held it can be noted that in 1523 he was twice sent by the city to intercede for Stephen Agricola, who was imprisoned in Upper Bavaria. On April 20, 1525, he was appointed as *Bergrichter* (magistrate for the miners) in which position he was responsible for the payment of the miners, the quality of the ore, the general well-being of the miners, and the arbitration of all disputes between the miners. He was authorized to dispose of all matters up to the jurisdiction of capital crimes. He was paid sixty-five pounds a year, and amassed considerable wealth, for he was able to loan King Ferdinand 1,000 pounds at 5 percent interest and also to acquire two houses. Maximilian I (1459-1519) had elevated the post of Bergrichter, for he saw that the position had military significance.

While Marpeck was pursuing his professional career he was also being touched by the religious movements which were sweeping over all of Europe. The Tyrol also had been affected by Anabaptism as early as 1526. We do not know when Marpeck himself first had contacts with Anabaptists. The earliest evidence we have of the state of religion in his own life comes in the fall of 1527 when the correspondence between King Ferdinand and Rattenberg shows that Marpeck was reluctant to report Anabaptists to the authorities. The king appeared to consider it part of Marpeck's responsibilities to guard over the elements of unrest among the miners and to attempt to keep out all revolutionary or dissenting elements. Marpeck showed an unwillingness to cooperate and although there was a short period of time in which he vacillated, after the execution of Schiemer on January 14, 1528, he made an about face. He gave up his position and left Rattenberg in January 1528 before Schlaffer's execution on February 4, 1528. His property and presumably also his loan to the King became the property of the state.

During the time that Schleitheim (February 24, 1527) was debating the legitimacy of whether a Christian could be a judge, Marpeck was carrying out the duties of one. He was deeply influenced by the more mystical approach to Christianity found in Denck, Hut, Schiemer, and Schlaffer, although he never took over the fiery apocalypticism of Hut nor did he follow Schiemer or Schlaffer in their debt to either the ascetical monastic tradition or the priestly tradition. In that sense he clearly marks a middle road between Denck and the Swiss Brethren. He found Denck's lack of interest in the church uncongenial to his reading of the New Testament. At the same time the Swiss concern with spelling out details of life, whether one should wear homespun clothes, or what one should eat or where one could drink, all of this he, like Hans Hut, found foreign and rejected as a false approach to the new life. Paul's rejection of all asceticism in Colossians 2:16-23 was often quoted and applied by Marpeck to the quest for ascetic rules in his time. He saw that such rules could only foster a false pride and not genuine union with Christ. "It has an air of wisdom with its forced piety, its self-mortification, and its severity to the body; but is of no use at all in combating sensuality" (Col. 2:23, NEB).

During his years in Strassburg (1528-1532) Marpeck was given a rich opportunity to exercise his skills as an engineer for he worked for the city of Strassburg in the areas of supplying wood and dealing with drainage problems. The other side of his work was to struggle with the Anabaptists there in trying to find a common ground on which to stand. With Melchior Hoffman continuing Hut's apocalypticism and the opposing influences of Denck and Sattler, above all the serious threat posed by the radical spiritualizers like John Bünderlin and Schwenckfeld, (to say nothing of Sebastian Franck!) who desired to dissolve the church into an invisible fellowship of likeminded people, it was clear that Marpeck had much work to do within the Anabaptist brotherhood. He felt an affinity to Bucer and Capito and other leaders of the magisterial reformation but after several disputations Marpeck was ordered to leave the city of Strassburg in December of 1531. He requested a stay of that order so that he would have time to dispose of his property and eventually left the city in January 1532. While there he had published two small booklets in 1531, one was directed against the Schwenckfeldian emphasis on suspending churchly functions until God should give further orders. The other was directed against Bünderlin and his radical program of omitting churchly functions, an attempt to see the essence of religion not in any outer expression but in inner attitudes and feelings. He also left behind in the Strassburg council minutes extensive evidence of his arguments with Bucer.

From Strassburg Marpeck went to Switzerland where he worked in the Grisons from 1532-1544. Most likely he made his headquarters in Chur for a letter is written from that place in 1544. He worked here again as an engineer, this time contributing to the success of the weavers by providing them with a source of water. At the same time he had abundant opportunity to work with Leupold Scharnschlager whom he had met in Strassburg, and also to become acquainted with Joerg Propst Rothenfelder, the one called Maler, who is most likely to be identified with the Gregor Maler who attended the Martyrs' Synod in Augsburg in 1527. At any rate although his work as an engineer was successful, he ran into repeated failures of communication with the Swiss. They, following the lines of Schleitheim, showed no reluctance in using the ban, and appeared to be concerned with spelling out ascetic rules of how the Christian was to live. For Marpeck, standing in the ethical tradition of Denck, the importance of love was increasingly stressed. At the same time Marpeck insisted on church discipline and separation of church and world. To be united with Christ meant for Marpeck to be separated from the world.

His years of working in Switzerland also brought him into increasing contact with the Hutterites and he developed a conviction that the Brethren were too divided. The body of Christ, he believed, could not be divided. His attempts to associate with the Hutterites failed when they refused to allow him to pray in their assemblies. His associate in Strassburg, Wilhelm Reublin, had rejected the authoritarian refusal of the Hutterians to allow group decisions to be made. Likewise, Marpeck who was always indebted to Reublin for the support of the Strassburg years saw the authoritarianism of the Hutterites as inimical to the freedom of the gospel. He in particular rejected the Hutterian insistence on community of goods, a position taken already by the Swiss Brethren during the days of Schleitheim.

The most important disagreement of these days, however, was with the Münsterites who attempted to establish an Anabaptist kingdom. During the latter half of the decade 1530-40 Marpeck and his associates were looking about for a confessional statement which would deal with baptism and the Lord's supper and which would then form a rallying point for those drawn to Schwenckfeld or drawn back into the magisterial reformation. When they discovered Rothmann's *Bekentnisse von beyden Sacramenten* they decided after it had been "tested, and its errors ... cleansed, corrected, and eliminated" to publish it as the *Taufbüchlein* of 1542. Thus they borrowed more than they criticized. It is an important confessional statement, coming as it does nearly twenty years after the beginning of the Anabaptist movement and correcting as it does the excesses of Hutterian insistence on community of goods and the use of violence by Müntzer and Münster. The changes made in it are far-reaching and show clearly what

Arrested Anabaptists are led to Zürich.

Marpeck and his collegues saw as important in 1542. Scharnschlager had taken the Swiss Church Order of 1527 and reprinted it with important revisions and additions of his own in about 1543. Marpeck and his associates saw themselves as taking the best of the Anabaptist tradition and adapting it to the struggles and issues of their time.

In 1544 with a change in the political climate of Augsburg, Marpeck was invited to become the city engineer in that city. He lived there from 1544-1556 when he died a natural death as a city employee. He rendered valuable service to the city as engineer and was hampered in his work as an organizer of Anabaptist churches only by the restriction of the authorities that no mass meetings be allowed and by their continuing admonitions that he cease publishing—all of which he ignored. His publishing continued unabated and above all he carried on a lively correspondence with Anabaptists in the Grisons, Moravia, and in Strassburg. In these discussions the question of the relation of Old and New Testaments resulted in the publication of a concordance, the *Testamentserleutterung* (Clarification of the Two Covenants). At the same time along with others he wrote a detailed reply to the criticism of Caspar Schwenckfeld. He wrote essays on Christology and on love, but these were never published, addressed as they were to certain congregations. In 1561 Maler gathered many of them together in his *Kunstbuch*, which was never published or even known until modern times.

The theological concerns of Marpeck and his group were essentially those of the Anabaptists led by Hans Hut and Hans Denck. Thus the Marpeck fellowship was characterized by an unswerving devotion to the principle of a new life which was a gift of God's grace, appropriated by faith, over against every attempt by Anabaptists or others to institute a works righteousness. The polemics in the correspondence of Marpeck, Scharnschlager, Veh, and Maler himself, were often directed against the tendency of a literalistic faith in the Anabaptist movement. At the same time there were those among the Anabaptists who heard only the call to freedom and thus Marpeck also wrote to the libertarians. He himself was accused by the Swiss of stretching the freedom of Christ too far or of using it as a "cloak for wickedness." All of this goes back to the rejection of Schleitheim by Denck, Hut, and Maler, who were not comfortable with the narrow way in which nonconformity and separation were defined there.

The most important theological contribution of Marpeck and his fellowship was their insistence that the humanity of Christ had relevance for the structuring of the church and its common life as well as for the shape of the ethical life. Freedom was important because Christ was free and had died to make others free. Marpeck and his colleagues insisted that the human and the divine Christ exist side by side and that by his becoming man in Christ God had spoken a definitive word which people reject at their own peril. While some Anabaptists made of the human Christ a model which people were slavishly to follow, for Marpeck the potential for human freedom opened up for humanity through the human Christ was a value which dare not be lost. The fact that God was incarnate in Christ also meant that if the church is to be the body of Christ then the external aspects of the church's life (e.g., baptism, proclamation, ban, Lord's supper., etc.) all had to be externally expressed. When that happened they became living realities. They called for a co-witness as the church gave testimony to the Scriptures that it was in fact the Word from God, that baptism was a co-witness to the fact that God had brought new life to the one entering into the covenantal experience of baptism.

During the second generation of Anabaptism Marpeck and his close coworkers stand as a tower of strength. Because they worked as a group the literary style of their legacy leaves much to be desired. Nevertheless, even though they parted ways with their colleagues within and without the Anabaptist group, they always did so by treating even their opponents with courtesy and respect born out of Christian love. Judged by the level of polemics of the 16th century, as displayed, for example, in Luther's contempt for Schwenckfeld, the communal theology of the Marpeck people breathes the same peace and love which formed the center of their reason for being.

Marpeck refused to allow the church or any of its ceremonies to be merely a symbol. For if history was to be taken seriously, then the scandal of divine intervention in history could not be avoided. He frequently referred to the desire of the contemporaries of Jesus that the Messiah might come in the form of glory. Instead, he came in the form of a humble man from Nazareth who asked a man born blind to go wash the mud from his eyes. As Luther was fond of referring to the majesty and sublimity of God incarnate, wrapped in a diaper, so Marpeck saw the church as the locus of Christ's presence and gave his considerable energies to the task of keeping that church strong. His passion was that the church might never lose the warmth of Christ's love, that it might never become so enamored by the world that it would lose its union with Christ. At the same time he spent no energy in defining the external boundaries between church and world, for he knew that those who remain united with Christ can go forth and eat and drink with sinners even as Jesus did. He remained free in Christ without violence and he followed the call of Christ even when, as a loyal citizen, he served his city. He was an Anabaptist of unique stamp.

For further reading:

J. Loserth, *Pilgram Marbecks Antwort auf Kaspar Schwenckfelds Beurteilung des Buches der Bundes-*

bezeugung von 1542, Wien und Leipzig, 1929.

Chr. Hege, "Pilgram Marbecks Vermahnung. Ein wiedergefundenes Buch," in *Gedenkschrift zum 400jährigen Jubiläum der Mennoniten oder Taufegesinnten, 1525-1925,* Ludwigshafen 1925, 178-282.

W. Klassen and W. Klaassen, *The Writings of Pilgram Marpeck,* Scottdale, Pa., 1978.

H. Fast, "Pilgram Marbeck und das oberdeutsche Täufertum. Ein neuer Handschriftenfund," *Archiv für Reformationsgeschichte* 47, 1956, 212-242.

T. Bergsten, "Pilgrim Marbeck und seine Auseinandersetzung mit Caspar Schwenckfeld," *Kyrkohistorisk Arsskrift,* 57, 1957/58, 39-100 and 53-87.

J. J. Kiwiet, *Pilgram Marbeck,* Kassel, 1957.

W. Klassen, *Covenant and Community. The Life and Writings of Pilgram Marbeck,* Grand Rapids, Michigan, 1968.

J. C. Wenger, "Life and Work of Pilgram Marpeck," *Mennonite Quarterly Review* 12, 1938, 137-166.

H. S. Bender, "Pilgram Marpeck, Anabaptist Theologian and Civil Engineer," *Mennonite Quarterly Review* 38, 1964, 231-265.

W. Klaassen, "Church Discipline and the Spirit in Pilgram Marpeck," in I. B. Horst (ed.), *De Geest in het Geding,* Alphen aan den Rijn, 1978, 169-180.

Klaus Deppermann

14. Melchior Hoffman

Contradictions Between Lutheran Loyalty to Government and Apocalyptic Dreams

Of the lay preachers of the early Reformation period who proclaimed to the common people the end of the old, unjust world and the beginning of a new, better future, none had so far-reaching an effect as Melchior Hoffman. He succeeded in transmitting Anabaptism from South Germany to East Frisia and the Netherlands, where in contrast to other areas of Europe it gained mass support. His militant apocalypticism made him the ideological precursor of the Anabaptist kingdom of Münster. By means of his fanciful prophecies, he gave birth to the mood of expectation which was converted into revolutionary action by Jan Matthijs and Jan van Leiden. Hoffman thus shared the responsibility of plunging Anabaptism into the greatest crisis of its entire history—the rise and fall of the "kingdom of God" in Münster 1534/35.

However, the miscarriage of that adventure did not spell the end of the movement initiated by him. After the catastrophe, Menno Simons gathered the scattered and confused Melchiorites, winning them for a fundamentally pacifist position. Out of the militant "Melchiorites" evolved the peaceful "Mennonites" who preferred not to be reminded of their founder and their own revolutionary past. Around 1550 approximately one quarter of the population in the Northern Netherlands were considered to be Mennonites. They prepared the basis on which the Reformation—although after 1550 under Calvinist leadership—prevailed. Thus, in spite of the failure of his utopia, the work of Hoffman's life did not vanish like sound and smoke.

Melchior Hoffman came from the free imperial city of Schwäbisch Hall. He was probably born between 1495 and 1500. Of his early development, we know only that he learned the trade of furrier, a vocation in which he took great pride throughout his life. He burst onto the historical stage in 1523 as one of the Lutheran lay missionaries of Livonia. During the next ten years of wanderings and until his imprisonment in Strassburg (1533), Hoffman sought those areas and cities in which the struggle between the old and the new faith remained in the balance, or where, in spite of a fundamental decision for the Reformation, the form of confessional commitment was still undecided. These were Livonia (1523-26), Stockholm (1526-27), Lübeck (spring 1527), Schleswig-Holstein (1527-29), East Frisia (spring 1529, summer 1530, winter 1532-33), Strassburg (summer 1529, December 1531, 1533), as well as the Northern Netherlands, including Amsterdam (summer 1531, 1532).

Again and again Hoffman sought to win the disputed territories for the truth he had embraced. At first it was the truth of Luther's cause as he understood it, thereafter the truth of his own apocalyptical-Anabaptist theology. Strife with opponents became a law of life. The most prominent features of Hoffman's character were the ability to sustain boundless hope for a better world, the capacity of unlimited hate against the established "parsons," irrespective of their creed, and in whom, as Müntzer before him, he saw the main obstacle for the arrival of the true faith, fearlessness, and a restless, almost superhuman energy, which his adversary, Martin Bucer, was able to explain only as a gift of Satan himself.

Hoffman was probably attracted to Livonia because of its flourishing fur trade, and because the Reformation was obliged to fight against the embittered resistance of the prince bishops. He proclaimed Luther's gospel of the righteousness by faith alone first in Wolmar, a small city of the Teutonic order, combining this message with threats of imminent judgment on the monks, knights of the order,

Milchior Hoffman

and on the prelates who governed extensive parts of the territory. This led to his expulsion from Wolmar after a short time by Wolter von Plettenberg, the grand master of the Teutonic knights, but Hoffman found asylum in the Hanseatic city of Dorpat, where the magistrates supported the evangelical movement. The journeymen's guild of German merchants, known as the "Schwarzhäupter" became his passionate supporters. Members of the lower class of Latvians also joined his cause.

The attempt by John Blankenfeld, then archbishop of Riga and bishop of Dorpat, to arrest Hoffman failed due to the resistance of the Melchiorites. The whole city revolted because in the futile attempt to arrest Hoffman the mercenaries killed four of his followers and wounded twenty others. In revenge, armed masses stormed every church in the city on January 10, 1525, demolishing images and altars. Then they plundered the houses of the canons of the cathedral. The provost of the bishop was forced to leave Dorpat with his mercenaries. Among the ten iconoclastic riots that swept through Livonia between 1524 and 1526 the one in Dorpat proved to be the most significant. It had disastrous consequences for the course of the Reformation in Livonia. Fearing that the simmering social revolution in the cities might spread to the peasants, the landed aristocrats, who in principle had sided with the Reformation in 1524, now withdrew their support. Riga, Dorpat, and Reval, the three great Protestant cities, found themselves again confronted by a united feudal Catholic opposition. The hope that the province, divided into six ecclesiastical principalities, might be united into a single territory with the aid of the Reformation by means of secularization proved an illusion.

The councillors of the cities and the official Lutheran preachers concluded that, in order to save both the Reformation and the minimal unity of the country, threatened further by Russian intervention, the religious radicalism in the cities kindled by the lay preachers needed to be suppressed. The magistracy of Dorpat, therefore, made Hoffman's future ministry dependent on a certification of his orthodoxy by Luther. Luther indeed acknowledged the furrier as his legitimate representative on the basis of the latter's commitment to justification by faith alone, nonviolence, and the bondage of the human will. Hoffman had been in Wittenberg during June 1525. Returning to Dorpat with an inflated self-image he now challenged the Lutheran ministers of Livonia, in particular Sylvester Tegetmeier, one of the pastors of Riga.

The following questions were under dispute:

(1) Hoffman's teachings about the imminent end of the world, according to which the present aeon would last only another seven years. The last 3½ years were to be filled with apocalyptical tribulation, the persecution of the true believers and the destruction of the "outer Word." However, at the height of distress, Christ himself would appear and rescue his defenseless saints.

(2) Hoffman claimed for himself the gift of inspired "figurative"—that is, allegorical and prophetic—interpretation of Scripture. Because of this he believed himself vastly superior to the "slippery" servants of the belly who understood only the letter.

(3) He demanded the restoration of the original order of the Christian community. This included the right of the local congregation to elect its pastors (instead of having them appointed by the authorities), and the right of all Christians to prophesy publicly and to interpret the Bible.

(4) Appealing to Karlstadt, he rejected obligatory aural confession as usurpation by the clergy.

(5) He differed with his opponents in his teachings on the sacraments. He taught that Christ united himself only spiritually with the souls of believers and not physically with the bodies of all participants in the Lord's supper. Unlutheran was also his doctrine of the deified man, who "in true self-composure" loves God even when condemned to hell, as well as his dogma that conscious sins committed after "illumination from above" cannot be forgiven. Hoffman's hour had finally come when he accused the local government of misappropriating church property. The irritating prophet and admonisher was expelled, first from Dorpat and then from Reval.

Hoffman fled to Stockholm, the main exchange center for the European fur trade, at that time still under the control of German merchants. The Germans, however, found their authority and autonomy threatened by the politics of Gustav (Wasa) I, the first king of Sweden, who, after the successful war of independence against Denmark, wanted to free Stockholm from Hanseatic control. The differences between the king and the German merchants were heightened by the sovereign's very moderate, pro-evangelical religious politics, which were not sufficiently radical for the German patricians. In order to expedite ecclesiastical reforms, they supported Melchior Hoffman by financing his commentary on the book of Daniel (among other things). The king responded to Hoffman's apocalyptic sermons with orders of expulsion.

Our missionary found even less success in Lübeck. In 1527, its council and cathedral chapter were still solidly on the side of the old church. The vagrant preacher was to be silenced by imprisonment, but fled to Schleswig-Holstein. Surprisingly, he received a letter of safe conduct from Frederick I, king of Denmark. On recommendation of the sovereign, Hoffman was appointed deacon at the church of Nikolai in Kiel. With this position came permission to preach in the whole of Schleswig-Holstein. The king used the untiring itinerant preacher to undermine the Catholic church in the territory. Hoffman now temporarily attained riches and honor. He became the proprietor of the first printing press in Kiel, which he valued at a thousand guilders. He utilized the printing press to defend himself against the attacks of Nicolaus von Amsdorf. The latter had denounced him as a "false prophet" and attacked his apocalypticism. Hoffman visited Wittenberg in 1527 in a second attempt to settle the quarrel with Luther's help. It ended in failure.

During 1528, his dispute with the Lutheran theologians shifted to the topic of the Lord's supper. With increasingly

aggressive words, Hoffman rejected the real presence of
Christ in the sacramental elements of bread and wine. The
Lutheran understanding of the sacrament appeared to him
an attempt to mix the divine with the material in order to
reestablish the control of the clergy over the laity. The
parsons arrogated to themselves the power to conjure the
Lord and Savior into material substance by means of the
spoken sacramental formula, "like a sorcerer traps Satan
in a bottle." In contrast, for Hoffman there was only one
form of real presence, that is, in the consolation of forgiveness. Simultaneously, the fearless zealot attacked the
magistrates of Kiel for enriching themselves with secularized church property at the expense of the community—
a reproach that was probably correct. He thought it would
be best to "butcher or hang" the councillors and to elect a
new council. "To the ruin of the common peace," as his
opponents feared, Hoffman also established relations with
the peasants in East Holstein. After 1524, they had been
increasingly forced into serfdom by the nobility. In April
1529, on the urging of the crown prince, a staunch Lutheran, soon to be King Christian III, Hoffman had to
defend his teachings on the Lord's supper against Bugenhagen and the leading Lutheran theologians of
Schleswig-Holstein at the Disputation of Flensburg.
Karlstadt, whom Hoffman had called in for assistance, had
to leave the territory on orders of the king even before the
disputation. The condemnation of Hoffman was thus a
foregone conclusion. For the third time in his career, Hoffman was expelled. He lost his entire belongings, as well as
his valuable printing press through looting and confisca-
tion. As far as Hoffman was concerned, the Flensburg Disputation revealed the true colors of Lutheranism.
Henceforth the new "papacy" of the Reformers of Wittenberg appeared to him no less tyrannical and blasphemous
than the old church. However, he retained his faith in the
"pious king" who, like Pilate once upon a time, had been

misled by the "godless parsons." Subsequently, Hoffman dedicated his *Exposition of the Revelation of John* to the King of Denmark. He had earlier addressed his *Commentary on the Song of Songs* to the Danish Queen.

In June 1529 after a temporary stay with the Zwinglians of East Frisia where he gained the confidence of chief Ulrich von Dornum, the former chancellor of East Frisia, Hoffman journeyed to Strassburg, the meeting place of the nonconformists of Europe. Martin Bucer, the leading Reformer of the city, at first received him cordially. Hoffman appeared to be a comrade in arms against the Lutheran "magic" of the Lord's supper. Relations between Wittenberg and Strassburg had reached an all-time low. However, it was not long before the evangelical preachers realized what a disconcerting guest they had brought into their house. They advised him to stop preaching and to return to his profession. This signaled Hoffman's final break with the official Reformation. The Strassburg Zwinglians now appeared no better than the Wittenberg Lutherans, namely as unspiritual anti-Christian tyrants, traitors to the true gospel and despisers of the common man.

Hoffman now allied himself with the "poor in spirit lying in the dust." These included followers of Hans Denck and the small group of "Strassburg prophets" who had gathered around the married couple of Lienhard and Ursula Jost. Both groups extolled the "inner Word" far above the "outer Word." They insisted that man find in himself the basis for the certainty of divine knowledge. As heretics, they stood outside the integrated urban society. Under their influence, Hoffman's theology underwent far-reaching changes. He replaced Luther's doctrine of predestination with Denck's faith in a universal divine grace, illuminating all men. Accordingly, Hoffman endorsed the dogma of free will, now also rejecting Luther's teachings on the bondage of the human will formerly upheld by him.

Furthermore, he condemned pedobaptism. The only baptism worthy of a mature free human being was a baptism upon confession of faith. He now differentiated between a first and a second justification. The first consisted of the cancellation of the consequences of original sin through the redemptive death of Christ. It was a gift of pure grace. Through the power of the Spirit, the second justification engendered "a sinless, heavenly man." This was to be earned through serious moral effort and free cooperation with God. If one fell on the straight and narrow path to eternal salvation, consciously committing a mortal sin, one could not be forgiven this sin against the Holy Spirit.

In discussion and debate with Schwenckfeld, Hoffman developed his new doctrine of the "heavenly flesh of Christ," according to which Christ did not take his flesh from the Virgin Mary. Only thus could he become the sacrifice for the sins of mankind. The most significant change, however, occurred in Hoffman's apocalypticism. He accepted the idea held by the Josts that the world had to prepare itself for the return of Christ through an act of great cleansing. Specifically, Hoffman described the cleansing as follows: during the final apocalyptic struggle the free imperial cities would defend the true gospel against the "divinity of hell"—emperor, pope, and false teachers. Although the Anabaptists themselves would not bear arms, they were to support the struggle by prayer and by building fortifications. After a testing period of a difficult siege, the attacking enemy would collapse. Led by the "two witnesses" of the Apocalypse, the 144,000 "apostolic messengers" would then proclaim the joyous message of the universality of divine grace in the whole world, dispensing the baptism of faith. The entire host of false parsons, including the "bloodsucking anti-Christian Lutheran and Zwinglian preachers," would perish. A new theocracy would emerge after the destruction of Babylon. The pious king and the Spirit-filled prophet would work hand in hand as once in the old Israel under Solomon.

This coming reign of peace was to be the necessary precondition for the return of Christ. With the idea that the extermination of the godless must precede the day of final judgment, and with the conception of an earthly reign of saints in a theocratic intermediate kingdom until the return of Christ, Hoffman had created the most important ideological presuppositions for the Anabaptist kingdom of Münster. Unlike Jan Matthijs, Hoffman wanted a revolution from above. The official authorities of the free imperial cities were to secure the military victory. Again and again, Hoffman reminded the magistrates of Strassburg to arm themselves to the teeth for the coming final struggle. He assured them at the same time of his unconditional loyalty. Not even during the holy war [with antichrist] were the Anabaptists to bear arms. Finally, he disapproved of polygamy as practiced by the Melchiorites of Münster.

Hoffman appears to have baptized his followers with believer's baptism on the strength of his own authority. In any case, he makes no reference to having received the true baptism from someone else. His disciples honored him as the second Elijah, one of the "two witnesses," who had butchered the 450 parsons of Baal at the brook of Kishon during his first ministry. In April 1530, Hoffman demanded that the council of Strassburg turn over one of the churches to the Anabaptists. However, since 1529 rebaptism had been punishable by death according to imperial law. The magistrates of Strassburg, therefore, replied to the request with a warrant for Hoffman's arrest. He escaped to East Frisia. Nevertheless, he revisited Strassburg secretly in 1531 and again in the spring of 1533. He was convinced that the events changing the course of world history and leading to the return of Christ would begin in Strassburg during 1533. A considerable following had been won in East Frisia, especially Emden, in the duchies of Holland and Frisia and in the city of Groningen and its surroundings.

A sequence of poor harvests and the paralysis of Baltic trade resulting from the war between Charles V and Denmark produced a severe economic depression from 1529 to 1535. The Melchiorites were primarily recruited from distressed unemployed artisans who suffered from the consequences of an enormous rise in the price of foodstuffs. Similarly, the large Anabaptist community of Strassburg consisted primarily of socially displaced artisans. About 80 percent were refugees. They had sought asylum in Strassburg because of its exemplary social welfare system. The Anabaptist movement in Strassburg was divided. The group around Reublin and Marpeck rejected the Melchiorites and especially Hoffman's teachings on the sword and his elitist demand for leadership by the "apostolic envoys" which amounted to placing the congregation under tutelage.

The evangelical preachers, with Martin Bucer in the lead, feared that the Hoffmanites planned a political revolution. Finding no concrete evidence, they condemned Hoffman for his theological "errors" at the Synod of June 1533. In particular these were his monophysite Christology, his insistence on free human volition, his rejection of pedobaptism, and his doctrine that conscious sins committed after conversion could not be forgiven. Hoffman spent the rest of his life in prison where he died in 1543. A helpless prisoner, his followers in the Netherlands and Westphalia emancipated themselves from his leadership, creating their own state in Münster. Under the influence of these events, Strassburg abandoned its policy of tolerance against the nonconformists.

Four years later in 1538, Johannes Eisenburg and Peter Tasch, his most significant followers, deceived Hoffman. They spread the false report that the master had totally recanted in their presence, thus inducing the majority of Melchiorites in Strassburg to fall away. Hoffman's end was gloomy. He died in absolute loneliness, almost forgotten by the world, banned by the Swiss Brethren as traitor to his own faith, no longer convinced of his own apocalyptic prophecies, suffering from terrible headaches and dropsy, and half blind after lying for months critically ill on the bare floor. During a merciless ten-year process of disillusionment, the second Elijah, who once debated with kings, aristocrats, and Reformers, had been reduced to an object of pity and scorn.

Hoffman had given voice to the expectations of the religiously interested "common man," awakened but disappointed by the Reformation of Wittenberg. Appealing to the priesthood of all believers proclaimed by Luther, he sought to restore the original Christian order of the church. According to 1 Corinthians 14, all believers possessed the right to interpret Scripture. The ministers were to be elected by the autonomous congregation. Secularized church property was to be set aside for the well-being of the poor. The hierarchical territorial church had fulfilled none of these hopes.

Beside this, however, late medieval moods and conceptions surfaced in Hoffman's teachings. Among these were his radical anticlericalism, the belief in the "deified, heavenly, sinless" man, who stands above the law, the doctrine that conscious sin committed after illumination cannot be forgiven, the conception of progressive divine revelation by means of dreams and allegorical prophetic interpretation of Scripture, and finally the expectation of an imminent return of Christ the date of which could be determined. Hoffman's intellectual world was filled with contradictions.

The concept of the universal priesthood of all believers stood in harsh contradiction to the claims of the inspired "apostolic envoys" that they alone possessed the full truth. The Lutheran conception of obedience to government stood in opposition to the idea of exterminating the parsons of Baal. It was impossible to harmonize Anabaptist nonresistance with a military struggle of the spiritual Jerusalem against the forces of hell. His expectations that the evangelical magistrates, who had come to power by legal means, would carry out Hoffman's program of [end-time] purgation were a total illusion.

Remarkable disparity existed also among Hoffman's group of promoters and followers. The rich merchants of Stockholm, the king of Denmark, and the aristocracy of East Frisia used him temporarily to combat the old church as well as the Lutheran hierarchical state church. On the other hand, Hoffman remained the prophet of the impoverished, socially uprooted masses whom he inspired with new hope. The internal contradictions of Hoffman's thought contributed eventually to the breakup of the Melchiorite movement into a peaceful Strassburg wing and the militant Münsterites. The contrasting deaths of Hoffman as a nonresistant prisoner in the jail in Strassburg and of Jan Matthijs as the new Gideon with the sword in his hand outside the gates of the besieged city of Münster function as symbols of the internal rift.

For further reading:

F. O. zur Linden, *Melchior Hoffman*, Haarlem, 1885.
P. Kawerau, *Melchior Hoffman als religiöser Denker*, Haarlem, 1954.
A. F. Mellink, *De Wederdopers in de Noordelijke Nederlanden*, Groningen, 1953.
C. Krahn, *Dutch Anabaptism*, Den Haag, 1968.
J. M. Stayer, *Anabaptists and the Sword*, 2 ed., Lawrence, Kans., 1976, Chap. 10.
K. Deppermann, "Melchior Hoffmans Weg von Luther zu den Täufern," in *Umstrittenes Täufertum*, 173-205.
_____, *Melchior Hoffman: Soziale Unruhen und apokalyptische Visionen im Zeitalter der Reformation*, Göttingen, 1979.
W. Klaassen, "Eschatological Themes in Early Dutch Anabaptism," in *The Dutch Dissenters*, Leiden, 1982.

Willem de Bakker

15. Bernhard Rothmann

The Dialectics of Radicalization in Münster

As a historical figure, Bernhard Rothmann is totally bound up with the Reformation in Münster. Apart from his activities there between 1529 and 1535 we know almost nothing about him. Born about 1495 in Stadtlohn, he may have attended the Cathedral school in Münster, and, possibly, the Deventer school of the Brethren of the Common Life. After a stint as schoolmaster in Warendorf he took a master's degree in Mainz. Then he dropped from sight. In 1529 he resurfaced as preaching assistant at St. Mauritz—a church on episcopal territory just outside Münster—and began to preach the gospel.

Rothmann's career, like the Reformation which he led, fell into two distinct phases. During the first he was a civic Reformer in his own right; during the second he was ideologue and propagandist for the Melchiorite leaders who replaced him. Although he is thus only indirectly responsible for the spectacular finale of his Reformation, his impetuosity and intransigence during the three years he was the major Reformer in Münster did much to set the stage for this finale. The major problem with Rothmann is to decide whether the pattern of ever-widening circles of opposition that characterizes the Reformation he led [first he fulminated against the Catholics, then against Lutheranizing evangelicals, and, finally, against the whole wicked world] was a function of the religious psychology of the man or whether it was due to the ambiguous constitutional arrangement of Münster.

191

At first glance, the situation in Münster when Rothmann arrived with the gospel was not unlike that in many another Reformation city. The institutional structure was broadly determined by three mutually antagonistic forces: the regent class, which traditionally constituted the city council; the more popularly based guilds; and the clergy, headed by a bishop who was titular ruler of the city and surrounding territory. The ideological pendant of this structure had two facets. The first reflected the traditional lay resentment of episcopal authority and clerical privilege in the city. The second reflected the split among the laity over the increasing tendency of the magistrates to constitute themselves into a closed corporation. This oligarchical tendency threatened not only the sense of civic solidarity by means of which the city had won its partial independence from the bishop, it also undermined the legitimacy of the institutional checks that the nonpatrician citizens, through their guilds, had established against the council. The guilds, naturally enough, resisted encroachments aimed at maximizing the council's power and, in response, promoted ever more stridently the slogan of "one community under God" which was their own legitimating ideology. Behind a facade of almost Polybian constitutional harmony—the bishop reigned, the council ruled, and the guilds acted as the tribunes of the people—a persistent three-cornered power struggle dominated political developments in Münster. It also, as we will see, determined the course of the Reformation.

Like everywhere else, the initial effect of the Reformation message in Münster was to give religious moment to traditional lay hostility to the clergy. Long resented as an alien entity and as an affront to civic pride, the clergy—their prestige undermined by Lutheran propaganda about the exclusive authority of the Word—were now said to be deceivers in their most fundamental self-justification, as necessary intermediaries between God and man.

Rothmann's earliest sermons attack the Catholic clergy on just this point. He preached against priestly deception, masses for the dead, purgatory, good works, the intercession of the saints, and images. On the eve of Good Friday 1531, Rothmann's rabble-rousing precipitated an outbreak of sacrilege and iconoclasm at St. Mauritz and his alarmed superiors suggested he go study theology at Cologne for a while. He left Münster but instead of going to Cologne where, his superiors hoped, he would be instructed in the error of his ways, he went on a tour of the major evangelical centers. In July he was back at St. Mauritz, spiritually replenished and still preaching reform.

Since the indirect approach had not rid them of Rothmann, his superiors now appealed directly to the bishop. This resulted in an order forbidding him to preach. Rothmann not only ignored this, but also challenged the Catholics to an open disputation on justification using Scripture as the sole authority. Since authority was the issue in the first place, the Catholics refused to debate on these terms. This left Rothmann free to charge that the Catholics were afraid to debate because their doctrines were false. It also gave him an opportunity to complain to the city council about the false prophets they tolerated in their midst. Such a complaint amounted to telling the city fathers that they and the community they represented had the ultimate responsibility for deciding questions of religion. Here was the kind of legitimation for controlling the religious life of the community that the lay rulers of Münster had always sought. Still, the council was not overly anxious to antagonize the bishop. They made the appropriate noises to express disapproval of religious innovations. They did not, however, try to impede Rothmann in any serious way.

The actual tactics of reform were quite simple. Rothmann was allowed to stir up popular enthusiasm for the gospel. The bishop's threatening response would antagonize the population. The council would then use the civic and religious outrage as an excuse for not acting more energetically against Rothmann who, of course, capitalized on this combination of popular indignation and governmental vacillation to spread his message. After a few cycles in this process of escalation the council, pressed by the guilds, announced that henceforth only the gospel as taught by Rothmann would be tolerated in the city's churches (July 1532). This action of the council hardly mollified the bishop, and his threats throughout the summer and autumn increased Protestant militancy and set the council to exploring the possibilities of a Lutheran alliance. The Münsterites finally forced the issue by taking hostage a number of the bishop's entourage. This prompted him to recognize the religious changes (Treaty of Dülmen, February 1533).

The triumph of the Reformation in the city and its reluctant recognition by the bishop had shifted the locus of religious authority from the clergy to the laity; it had not resolved which laymen should exercise this authority. The regents dominating the council naturally assumed that the authority would be theirs. The guilds, equally naturally from the standpoint of their communal ideology, presumed that it would reside in the community as a whole. This immediately swept the problem of religious authority into the sphere of the political power struggle, and gave Rothmann, as undisputed religious leader of the city, tremendous leverage in legitimating the position either of the council or the guilds.

Rothmann's political ethic, which set the magistracy squarely within the religious life of the community, knew nothing of the Lutheran separation of religious and temporal authority. His doctrine of justification, moreover, put much less stress than Luther's on the internal, personal meaning of faith and much more on its active realization through works of the law. Both in theology and in

political ethic, then, Rothmann's doctrine had a
Reformed—not a Lutheran—flavor. It thus fit very well

Title page of a polemic against the Anabaptists of Münster

with a "people of God" conception which was, of course, but the religious articulation of the guilds' communal ideology. The social implications of Rothmann's religious doctrines thus suggested a natural alliance with the guilds in the civic power struggle.

That this alliance actually came about was perhaps due less to Rothmann than to the atmosphere of tense confrontation during the summer and fall of 1532, and to the arrival, with a fully articulated Zwinglian conception of the sacraments, of Heinrich Rol. First covertly and then more and more openly, Rol repudiated the real presence and argued for a covenantal understanding of the sacraments. He presented them as the symbolic forms through which a Christian testified to God and his fellows that he had forsaken sin and had been reborn in Christ.

In a community whose ideology was already proto-Reformed and which was looking for a religious form to concretize the heightened group consciousness created by the bishop's threats, Rol's sacramental theology, with its suggestive stress on a new people of Israel and its obvious affinities to the civic oath, found a ready audience. Rothmann, who was still encouraging Lutheran preachers to come to Münster and backing efforts for a Lutheran alliance, was thus—so long as he refused to draw the Reformed implications of his own theology—in danger of losing his most enthusiastic followers. After some hesitation—sacramental theology was something about which the prospective Lutheran allies were especially sensitive— he curbed the threat on his left by adopting Rol's position.

For the city council this new religious development was most distressing. They had every reason to suspect that, once the Lutherans heard of it, their already tepid enthusiasm for supporting Münster against its bishop would vanish altogether. Moreover, the Reformed theology that Rothmann was now propounding undermined their authority as magistrates. As long as the Reformation had been a means for winning further independence from the bishop the council had winked at it. Once it became the expression of guild ideology the council's opposition was more energetic.

Despite this new opposition, it seemed likely at first that Rothmann would be able to consolidate his Reformed Reformation. The sudden victory over the bishop just before the annual elections set the stage for an evangelical sweep of the council positions, and there was every reason to expect that the new council would be more tractable. Unfortunately, the new council turned out to be just as jealous of its prerogatives and just as conscious of the external dangers to which Rothmann's eucharistic doctrines exposed the city as the old one had been. When first the Lutherans started to demand they be allowed to examine Rothmann's doctrines for orthodoxy, and then the bishop started to claim that the treaty of Dülmen sanctioned only the religious innovations adopted as of January 1533, the council, afraid of isolating the city from its potential allies, began to put pressure on Rothmann. This rekindled the religious strife and the population divided into three mutually antagonistic groups: the remaining Catholics; the Lutherans, backed by the council; and the Reformed Rothmannists, backed by the guilds. Since neither evangelical party was strong enough to dominate the other, and since the council party did not dare appeal to the Catholics for fear of reviving episcopal authority over the city, this situation resulted in an uneasy stalemate.

The city exploded into violent agitation again when some of Rol's associates, recently expelled from Wassenberg, came to Münster and publicly extended the covenantal implications of his sacramental theology to baptism. Infants, unable consciously to repudiate sin and embrace Christ, should not, they argued, be baptized. Although logical enough, this view encountered the strongest possible opposition from parents who believed that their children would go to hell if they died unbaptized. In addition, antipedobaptism, like Anabaptism, was against imperial law and the council had no desire to add the emperor to Münster's growing list of external enemies. Rothmann was thus ordered to restrain the Wassenbergers. When he not only refused, but joined them, and denied the jurisdiction of temporal authority in religious affairs, the council sought to remove him, at first indirectly and finally—by means of an informal alliance with the Catholics—through force (Nov. 5, 1533).

Because an armed quarrel between the two evangelical parties increased the risk of a Catholic restoration, the guilds, at the last possible minute, persuaded the council to settle for a compromise. Rol and the Wassenbergers were expelled; Rothmann was allowed to stay but forbidden to preach. Of course, this solved nothing. With the chief rabble-rouser still in town, the religious agitation continued. At the end of December the Wassenbergers suddenly reappeared in the city. Rioting followed, after which—the council-Catholic alliance having fallen apart—a new stalemate, infinitely more tense, prevailed. This, then, was the situation that the apostles of Jan Matthijs encountered when they arrived in early January 1534.

Why Rol and Rothmann accepted the apostles' message and submitted to baptism is unclear. Most likely they had given up hope of transforming Münster into an apostolic community and were retreating into a psychology of separation. Be that as it may, by accepting baptism they had fundamentally changed the character of their Reformation from legitimist Reformed to illegitimist Anabaptist.

Since the Münsterites were acutely aware that the toleration of Anabaptism would give the bishop a *casus belli*, apprehension about his reaction dominated the city. When, in the early morning of February 9, it was rumored that the bishop's army was at the gate, the Anabaptists flew to arms and assembled on the market. The other citizens armed also; however, not to defend the city but to hand over the Anabaptists and, in so doing, to save their own skins. In the end, the discovery that the rumor was false and a general distrust of the bishop brought about another compromise. Nevertheless, the damage of the February 9 episode was irreparable. The willingness of the other Münsterites to hand over their Anabaptist fellow citizens in a moment of crisis had fatally undermined civic morale; and when the bishop was seen to make serious preparations for a siege the non-Anabaptists, having less to lose, began to leave. The Anabaptists themselves, giving an apocalyptic interpretation to the crisis, began to send out messengers urging outside brethren to come to Münster, where they would be safe when God's punishment began.

With most of the able-bodied non-Anabaptist males out of town, the Anabaptists had no trouble gaining control of the city council when the annual elections were held on February 23. On that same day the prophet Jan Matthijs with several hundred other Melchiorites arrived to fulminate against the remaining godless. On February 27, the siege began. In response the godless were driven out. Rothmann had attained his holy, apostolic community, though perhaps under different circumstances than he would have wished.

The arrival of Jan Matthijs permanently swept Rothmann from center stage. He lost the ability to influence developments directly and was reduced to articulating and propagandizing the religious ideology of the besieged community. His first efforts in this line were quite restrained and legalistic. Then, as the siege tightened and the Anabaptists fixed their hopes on divine deliverance, the tone of his pamphlets became more shrill.

As propagandist Rothmann was charged with sustaining morale at home and promoting aid from abroad. As Müns-

terite apologist he had to rationalize polygamy, communism, and the assumption of Davidic kingship by Jan van
Leiden. Against a darkening eschatological sky, the
natural way to do all this was to play on the religious
reorientation that had occurred in his audience. The
Anabaptists, with their emphasis upon following Christ in
obedient discipleship, had a distinct New Testament
orientation focused on the synoptic Gospels. However, to
the degree that the present crisis fixed their attention on
divine deliverance, their religious consciousness shifted
from New Testament imitation to Old Testament anticipation of the Messiah. A group that had formerly consciously
perceived of itself as a New Testament holy people of God
now found itself, both in external circumstances and in religious psychology, in much the same situation as the embattled Israel of the prophets.

This psychological shift to the Old Testament made it
possible for Rothmann to claim that, contrary to the
conventional interpretation, Christ in his first advent had
not fulfilled all the promises of the prophets, but that, as
was written, he would do so before his second coming.
World history Rothmann interpreted as a series of restitu-
tions and falls. Christ's, the greatest previous restitution,
had been followed by a decline in which the biblical
measure of wickedness would be filled. The recovery of the
Word marked the end of the decline and thus the beginning
of the glorious final restitution. In these final days, then,
all that had yet to be fulfilled would be fulfilled: both the
promises and the wickedness. Apart from making possible
this understanding of history, the Old Testament provided
happy models for the Davidic kingship, polygamy and communism.

At first Rothmann ascribed to the Münsterites a passive
role in these last days. Then, as the siege tightened and
persecution elsewhere became fiercer, the mission of the
Anabaptists was conceived as active. The Davidic kingdom

was now no longer a place to gather the saints in anticipation of the new Solomon but a crusading kingdom to cleanse the world of the godless and to prepare the way for the second coming.

Unfortunately, words alone did not conjure up troops and, as human and divine aid failed to materialize, morale in the besieged city started to sag. In the end not even Rothmann believed that God would come to the rescue. In his last pamphlet and letter he brooded about the possibility that perhaps Münster's historical significance lay in giving the godless the occasion for completing the measure of wickedness. Münster's fall would thus inaugurate the second coming. Cold comfort perhaps to the thousands of desperate people in the city, but at least Rothmann and the other leaders could expire in the serene conviction that the godless would get their deserved punishment in the end.

Münster fell on June 25, 1535. Rothmann is generally believed to have been killed in the final assault or subsequent slaughter. Although there is some plausible evidence that he may have survived, his historical role ended when the curtain rang down in Münster.

The process of radicalization in Münster, after the initial success of the Reformation there, was the product of a conflict over religious authority in a context of increasing external pressure on the city. Rothmann, with his sense that God had directly chosen him to transform Münster into an apostolic community, was unwilling to have the council dictate to him the nature and extent of this transformation. The council, in its turn, was equally unwilling to have Rothmann's religious innovations jeopardize the security of the community. This conflict led Rothmann to claim that the council's authority in matters of religion was legitimate only to the extent that it coroborated and reinforced his authority as the community's prophet. This claim, being the exact analogue of the guilds' long-standing claim that the council's authority was legiti-

mate only in so far as it was corroborated by them as the
people's tribunes, found a ready support among the guild
membership. This support, together with the mood of
intransigence evoked by the bishop's threats, emboldened
Rothmann at the critical moments to claim that his "truth"
transcended all earthly considerations and to override temporal authority completely. The result was Anabaptism.

For further reading:

R. Stupperich, *Die Schriften Bernhard Rothmanns. Die Schriften
    der Münsterischen Täufer und ihrer Gegner I*, Münster, 1970.
C. A. Cornelius, *Geschichte des Münsterischens Aufruhrs*, 2 vols.,
    Leipzig, 1855 and 1860.
G. Brendler, *Das Täuferreich zu Münster 1534-35*, Berlin, 1966.
K. H. Kirchhoff, *Die Täufer in Münster. Untersuchungen zum
    Umfang und zur Sozialstruktur der Bewegung*, Münster,
    1973.
H. Schilling, "Aufstandsbewegungen in der Stadtbürgerlichen
    Gesellschaft des Alten Reiches. Die Vorgeschichte des
    Münsteraner Täuferreichs, 1525-1534," in H.-U. Wehler, *Der
    Deutsche Bauernkrieg 1524-1526*, Göttingen, 1975, 193-238.
J. M. Stayer, "The Münsterite Rationalization of Bernhard
    Rothmann," *Journal of the History of Ideas*, 28, 179-192.
R. van Dülmen, *Reformation als Revolution. Soziale Bewegung
    und religiöser Radikalismus in der deutschen Reformation*,
    München, 1977.
W. J. de Bakker, "De Vroege Theologie van Bernhard Rothman.
    De Gereformeerde Achtergrond van het Munsterse Doper-
    rijk," *Doopsgezinde Bijdragen*, 3, 1977, 9-20.
J. M. Stayer, "Vielweiberei als 'innerweltliche Askese': Neue
    Eheauffassungen in der Reformationszeit," *Mennonitische
    Geschichtsblätter* 37, N.F. no. 32, 1980, 24-41.
K.-H. Kirchhoff, "Was There a Peaceful Anabaptist Congregation
    in Münster in 1534?" *Mennonite Quarterly Review* 44, 1970,
    357-370.

16. Menno Simons

The New Man in Community

In a letter by Menno Simons about 1545 to a group of Anabaptists at Amsterdam, the problem of the new man and his commitment to community is thrown into sharp focus. Here within the compass of a pastoral document we catch a glimpse of the church—in this case the emergent brotherhood eventually to be known as Doopsgezinden and Mennonites—calling for the allegiance of the newly awakened man of the Reformation period. The more exact time was the first decade following the uprisings at Münster, Oldeklooster, Amsterdam, and elsewhere in the Netherlands, a time of disillusionment and uncertainty. The executions and suppression, awful and severe as they were, tried men's souls and led to much discernment of spirits. Was it really necessary to break with the existing order? Was public worship not a matter indifferent to true faith? Could one not conform outwardly and nonconform inwardly? Men and women of the spirit always find their likes, do they not? The answers were not always apparent. Good men differed in their views. A spiritual leader such as Obbe Philips, who had baptized and ordained Menno Simons along with many other believers, questioned the authority of his own calling and forsook the brotherhood. Menno and his supporters however took a firm stand in favor of open dissent, calling for a separated and disciplined church.

The letter is addressed to a group of secret believers who concealed their faith and thus avoided persecution. Menno writes to them in affectionate terms—at one place he calls them "beloved brethren and sisters in Christ Jesus"—but chides them for attending services, receiving the mass (at least at Easter), and permitting the baptism of infants in the Roman Catholic Church, that is, in the established church of the town. These compromises, Menno states, are not in line with scriptural teaching; neither can they be justified with innuendos about Christian liberty. How can you, he asks, partake of the antichrist's table and neglect the Lord's supper? As for baptism, Christ commanded his church to baptize believers on confession of faith. As for any kind of community, you know, Menno writes, "wherever there are two or three stones together, held together with the mortar of love, there they hasten to destroy them." This reference to believers as living stones in a spiritual house (1 Pet. 2:5) is a favorite figure of Menno. Here, no doubt, he alludes to the action on the part of the authorities to destroy not only the dissenting congregations but also the secret fraternities. In sum, the letter admonishes the Amsterdam brethren to declare their faith openly to the world.

We have chosen this letter as a way to approach an estimate of the life and work of Menno Simons not only because it brings some of his ideas into relief but also the man himself. In it he relates to a specific group of people in a precise historical situation. It would be possible to look at one or more of his chief writings in order to investigate our subject but here we can see it focused on a life situation. Menno, it seems, has rapport with his audience, is able to identify with them, probably because he struggled with the same problem in his own life. Also the issue has some relevance for us today and our hopes and needs for faith and community. Furthermore, this particular letter has been neglected in recent Menno Simons studies.

Our subject about the new man in community offers a perspective on the Christian view of man in the world. In

Menno's writings the new man has turned away from sin in his own life and in the world and is renewed in Christ with the result that he manifests the spirit and nature of Christ in all of his conduct. The new man, however, cannot live in

Menno Simons

isolation. As a man in Christ he finds his identity and fulfillment in the body of Christ, that is, the community. In this view the community is seen as an extension of the new man. The individual as well as the group is identified with Christ. As the believer is in Christ and Christ in him, so the community is in Christ and Christ in the community. In the theological as well as in the existential sense we can speak of "Christ existing as community" (Bonhöffer). The most recent study of Menno emphasizes the central significance of the new birth in Menno's concept of faith. This interpretation is justified. Not only is it documented in the writings of Menno, but it is illuminated by the fact that teaching about the salvation of man was central to the controversies of the Reformation period. It is important to notice that Menno's understanding of the community is entirely dependent on his concept of the new man.

It is not altogether arbitrary to divide Menno's writings into two groups: those that deal with the new man in discipleship, and those which describe the church or the community as the bride of Christ. To avoid misunderstanding, we emphasize that Menno never claimed to be a theologian. He was concerned more to be a Christian than to define dogma. Whenever he allowed himself to be drawn into controversy such as, for example, the dispute with Jan a Lasco, it happened because of the consequences which flowed from the subject of the debate for the actual life of the Christian, in this case the incarnation. He would admit only one standard of truth, namely the authority on which he drew—the Bible—and in it primarily the New Testament.

Menno's conception of the new man in the community appears to have been theologically based. For nearly two decades, under extreme oppression, the brotherhood in the Netherlands gradually developed into a viable alternative to the existing church. It was determinative for the faith and confession of a significant branch of the Reformation.

Nevertheless, even before Menno's death this brotherhood withdrew from the world and degenerated into a narrow sectarianism. One other fact was also important: the internalization of the radical faith of the 1530s as it occurred in the sectarian phase prepared the way for outward conformity. Barred from public life and the professions the hardworking and thrifty Doopsgezinden soon became prosperous merchants and traders. By the end of the sixteenth century the sluices against conformity in general had opened and the "world" came in with a flood.

The Amsterdam letter, as already noted, has a pastoral character. Menno writes as a spiritual father concerned about the well-being of spiritual children. However, he does not call them "elect brethren and sisters," the name reserved for members of the dissenting community. Still he does not question their new birth but warns that unless they forsake the false shepherds who do not pasture the sheep of Christ aright they will die spiritually. This letter was evidently written to a group of Melchiorites, rather than followers of David Joris, and its date of composition is likely early in the 1540s. It is far too brotherly and even conciliatory to be intended for Davidjorists. One need only compare the condemnation and severe censure Menno heaps on this latter group in his writings; they are included, for example, under "the corrupted sects" in "The Foundation of Christian Doctrine" (1539-1540). Also Amsterdam became the chief center of the Melchiorites during the early 1530s when Hoffman appointed Jan Volckerts Trijpmaker as his successor.

The Melchiorites, as the earliest Anabaptists in the Netherlands, were particularly inclined to compromise the public profession of faith. This was partly due to their roots in the Sacramentarian movement in the Netherlands. The Sacramentarians were nonseparating dissenters who held their faith in secret. At the time of the breakthrough of Anabaptism in Northwest Europe in 1530 under the impetus of Melchior Hoffman's preaching at Emden, some of them were in the town as exiles and joined the new movement. When "zendboten" (emissaries) went through the land and preached the imminent return of Christ and baptized the new believers, the authorities acted swiftly against them. But Melchior Hoffman, rather than face the persecution, declared a moratorium on further rebaptism and the Anabaptist preachers temporarily halted their activities. It must be said too in regard to secret belief—Nicodemism as it was called after Nicodemus of John 3—that it was a common position held at the time of the Reformation. Free spirits such as Sebastian Franck and especially Otto Brunfels worked out moral justification for a wholly spiritual and interior view of religion. Consistent with this they regarded all ceremonies and outward observances as nonessential to true faith. Both of these authors were known and influential in the Netherlands.

It was in the Melchiorite form that Menno first encountered Anabaptism. He tells us how he was stunned to hear about the execution of his fellow countryman Sicke Freerks (1531) for being rebaptized. The area in which Menno resided in Friesland was in fact a hotbed of Anabaptist activity during the early 1530s which came to a head in the seizure of the Oldeklooster, a Cistercian abbey near Bolsward, on Easter of 1535. Menno resorted to an intense study of Scripture to learn for himself the truth about baptism but found nothing about infant baptism. Sicke Freerks he says was a "God-fearing, pious hero." As for "the zealous children" of the uprisings he feared that his disclosure "to some of them [of] the abominations of the papal system" had influenced them. The authorities too blamed the preachers for inciting the uprising.

The evidence that Menno was a Melchiorite is not explicit. He certainly rejected infant baptism shortly after 1531, and about eight years earlier he rejected the real presence in the mass and thus stood in the Sacramentarian camp. As we have observed he knew the Melchiorite position and was kindly disposed toward its members. Menno evidently had a likable personality, for he tells us that people liked him and said he was a good fellow. His popularity, however, as well as his position as a parish priest stood in the way of a break with the existing order. Even though he had radical views about the Lord's supper and baptism, he continued in his frivolous way of life until about a year before the break came in 1536. To say with K. Vos that Menno had his Melchiorite period is a convincing way to explain the many years of standing still, but then it must have been a matter of attitude or as a fellow traveler rather than a member of the party. After the break he seems to have had contacts with Melchiorites, although he did not attend the Bocholt Conference (1536) when Anabaptists leaders conferred after the Münster debacle. Certainly many of his own supporters came from the Melchiorites, and the Amsterdam letter suggests that in the early 1540s he assumed pastoral responsibility for members of the group.

Menno's earliest writings are devoted to the subject of the new man of which "The New Creature" is the most important. It first appeared in 1539 and was reprinted more often than any other one of his writings during his lifetime. A look at these first expressions of a changed life offer no doubt the best cue to what happened when in 1536 he laid down his priestly office, forsook his former way of life, and "willingly submitted to distress and poverty under the heavy cross of Christ." What we are suggesting is that Menno's renunciation of Rome, as it has been called—he spoke of "my illumination, conversion, and calling"—and his writings about the new man should be placed side by side in order to see the cause-and-effect relationship in a right perspective.

First of all the illumination. In Menno's own account of the influences which brought him to a knowledge of the truth in God's Word (Scripture) he mentions Luther but discounts "the instrumentality of the erring sects." His view of baptism and the Lord's supper, he tells us, were obtained through the illumination of the Holy Spirit and through the reading and pondering of Scripture. In this connection Menno says he hopes he is telling the truth for he desires to give thanks to those who helped him. Writing this to Gellius Faber by way of defense in 1554 he discounts the influence of the Melchiorites. One is also reminded that his insights about baptism and the Lord's supper were gained in the years he still lived in carelessness and carnality. There can be little question that Menno was a child of early Anabaptism in the Netherlands. Still the statements about his own searching of Scripture should not be discounted, for the Bible and the Bible only was the source as well as the authority for divine truth. In "The New Creature" also Menno emphasizes that the knowledge leading to regeneration can only originate in the Word of God (Scripture) and be received in the heart by faith through the Holy Spirit.

The experience of regeneration Menno considers in terms of conversion and the new birth. The accent is primarily on a new state of being, a qualitative change, rather than on an experience as verification in time and place (pietism). The new state of being is a Christ-relationship: "You must be so converted and changed that you become new men in Christ, so that Christ is in you and you are in Christ." The new man then lives in the spirit of Christ and bears good fruit.

Complimentary to illumination and regeneration is the call into the communion of saints. In Menno's account of his call he stresses that he was rightly chosen for the work of minister or shepherd in the brotherhood by men sound in doctrine and irreproachable in life, separated from the world, and living under the cross. While these remarks were written in reply to Gellius Faber, they allude to the new developments in Dutch Anabaptism in regard to the place and character of the new community. Menno's 1536 decision not only involved a break with the Roman Catholic Church, but also with the Melchiorites and all other parties who had compromised with the world. As we have observed in the case of the Amsterdam Melchiorites, Menno called for an open testimony before the world and separation from the established churches. "Flee from Babylon and go to Jerusalem" he wrote in the Amsterdam letter by which he meant that the brethren were to depart not only from the Roman Church but also to forsake the world.

Menno's call, interestingly enough, had in it the echoes of the Münster kingdom. What was Menno's "Jerusalem" to be like? In the first place there was a continuity with the past. The elders who ordained him and thus confirmed his own divine call had come out of the early Melchiorite movement. We know that Obbe Philips was among them and commissioned Menno for his office as elder. Did Menno find in a select group of Melchiorite Anabaptists a prototype for the biblical example of the Christian community as he understood it? That is, a group of peaceful Anabaptists who kept themselves apart from Münsterites, Batenburgers, and Davidjorists, who had lived openly before the world and avoided the compromises of the main group of Melchiorites? That such a group existed we know for certain, but its strength and patterns of life and practice often seem unclear. When did the Anabaptist community begin? It is a question that cannot be answered clearly.

The idea of the Christian community as a fellowship of covenanted Christians is common to all groups of Dutch Anabaptists. When Menno left the official church in 1536 the government in Friesland reported that he had gone over to "the covenant of the Anabaptists." While the name refers specifically to baptism, it also indicates the close-knit character of the Anabaptist brotherhood. After Münster there was the strong concern that the community should provide true shepherds to feed the flock but to guard against the false shepherds. In the Amsterdam letter the brethren are repeatedly reminded of the futility of seeking spiritual nourishment under the false shepherds and the need for the sheep to seek the protection of the community. In his writings but also in his work in the brotherhood Menno was intensely preoccupied with the community as the bride of Christ. He envisioned the community as a chaste virgin to be presented to the one husband Christ (2 Corinthians 11:2). The community, he says, must be so pure that those who taught wrong doctrine or caused offense or divisions were to be avoided. The failure of Menno and his close colleagues to maintain a strictly disciplined community led to a centralization of power and authority; decisions passed into the college of elders. No longer was the community the place where the continuity of Christ's work and revelation found expression. The rightful character of the church as the community of the new man, as earlier envisioned by Menno, was lost sight of. Over against what Bornhäuser calls an "oligarchic community leadership" one might place the fully independent order of the local congregation in the Baptist churches, in some ways the English version of the Doopsgezinden (Mennonites) and which today has gone on to number 64 million members.

It is sometimes stated that from an historical point of view Menno Simons was a second-generation figure, more Doopsgezind than Anabaptist. Actually he was the same age as Michael Sattler and Melchior Hoffman. In Friesland he lived in an area where Anabaptism first took hold in the Netherlands and was related to the developing movement, sometimes obliquely, until five years had passed and he decided to join it. He was rather a transitional figure, and although much was transmuted under his leadership it would be wrong to give the impression that the vital forces of Dutch Anabaptism were spent in the early 1530s. As the Netherlands continued under Habsburg rule the Anabaptists were compelled to live under the cross. Nevertheless the movement grew in numbers as well as in spiritual strength and permanence. In all of this Menno played a leading role.

For further reading:

Menno Simons, *Opera omnia theologica*, Amsterdam, 1681.

Menno Simons, *Die vollständigen Werke*, Elkhart, Ind., 2 vols., 1876 and 1881.

J. C. Wenger (ed.), *The Complete Writings of Menno Simons*, Scottdale, Pa., 1956.

K. Vos, *Menno Simons*, Leiden, 1914.

A. F. Mellink, *De Wederdopers in de noordelijke Nederlanden*, Groningen, 1953.

C. Krahn, *Dutch Anabaptism*, Den Haag, 1968, Scottdale, Pa., 1981.

H. W. Meihuizen, *Menno Simons*, Haarlem, 1961.

Chr. Bornhäuser, *Leben und Lehre Menno Simons, Ein Kampf um das Fundament des Glaubens*, Neukirchen-Vluyn, 1973.

H. J. Hillerbrand, "Menno Simons: Sixteenth Century Reformer," *Church History* 31, 1962, 387-399.

C. Krahn, *Menno Simons*, Karlsruhe, 1936.

G. K. Epp, "The Spiritual Roots of Menno Simons," in Harry Loewen (ed.), *Mennonite Images*, Winnipeg, 1980, 51-59.

17. Caspar von Schwenckfeld

Proclaimer of the Middle Way

One of the most controversial figures of the Reformation is without doubt the Silesian nobleman, Caspar von Schwenckfeld von Ossig. Disagreement over him is not recent. It preceded the relatively early beginning of modern Schwenckfeld research at the end of the nineteenth century. Indeed, it is evident in the literature of his contemporaries. Whereas some listed this lay theologian among the heretics and twisted his name into "Stenckfeld [stinking field]," others identified him with one of the two witnesses in the book of Revelation (11:3), the prophesied forerunners of the Messiah. Who was Schwenckfeld and what theological concerns were pursued by this man whose name still lives, institutionalized in the "Schwenckfelder Church"?

Schwenckfeld was born in 1489 at Ossig near Lüben in the principality of Liegnitz to a noble Silesian family which traced its heritage back to the thirteenth century. It is certain that, following his early education, he attended the University of Cologne, and the Viadrina (an institution strongly influenced by humanism) at Frankfort on the Oder. It is possible that he studied canon law in addition to the liberal arts. He never received an academic degree. Following court service in the principalities of Münster-berg-Oels and Brieg, he entered the service of the Piast, Duke Frederick II of Liegnitz, as court counselor about 1518 or 1519.

Under the influence of Luther's works, in particular the

latter's commentary on the seven penitential psalms, Schwenckfeld experienced a religious awakening. Thereafter, until the end of his life, he felt himself under obligation to Luther. Because of his position of trust at the court of Frederick II, he was able quickly to gain acceptance for the Reformation movement in the city and principality of Liegnitz and to gather about himself numerous followers. Among these the one who was to become the most significant was Valentin Crautwald. Trained as a humanist and belonging to the Silesian Reuchlinists, Crautwald was a canon at the richly endowed Liegnitz chancellery of the Holy Sepulcher.

Schwenckfeld and his friends immediately sought to bring all of Silesia to the new faith. The bishop of Breslau, Jakob von Salza, took a posture of waiting, as his predecessor had, but in the end did not agree to a reform of his diocese when the cathedral chapter stood stoutly against the concerns of the Reformation. As a result Schwenckfeld and his friends endeavored, this time successfully, to move the temporal authority, Duke Frederick II, to issue a mandate for the Reformation. Furthermore, they concerned themselves with an intensification of preaching. Schwenckfeld himself, as a layman, preached publicly "for some years before lords, bishops, princes and a great multitude of the people." Moreover, they endeavored above all to renew the catechumenate, particularly for adults, and began as a result to produce a practical catechetical literature. Since Schwenckfeld and his circle felt themselves part of the Wittenberg movement, they exchanged ideas with other Reformation centres inside and outside Silesia, for example, with Breslau and Königsberg in Prussia.

Since about 1522, however, a cautious critique of the Reformation is to be noted in Schwenckfeld. Gradually he came to the conviction that the absence of the general religious awakening ardently awaited by him had a double cause: the Reformation doctrine of justification was misunderstood, and it was partly false. It based the reception of grace on no condition (namely asceticism), completely denied the freedom of the human will, and totally eliminated the significance of works for justification. Schwenckfeld was convinced, on the other hand, that by the communication of the Spirit, the sinner experienced a saving righteousness and progressively became a "new man," reflecting his new state in ethical behavior. This position was shaped, in addition to the undoubted role of Luther's thought, by humanistic and mystical influences.

In 1525 Schwenckfeld developed his own doctrine of the Lord's supper, since he believed he could not ascertain any ethical improvement in Lutheran communicants after they had taken the sacrament. Basing his approach on the Johannine treatment of the bread of life, he constructed with others, and particularly with the trilingual Crautwald, a new understanding of the Lord's supper, which was certainly influenced by Zwingli. Referring to the logion of the bread of life in John 6 and basing their position on their own headstrong philological-grammatical exegesis of the New Testament texts on the Lord's supper, Schwenckfeld and Crautwald taught that believers ate the bread of heaven, namely Christ, in a spiritual-essential manner at the celebration of the Eucharist but at other times as well. Since they were convinced of the truth of their conception of the Lord's supper, they endeavored to win Luther and his associates to their side. With this in mind Schwenckfeld traveled to Wittenberg at the end of 1525 and held discussions with Luther, Bugenhagen, and Justus Jonas. The endeavor foundered, however. As a result, with the agreement of their prince in Liegnitz, Schwenckfeld and Crautwald provisionally suspended the celebration of the Lord's supper and were soon charged as despisers of the sacrament.

After the final break with Wittenberg in 1526, the

Liegnitz brotherhood drew closer to the Swiss and Upper German Reformers since, not without justification, they saw themselves as theologically related to them. Because the Swiss and Upper Germans also rejected the real presence of Christ in the bread and wine, the Silesians only needed to interpret their concept of the spiritual-essential eating of the bread of life more clearly in the sense of an eating in "faith" to secure a consensus. Although the Swiss and the Upper Germans were able to rejoice in the new association, Schwenckfeld and his followers were, above all because of this association, soon faced with a decisive opponent in Johannes Fabri, the court preacher and ecclesiastical counsel of King Ferdinand I. Fabri soon began a literary campaign against them. His attack was directed in particular against Schwenckfeld's understanding of the sacrament which in fact approached that of Zwingli and the Upper Germans at this time. King Ferdinand I finally issued a number of mandates against the despisers of the sacrament in the year 1528. To spare Duke Friedrich II personal unpleasantness and, above all, not to endanger the reform program in Liegnitz, Schwenckfeld voluntarily went into exile at the beginning of 1529. He never returned to his homeland, although he later repeatedly investigated possibilities to do so.

Schwenckfeld went to Southwest Germany to the famous imperial free city of Strassburg where he was taken in as a guest first by Wolfgang Capito and then by Matthäus and Catharina Zell. Capito praised Schwenckfeld to Zwingli as a "Vir vere nobilis. Totus Christum spirat [a man truly noble; as a whole being he breathes Christ]." Initially a peaceful harmony existed between the Silesian nobleman and the Strassburg theologians. Schwenckfeld shared fully in the life of the community and took part in dealing with the ecclesiastical as well as the theological problems which arose. Relatively early, however, his first differences and disagreements with the preachers of the city, especially with Martin Bucer, developed. In particular, these concerned the problem of the significance of the external word and the sacrament for salvation. Because of his spiritualist position it was inconceivable to Schwenckfeld that salvation should be bound to the external spoken word. Sharply distinguishing between Holy Scripture and the Word of God, he insisted that salvation is never given through the "external." Associated with this problem was the question of the theological evaluation of and the pastoral relationship toward the Anabaptists in Strassburg who were growing ever stronger. Schwenckfeld, who was little interested in the question of baptism, was first encouraged to deal with it by Bucer himself.

In the fall of 1533 Schwenkfeld went on a long journey to Augsburg, where he wished to visit with friends and to take care of some financial matters—he received an annual rent from his lands in Ossig. His journey took him by way of Speyer, Esslingen, and Ulm. Because of his modesty and learning he was able to make close contacts and lifelong friendships with important persons everywhere, such as Hans-Friedrich Thumb, the chief magistrate in Kirchheim-unter-Teck not far from Esslingen. In Augsburg Schwenckfeld was taken in by the pastor Bonifacius Wolfhart, whom he had come to know some years earlier in Strassburg. In Wolfhart's home he completed his knowledge of Hebrew. The Strassburg theologians, above all Bucer, had in the meantime endeavored to discredit Schwenckfeld in Augsburg and in all of South Germany, sending out warnings against him as one who stirred up controversy. Nevertheless, he was able to win numerous loyal followers among the residents of Augsburg.

In July 1534, Schwenckfeld returned to Strassburg, going by way of Ulm, where he was soon embroiled in a spirited discussion with the cathedral preacher, Martin Frecht. When Schwenckfeld arrived in Strassburg, a bitter controversy developed between himself and the theolo-

gians. Bucer increasingly played a leading role in the attack on Schwenckfeld and finally succeeded in winning
over the city council against the Silesian nobleman. As a

Caspar von Schwenckfeld

result Schwenckfeld was requested to leave the city. So as to avoid official banishment, Schwenckfeld left Strassburg in 1534 of his own accord, and following brief stays over several months in various locations in south Germany, he went to Ulm in Württemberg.

Here Duke Ulrich I, after his lands had been returned to him as a fief of Austria in 1534, began to carry out a reformation. One year later he issued a mandate against clandestine preaching. The mandate indirectly affected Schwenckfeld and his followers in Württemberg, and because of this Schwenckfeld's influential friend, Hans Conrad Thumb von Neuberg, the Duke's hereditary marshal, arranged for a meeting in Tübingen between the Silesian nobleman and some theologians: Ambrosius Blaurer, who represented the principality of Württemberg; Bucer, who represented Strassburg, where the controversy with Schwenckfeld had arisen; and Frecht, as leader of the Ulm church. In spite of clear theological differences at this so-called Tübingen Colloquy, a concord was reached in which each of the two parties agreed to cease further attack on one another. Schwenckfeld nurtured the mistaken hope that this agreement would serve as the basis for a continuing peaceful coexistence.

Schwenckfeld was in fact able to live in Ulm for almost two years unmolested. During this period he dwelt with the mayor, Bernhard Besserer, and won to his case a number of followers, particularly women. He also found patrons and friends among the city's nobility. After two years, however, Frecht, regretting and ignoring the Tübingen agreement, began to intrigue against Schwenckfeld, asserting that the latter not only did not hold to the union of the Upper Germans and Wittenberg reached in the Wittenberg Concord, but that he opposed it. At the beginning of November 1536 Schwenckfeld defended himself ably against these charges before the city's five privy councillors. However, as the Ulm preachers' opposition nevertheless continued, Schwenckfeld undertook ever more regular and lengthier journeys, some of which lasted several months, so as to pacify the irate theologians.

The opposition of the Ulm preachers against Schwenckfeld escalated in 1537-38 with the beginning of a Christological controversy. Schwenckfeld insisted at this time in an evermore pronounced way that the humanity of Christ was not created. Consistent with his Spiritualist position he rejected the concept of creature as applied to Christ's humanity. Christ, he insisted, had taken his flesh from Mary (thus Schwenckfeld distinguished his position from the Valentinian Christology of Melchior Hoffman); thereafter, Christ's flesh underwent a continual process of deification through suffering and the cross. Following the resurrection and the ascension, the humanity of Christ was "completely clothed, penetrated, and irradiated with the glory of God." If the flesh of Christ was not divine, Schwenckfeld argued, we could not eat of it in a spiritual-essential manner, nor could we receive a substantive share in the divine nature, i.e., become new men. Christ's humanity was therefore deified so that through this "divine flesh all other creaturely flesh might be helped." Thus Schwenckfeld's Christology is certainly shaped by his soteriological interest.

In the summer of 1538, fourteen Christological theses in manuscript of Schwenckfeld opposing the creatureliness of Christ's humanity were circulated by him in Ulm. As a result Frecht denounced Schwenckfeld to his host, the mayor Besserer, and thus indirectly to the secular authority. A short time thereafter Frecht informed the South German and Swiss Reformers (Heinrich Bullinger, Joachim Vadian, Johannes Brenz, Blaurer, Bucer, and others) of Schwenckfeld's Christology. Frecht wished to banish the Silesian nobleman, and to reach this goal more easily he attempted to link Schwenckfeld with Sebastian Frank, who

had printed two Crautwald pieces a few years earlier at
Schwenckfeld's request, and who had been banished by the
Ulm magistracy early in 1539. Schwenckfeld defended his
Christological views before the Ulm council on January 13,
1539. When the councillors hesitated to move against the
"heretic," the preachers themselves petitioned for their dismissal.

Concerned for his host Besserer and wishing to avoid
possible banishment, Schwenckfeld voluntarily left the
city in September of the same year. It is astonishing that in
spite of his many travels, he still found time to carry on an
extensive correspondence and to compose numerous
theological, catechetical, and ascetic treatises. In the
following year after visiting followers in Augsburg, Esslingen, and the surrounding area, Schwenckfeld went to
stay at the castle of his friend and patron Ludwig von
Freyberg at Justingen on the Swabian Alb west of Ulm.
Thanks as well to the protection of the landgrave Philip of
Hesse, whom Schwenckfeld had first visited in the summer
of 1535 and with whom he had corresponded thereafter, he
was able to live in Justingen unhindered for seven years, to
carry on a continually growing correspondence, to edit
several works, and to compose many theological treatises,
concerned for the most part with the Christological question.

In these years, the controversy over his Christology
reached its high point. In March 1540 it was condemned by
the theological gathering at Schmalkalden; Schwenckfeld
was not given the opportunity for a defense. Now finally
standing outside reformed Christendom, he movingly complained: "Alas, how almost all the shelters throughout the
world are closed to me." He did not give in, however, but
defended his Christology in a number of treatises, and in
particular detail in his *Confession and Declaration of the
Knowledge of Christ and His Divine Glory* which he wrote
a year after the condemnation of his position. To prove his

orthodoxy he supported his contentions with citations from the Fathers. Nor did he refrain from pointing out the differences in the Christological conceptions of Wittenberg and the Swiss and to play them off against one another. Because of his peculiar Christological position a long and fierce controversy arose between himself and the Zwinglians, first with Vadian and Bullinger, and later also with the Lutherans, above all with Sebastian Coccius and Brenz. The controversy centered particularly on Schwenckfeld's eutychian position that the humanity of Christ even in the state of humiliation (*status exinanitionis*) was not a creature, and on his patripassian formulation that Christ in the state of humiliation also suffered in his divine nature.

In all these battles Schwenckfeld enjoyed external peace and security at the castle in Justingen. It is interesting to note that he gained influence in the Freyberg territory and its pastorate only after the death of his protector through Ludwig's heir, his son George Ludwig. He often went on visits with friends in Augsburg and Speyer, carefully obscuring his route so as to protect himself and his followers against persecution. However, when George Ludwig refused, among other things, to reestablish Catholicism in his domain, the emperor, Charles V, took action at the beginning of 1547. A small war began, the so-called "Schwenckfeldian War." The area was taken over and Schwenckfeld with his lord had to leave his refuge. For the following three years he lived incognito in a Franciscan monastery in Esslingen. From there he wrote to his friends, for the most part under the pseudonym Eliander.

The last decade of his life was marked by continual wandering, by long or short stays with followers and friends in imperial free cities or in the castles of noble patrons. Nevertheless, he remained true to his Spiritualist position not to organize his followers in any way into a "separate church"; at most, he brought the circles of his friends into a rather loose association. In spite of continual disturbance he still found time and leisure to publish a not insignificant number of compositions. Among these are to be noted several polemical treatises against Matthias Flacius, the most determined leader of the Gnesio-Lutherans.

Schwenckfeld had long suffered from arthritis and for this reason sought the baths. In the summer of 1561 he became seriously ill in Memmingen, where he was staying with his fellow countryman Jakob Meretzki of Jägerndorf, and followed the urgent request of his longtime follower, the Ulm physician, Agathe Streicher, to come to her home to be treated. There on December 10, 1561, at seventy-two years of age he died among his most loyal friends—a man who had given all to propagate "the true mean between Papists and Lutherans which is the ruling king Jesus Christ with his justification."

The story of Schwenckfeld's influence did not end with his death. This influence is particularly apparent in mystical Spiritualism and Pietism, and to a lesser extent elsewhere, although it is more indirect than direct and more theological and spiritual than historical. Especially to be noted are the ties to radical Pietism with its Spiritualist, individualist, and ethical tendencies. On the other hand, there is more historical than theological continuity between Schwenckfeld and the conventicle-like communities which arose in Württemberg and Silesia, in the county of Glatz and especially in the region of the Bober-Katzbach Mountains. Even if these groups, in part under the influence of Anabaptist ideas and in part under the renewed reception of the mystical inheritance, substantially modified Schwenckfeld's theology, they, nevertheless, kept alive the memory of the Silesian nobleman, the proclaimer of the "middle" way.

For further reading:

Corpus Schwenckfeldianorum, Vols. 1-17, Leipzig, 1907-1960.

K. Ecke, *Schwenckfeld, Luther und der Gedanke einer apostolischen Reformation*, Berlin, 1911.

G. H. Williams, ed., *Spiritual and Anabaptist Writers*, Philadelphia, 1957, 163-181.

S. G. Schultz, *Caspar Schwenckfeld von Ossig (1489-1561). Spiritual Interpreter of Christianity, Apostle of the Middle Way, Pioneer in Modern Religious Thought*, Norristown, Pa., 1946. Reprinted with a bibliographical introduction by P. Erb, Pennsburg, Pa., 1977.

J. Wach, "Caspar Schwenckfeld: A Pupil and a Teacher in the School of Christ," *Journal of Religion* 26 (1946), 1-29.

P. C. Erb, *Schwenckfeld in His Reformation Setting*, Pennsburg, Pa., 1978.

T. Bergsten, "Pilgram Marpeck und seine Auseinandersetzung mit Caspar Schwenckfeld," *Kyrkohistorisk Arsskrift*, 57, 1957-58, 19-100.

P. L. Maier, *Caspar Schwenckfeld on the Person and Work of Christ*, Assen, 1959.

G. Maron, *Individualismus und Gemeinschaft bei Caspar von Schwenckfeld. Seine Theologie, dargestellt mit besonderer Ausrichtung auf seinen Kirchenbegriff*, Stuttgart, 1961.

H. Weigelt, "Sebastian Franck und Caspar Schwenckfeld in ihren Beziehungen zueinander," *Zeitschrift für bayerische Kirchengeschichte* 39, 1970, 3-19.

H. Weigelt, *Spiritualistische Tradition im Protestantismus. Die Geschichte des Schwenckfeldertums in Schlesien*, Berlin and New York, 1973.

A. Sciegienny, *Homme charnel-homme spirituel. Etude sur la christologie de Caspar Schwenckfeld (1489-1561)*, Wiesbaden, 1975.

D. C. Steinmetz, "Caspar Schwenckfeld (1489-1561): The Renunciation of Structure," in *Reformers in the Wings*, Philadelphia, 1971, 186-196.

R. E. McLaughlin, "Caspar Schwenckfeld von Ossig (1489-1561): Nobility and Religious Commitment—Crisis and Decision in the Early Reformation," unpubl. PhD dissertation. Yale University, 1980.

18. *Sebastian Franck*

Critic of the "New Scholastics"

Sebastian Franck, a leading Spiritualist and critic of the Lutheran Reformation, is considered by some scholars to have been the most "modern" thinker of the sixteenth century. He was born in 1499 in Donauwörth and attended Latin school in Nördlingen. In March 1515 he matriculated at the University of Ingolstadt, where he received the Bachelor of Arts degree in 1517. While in Ingolstadt he made the acquaintance of the future South German Anabaptist leader Hans Denck, who enrolled in the university in 1517. After leaving Ingolstadt, Franck studied for the priesthood in Heidelberg, where he had among his fellow students such future Lutheran leaders as Johannes Brenz, Martin Bucer, and Martin Frecht, the latter two of whom were destined to become his chief persecutors during the last decade of his life. Franck also probably met Martin Luther during the famous Heidelberg Disputation in April 1518.

Following his training in Heidelberg Franck was active as a Catholic priest in the bishopric of Augsburg. Although the exact date and circumstances of his conversion are unclear, we know that he became a Lutheran by 1525 or 1526, while serving as chaplain in Buchenbach. In 1528 he assumed the position of chaplain in Gustenfelden and some decisive changes began to occur in his life. On March 17 he married Ottilie Beheim, a sister of the so-called "godless painters" of Nuremberg, who were punished for heterodox beliefs by the authorities there. Franck also performed his

first scholarly work in this year, a German translation of
Andreas Althamer's *Dialloge,* a strongly Lutheran tract
against Hans Denck and Anabaptist "fanaticism," to which
Franck added his own preface. In the latter he criticized
the "saints of the Word" and "mouth-Christians," whom he
accused of leading unchristian lives, while at the same time
protesting their faith in Holy Scripture. Franck's preface
was an obedient Lutheran criticism of sectarians, whom
the Lutherans considered to be both troublemakers and
heretics, but it was also a criticism he was soon to turn
against the Lutherans themselves.

Franck's ethical sensitivity and growing disillusionment
with the Reformation can be seen in his first independent
work, also in 1528, *Von dem greulichen Laster der
Trunkenheit* (On the horrible vice of drunkenness). Here
Franck cried out against what he described as a
widespread preference of Bacchus to God's truth and urged
strict enforcement of the ban against morally lax Christians in Gustenfelden. The work, dedicated to a magistrate
of Colmburg, was written in the naive hope of inspiring the
nobility to abstinence. Franck clearly was beginning to
suspect that the Lutheran belief in salvation by faith alone,
rather than by a life of suffering and good works, actually
encouraged lax, immoral behavior.

Franck forsook both Gustenfelden and the Lutheran
ministry in the following year to become a private citizen
in Nuremberg, where he worked as a translator. Among his
first accomplishments were a German translation of
Simon Fish's *Supplication for the Beggars,* a savage satire
on the English clergy, and a popular account of life among
the Turks, the *Chronicle or Description of Turkey.* Franck
may also at this time have made the acquaintance of
Paracelsus, who was resident in Nuremberg.

One of Franck's most important and controversial
works, composed in Nuremberg, was published in
Strassburg in September 1531: the *Chronica, Zeitbuch und*

Geschichtsbibel (Chronicle and History). This work contained a chronicle of kings ("Chronik der Keiser"), which repeated and elaborated in its preface two of Erasmus's most biting satires on political rulers, depicting them as being as faithless and predatory as their beloved symbol, the eagle. The *Chronicle* also contained a chronicle of heretics ("Ketzerchronik"), in which Franck praised as true Christians many whom the church had earlier condemned. In addition to these politically sensitive writings, Franck further aroused criticism by openly associating with the Spanish anti-Trinitarian Michael Servetus, whose *De trinitatis erroribus* (Errors of the Trinity) (1531) was beginning to create a Europe-wide scandal, and the controversial Spiritualist Caspar von Schwenckfeld. Not surprisingly Franck earned the undying hostility of Strassburg's leading Lutheran theologian, Martin Bucer, who inspired Franck's imprisonment and dismissal from Strassburg in 1532.

After a period of wandering Franck settled finally in Ulm, where he received citizenship on October 15, 1534. Because of his reputation as a critic of religious and political authority, his citizenship was made conditional upon his ability to avoid bringing either threat or embarrassment to the city by his past or future activity as a writer. Modestly subsidized by a Donauwörth patron, a former Anabaptist named Jörg Regel, Franck published in 1534 the first edition of his popular *Paradoxa* and a German translation of what he called *Four Royal Books*, the first selection of which was the *Moriae Encomion (Praise of Folly)* of Erasmus, who was perhaps the most important influence on his thought. His first year in Ulm ended, however, on an ominous note and it became clear that Franck's presence in Ulm was to be no less controversial than his residence in Strassburg had been. In a letter dated December 31, 1534, Philip of Hesse, writing at the instigation of Philip Melanchthon, Bucer, and Martin Frecht, the leader of the Ulm

Lutherans, warned the magistrates of Ulm against Franck, whom Philip described as an obvious Anabaptist and revolutionary. The charges led to months of investigation under Frecht's direction and ended with a negative ruling against Franck by the magistrates.

Faced with imminent dismissal from the city, Franck

Sebastian Franck

presented an eloquent self-defense in September 1535. In it he appealed to Erasmus, certain Church Fathers, and the German mystics Johannes Tauler and Meister Eckhart for support of his teaching. According to Franck, God communicated with men and changed their lives by means of the "inner Word," which was spoken directly without intermediaries into their hearts, and not conveyed by simply reading Holy Scripture or listening to the sermons of evangelical preachers. In addition to explaining his teaching, Franck also pledged to conform in every way to the city's religion and polity and promote law and order by his writings. Fortunately, he received the backing of the old mayor, Bernhard Besserer, who resented outside interference in the affairs of Ulm. Thanks to the latter's support, Franck won a conditional tenure in the city on November 5, 1535.

Franck's success did not cause his enemies to cease their vigilance. In 1538 it was discovered that he had published a work in Augsburg *(The Golden Ark)* without the permission of the Ulm authorities. This breach of the conditions of his tenure renewed the old charges against him. Martin Frecht, sensing a belated victory, accused Franck of having demeaned Holy Scripture and the external means of grace, subscribing to the heretical belief of the Donatists that immoral men had neither calling nor office as ministers of God's Word, and sharing the convictions of three contemporary heretics: the revolutionary Thomas Müntzer (who had been executed as a leader of the Peasants' Revolt of 1525), the Spiritualist and anti-Trinitarian Ludwig Haetzer (who had been executed in 1529 for bigamy), and the South German Anabaptist leader, Hans Denck. This time the charges, although highly exaggerated, stuck, and Franck was officially turned out of the city in July 1539, lucky to have escaped with his life.

Franck later settled in Basel, where he died in October 1542. The major work of his last years was a Latin paraphrase of the *Theologia Deutsch* (German Theology), an anonymous mystical tract that had previously been published by Luther (in 1516 and 1518) and the Anabaptists of Worms (1528). This was an appropriate scholarly conclusion to Franck's life, for he had become completely devoted to the teaching of the mystics, holding it to be both a critical alternative to Lutheran theology and a sure guide to an active moral life. Mysticism confirmed Franck's belief that the Word of God was absolutely free to speak authoritatively wherever and through whomever it chose. He found in the *Theologia Deutsch* a concrete example that God could speak as clearly through an unknown and uneducated German as through the canonical Scriptures themselves, and even more truly through such a writing than through all the learned Lutheran and Catholic theologians.

Franck's rejection of the Reformation had several sources. The quarrels between Luther and Erasmus over the bondage of the will and between Luther and Zwingli over the nature of Christ's presence in the Eucharist wearied him. He shared Erasmus's distaste for doctrines of original sin and predestination, as well as his belief in the freedom of man's will in salvation. Also, like Erasmus, Franck believed that the church had fallen away from its original mission of faith and love when, in the second century, it became preoccupied with defining orthodox doctrine and securing political support for its institutions. These seemed to him also to be the major concerns of the Lutherans. Although Franck was much closer to Zwingli's spiritual interpretation of Christ's presence in the Eucharist than he was to Luther's belief in a true corporeal presence, he found the entire debate a meaningless war of words. Like the Anabaptists, he was shocked by the growing control of the Lutheran churches by princes and urban magistrates, and his shock turned to bitter criticism after the treatment he received from the Lutherans of Strassburg and Ulm.

Franck's main criticism of the Reformation, however, was directed at what he believed to be its failure to transform society morally in accordance with its original promise. The Reformation had failed, he believed, for the same reason that the medieval church had failed: because it devoted all its efforts to disciplining and coercing the outer man rather than trying to renew the inner man. Franck's chief criticism of Luther was that he failed to distinguish between the outer word and the inner word, between the external man and the internal man. "Luther believes," he wrote in the *Chronicle*, "that anyone who separates the inner and the outer word and boasts that he has the Spirit and living Word of God within himself, is a fanatical Müntzerite or 'heavenly prophet.' He teaches that it is always wrong to distinguish the outer and the inner word and that the inner word comes to man only through the outer." The result of this emphasis, Franck believed, was the reduction of religion to an "opus operatum," just as the medieval church had done. Franck found Lutheran religion to be an external ritual of belief in the Bible, "bare faith in plain words," that failed to penetrate and change the heart. By contrast, the mystics taught about the divine spark of the soul *(synteresis, scintilla animae)* and the inner word, of Christ who teaches within man and is born in the depths of the soul, of deification and real ethical renewal. And, unlike the new Lutheran Scholastics, who used the Bible as a proof-text in debates over doctrine, the mystics treated the Bible as a guide to true inner piety.

Franck's own theology brought humanist criticism of external religion together with mystical-Spiritualist belief in God's direct presence to every individual. The important thing was not belief, but experience, not creeds, but deeds. This simple, yet highly idealistic, theology influenced many important later thinkers, among them Valentin Weigel, Jacob Boehme, Dirck Coornhert, and Gottfried Arnold. It is a religious point of view that is shared by many people in the modern world today.

For further reading:

G. H. Williams, *Spiritual and Anabaptist Writers*, Philadelphia, 1957, 145-160 (source).

R. M. Jones, *Spiritual Reformers of the 16th and 17th Centuries*, London, 1914, 46-63.

R. Kommos, *Sebastian Franck and Erasmus von Rotterdam*, Berlin, 1934.

J. Endriss, *Sebastian Francks Ulmer Kämpfe*, Ulm, 1935.

E. Teufel, *"Landräumig": Seb. Franck, ein Wanderer an Donau, Rhein und Neckar*, Neustadt a.d. Aisch, 1954.

A. Koyré, *Mystiques, spirituels, alchimistes: Schwenckfeld, Seb. Franck, Weigel, Paracelse*, Paris, 1955.

C. Ginzburg, *Il Nicodemismo. Simulazione e dissimulazione religiosa nell'Europe del 1500*, Turin, 1970.

H. Weigelt, *Sebastian Franck und die lutherische Reformation*, Gütersloh, 1970.

S. Wollgast, *Der deutsche Pantheismus im 16. Jahrhundert. Sebastian Franck und seine Wirkungen auf die Entwicklung der pantheistischen Philosophie in Deutschland*, Berlin, 1972.

St. E. Ozment, *Mysticism and Dissent: Religious Ideology and Social Protest in the Sixteenth Century*, New Haven and London, 1973.

H. J. Hillerbrand, *A Fellowship of Discontent*, New York, 1967, 31-64.

S. L. Verheus, *Zeugnis und Gericht: Kirchengeschichtliche Betrachtungen bei Sebastian Franck und Matthias Flacius*, Nieuwkoop, 1971.

C. Dejung, *Wahrheit und Häresie. Untersuchungen zur Geschichtsphilosophie bei Sebastian Franck*, Zürich, 1980.

19. Martin Cellarius

On the Borders of Heresy

A man of diminutive stature prone to extreme and overly enthusiastic pronouncements in his younger years, Martin Borrhaus, alias Cellarius, was born in Stuttgart to respectable parents in 1499. At the age of thirteen Cellarius enrolled at the University of Tübingen, where he began to study philosophy and Scholastic theology. But the theologians were, as he complains, uninspired men, and so he turned to the study of mathematics under Stoeffler and Aristotelian philosophy under Stadion. The latter was also Melanchthon's teacher patron. Brought together in this way, Cellarius and Melanchthon became close friends, shared similar interests, studied under the same men, and left the university about the same time. Nor did the fact that Cellarius considered himself a Scotist while Melanchthon favored Occam disrupt their relationship, for it was apparently during these years the two planned future studies on Aristotle. It appears that Cellarius initiated these plans and exercised a considerable influence over Melanchthon in this regard, inspiring the latter to develop a new approach to the understanding of Aristotle's works based on the ancient rhetorical rather than the dialectical method of the medieval Scholastics.

Awarded the Magister Artium at the ripe age of sixteen in 1515, Cellarius continued to reside in Tübingen until 1519 when a war between the Swabian League and Württemberg broke out. The war so disrupted life at the university and in the city that Cellarius declared the former to have become a place of desolation where spiritual and intellectual life had been virtually destroyed. As a consequence, he moved to Ingolstadt, where he came under the pervasive influence of Reuchlin on the one hand, and Johann Eck on the other. The move appears a calculated one since Duke Wilhelm had just called Reuchlin, whom Cellarius lauded as a man profoundly learned in the secret wisdom of the Hebrews, Pythagorians, and Platonists, to the university in Ingolstadt. Until the spring of 1521, when the plague struck the city and Reuchlin returned to Stuttgart, Cellarius studied Greek and Hebrew under the great humanist.

So greatly did university life in Ingolstadt appeal to Cellarius that he decided to pursue an academic career himself. As the first step in that direction, he defended a number of philosophical theses under the auspices of Johann Eck and was awarded the baccalaureate in theology at the age of twenty-two. An ardent admirer of Eck at this point, Cellarius would probably have continued his theological studies under the latter had not "divina providentia" intervened. Whereas divine providence had previously appeared in the form of war, it now intervened through the dread plague, the very plague that had driven Reuchlin to Stuttgart.

At the suggestion of Leonhard Eck, the lawyer and trusted confidant of Duke Wilhelm, Cellarius decided to seek sanctuary in a famous Bavarian monastery for the duration of the plague, only to be denied admission by Johann Eck, who had reserved the place for himself. Incensed by what he considered Eck's malevolence, Cellarius, as an act of spite, decided to transfer to the university of Eck's famous antagonist in Wittenberg. But before he departed, he paid Eck one final visit, informed him of his decision, and remarked that he intended to investigate the truth of Luther's theology at its most pristine source. He set off for Wittenberg and developments he could not have foreseen.

His old friend Melanchthon received him warmly in Wittenberg, even lodging him in his home for some time. Here Cellarius met former friends and associates such as Simon Grynaeus and the French nobleman Anemond de Coct. The first months in Wittenberg allowed considerable time for intimate fellowship with old friends during which the profoundly stirring events of the day were discussed, a time, as Cellarius remarks, which made it easy for him to embrace the new evangelical doctrine and forsake the "sophistry" in which he had thus far been trained. The decisive break with the old theology, however, came for Cellarius one day while on an afternoon walk as he was reading Luther's pamphlet on the freedom of a Christian man. It was there, he later told his companions, that the Holy Spirit had suddenly illumined his mind. From that moment on, he asserted, a growing love toward the new teaching and its author, Martin Luther, began to fill his heart. Perhaps this experience also predisposed him to the teachings of the Zwickau Prophets, who were about to appear in Wittenberg.

No sooner had Cellarius arrived in Wittenberg than Melanchthon set his old friend to work teaching mathematics at his school and preparing the students for the university. Apparently this position was eventually to lead to an appointment at the university, for on April 7, 1522, Cellarius was inscribed there as Martinus Cellarius Stuckardianus, Magister Tubingensis. But already on April 12 Luther wrote to Spalatin and Johann Lange that Cellarius had left the city. What caused this abrupt change in plans? Cellarius remarks that he had a disagreement with Luther over the way the latter treated several uneducated people who had asked him to explain some dogmas to them. These "uneducated persons" were the Zwickau Prophets who, as Paul Wappler has made clear, totally captivated Cellarius. He was drawn to their cause by one Marcus Stuebner. These prophets, led by Nicholas Storch, proclaimed three things in particular: first, that infant baptism was not biblical; second, that a new and glorious kingdom would be established on earth in which he, Storch, would be the most prominent personality; and third, that the Holy Spirit communicated directly with the elect, something that Cellarius may have thought he had already experienced.

Though these teachings captivated Cellarius, they so upset Melanchthon that he immediately wrote to the elector and Luther concerning them. When the latter returned from the Wartburg, Melanchthon, at the urging of the prophets, arranged a meeting in an Augustinian monastery between Luther and Stuebner. Cellarius attended as the friend and supporter of Stuebner. Luther at first listened calmly to what Stuebner had to say. When the latter had finished, Luther remarked that since he found neither their teachings nor their visions confirmed in the Bible, they had better give up such nonsense. Stuebner, taken aback, asserted that he would not even allow God to rob him of his teachings, while Cellarius, incensed at Luther's cavalier dismissal of his new friend's teachings, began to rant and rave, stamp his feet on the floor, and pound his fists on a small table before him. Never, wrote Luther, had he seen a man so enraged. Although Stuebner remained somewhat calmer, he too finally gave up trying to convince Luther of his high calling with the parting shot: "God curse you, you Satan!" Then, amidst boastful words, the two left the monastery, shook the dust of Wittenberg from their feet in prophetic fashion as they turned their backs on the city, pausing only long enough at the neighboring town of Kemberg to fire off a letter to Luther filled with abuse and imprecations as a final act of defiance.

Cellarius must eventually have turned his steps back to Stuttgart, whether or not in the company of one or more of the prophets is unknown. Here, like Karlstadt and others who had been illumined by the Spirit and convinced of the

vanity of all human learning, he lived a life alienated from
scholarship, probably eking out an existence by working as
a glass blower, as he was to do later in Basel. But by the
summer of 1524 other of the Saxon radicals began to come
south as well. In August-September Thomas Müntzer came
as far south as Basel and its environs where he met with
Oecolampadius. Karlstadt also came, meeting with the
Swiss Brethren in October of 1524. Rumor even had it that
Storch himself was to be in Strassburg in December of the
same year. Was it mere coincidence that so many of these
radicals came south toward the end of 1524? Did they
perhaps sense that a new beginning might take place here?

Some time during October of 1524 Cellarius too left Stuttgart to come south, appearing in Zürich during that month.
Here he met Dr. Gerhard Westerburg, whom he had
known since the turbulent Wittenberg days of 1521-22.
Surely Westerburg and Cellarius must have been drawn
together through their mutual attachment to the Zwickau
Prophets. In all likelihood Cellarius also came to know
Karlstadt rather well during this time. Could it be that
Grebel's correspondence with Karlstadt, Westerburg's trip
to Zürich—shortly to be followed by that of Karlstadt
himself—came to the ears of Cellarius? Was there still
contact between the various members of the group? It may
well have been since Cellarius arrived in Zürich in early
October, about the same time as Westerburg. The recorded
evidence confirms that it was Felix Mantz in particular
who assisted Westerburg and Karlstadt in their attempt to
publish some of the latter's pamphlets in Basel. And from
Cellarius' letter to Oecolampadius of August 1527, it is obvious that he too had intimate contact with Mantz. Apparently he also shared the latter's views on baptism at
this time, as his response to an inquiry from Hubmaier
makes clear. Zwingli was later to remember this interlude
in Cellarius' life with considerable ill-will.

Whether or not Cellarius had worked out all the implications of his new theology by this time—as the Swiss Brethren were in the process of doing—is not clear. It would appear, however, that he was attracted to the latter because of the similarities between certain of their teachings and those of the Zwickau Prophets which he had made his own—the question of infant baptism being perhaps the most important. It is to be lamented that Cellarius later felt compelled to pass over this encounter, as that with the Zwickau Prophets, in virtual silence.

From Zürich, which he also left abruptly, Cellarius appears to have traveled to Austria, Poland, Danzig, and Königsberg. He cannot have tarried long underway, for already on June 11, 1525, Paul Speratus informed Luther that Cellarius had arrived and that it was necessary to keep a close eye on him, for he seemed involved in the same incendiary activities as Karlstadt and Müntzer. As a consequence, Cellarius had been detained by the court in order to keep him from moving at will about the city and infecting its inhabitants with his poisonous doctrines.

Cellarius reports that he had been in Königsberg some time before he was cited to appear before the court. The citation was the result of the falsehood spread by some rumormonger that he was a seditious person. Yet he does not tell us precisely what he was up to, implying that, aside from the false accusations, he, together with Zwingli, Karlstadt, and Oecolampadius, were considered to be sacramentarians. He had refused to comply, he wrote, with the command to cease his propagandistic activity in Brandenburg.

What were these teachings? Reports from Königsberg revealed that they dealt more with the role of the Holy Spirit, infant baptism, and the glorious future kingdom of God than the incipient sacramentarian controversy. In response to a small tract of Cellarius entitled "In Evangelium Nicodemi," Speratus repudiated Cellarius' chiliasm and accused him of attempting—like Müntzer—to establish an earthly kingdom of the elect. Coming just after the events at Frankenhausen, these were teachings that did not sit at all well with the political and ecclesiastical establishment in Brandenburg.

So Cellarius was put under house arrest and asked to prepare a detailed written statement of his theological position for the court. Upon his complaint that a busy court was not the place to compose such a document, the prince allowed Cellarius to stay with the bishop of Polentz, who graciously offered his residence on the Baltic Sea. Here at the stately castle of Balga, with all the necessary books supplied, Cellarius composed his theological treatise. It was this document, he remarks in his autobiography, that was later published as the *De Operibus Dei* in Strassburg. In any case, the authorities were still not satisfied with his orthodoxy and so they made Cellarius promise to go straight to Wittenberg there to be instructed by Martin Luther himself.

From Luther and Melanchthon's report regarding their discussion with Cellarius, it is apparent that the latter had still not given up his radical views. Despite their disagreements, Cellarius was careful to note that he, the "little fellow," as Melanchthon called him, had impressed Luther, nevertheless. Luther had even asked Cellarius to stay on in Wittenberg, but the "little fellow" felt uneasy and decided, once more, to head south for more tolerant climes. This time the road led to Strassburg.

At some point between Wittenberg and Strassburg, or even in Strassburg itself, a change seems to have come over Cellarius. How radical the change was and who was responsible for it is difficult to say. Perhaps Cellarius was himself partially responsible, having been forced to sit down at the castle on the Baltic to organize his theological thoughts into a coherent whole. Perhaps he decided that discretion was the better part of valor, and so he at least partially disguised his more radical ideas. Or, perhaps it was a combination of the two. In the time that followed he noticeably moved away from Anabaptist positions.

Cellarius had left Königsberg shortly after February 6, 1526. By mid-November he had arrived in Strassburg where, after an initial period of aloofness, he was warmly received by both Capito and Bucer. In November already, Capito wrote Zwingli that although Cellarius had his theological idiosyncracies, he was a most likable fellow who held Zwingli in high esteem. Even Bucer, who was later to become somewhat more suspicious of Cellarius, wrote to William Farel in December: "Good God, what a genius he is and how pious! Truly his spirit is totally different from that of Denck." Denck had arrived in Strassburg about the same time as Cellarius. Here he had made contact with Capito and especially with Ludwig Hätzer, whom Cellarius knew from Zürich and who was now coming under Denck's influence. Apparently Hätzer was staying with Capito, whose house Cellarius also frequented on a regular basis, if he did not in fact lodge there at first. The Denck-Cellarius encounter, which took place as a result of these contacts, presents some interesting problems for the early history of the relationship between Anabaptism and the Reformation.

Whereas Hätzer and Cellarius had been a part of the radical group in Zürich during late 1524 and early 1525, in Strassburg the two came into conflict. As Hätzer came under Denck's influence, they must gradually have become aware of a basic disagreement. For Denck, who had just published his work against predestination *(Was geredt sei . . .)*, was an advocate of the freedom of the will, while Cellarius, who was about to publish his *De Operibus Dei*, was by now, if he had ever been anything else since he was or had been a Scotist, a strict predestinarian. At a meeting between these two on December 20, 1526, arranged by Capito, where the issue was discussed, Denck, probably fearing expulsion from the city, apparently had his own views on the subject and agreed completely with Cellarius' predestinarian perspective. Hätzer, however, refused to be a Nicodemite on the matter and began to denounce both Cellarius and his opinions.

This event was quickly followed by news from Zürich of Felix Mantz's drowning at the hands of the Zürich magistrates on January 5, 1527. And now the division between Denck and Hätzer on the one hand, and Cellarius on the other, once again became apparent. For while Cellarius, along with Capito and Bucer, defended Zwingli's role in the execution, Hätzer denounced Zwingli, and Cellarius along with him. Surely Hätzer, who had been in Zürich along with Cellarius during the last months of 1524, knew of the latter's intimate contacts with Mantz during these months. Now, however, Cellarius was on the side of Zwingli, whom he had disdained even to visit in 1524. In view of his subsequent stand against Calvin's involvement in the Servetus affair, Cellarius' attitude in this instance is difficult to explain unless we wish to assume that he was going out of his way to try to rehabilitate himself in the eyes of the orthodox Reformers.

In a letter to Zwingli of August 15, 1527, Capito delineated the change he believed had come over Cellarius. In it he states: "The cross has taken him to task and convinced him." Not only, apparently, had Cellarius changed his views, but the old explosive, militant temperament seemed also to have disappeared. Nearly everyone who came in contact with him remarked on this fact. Even this change, however, apparently did not convince Bucer. On April 15, 1528, he wrote Zwingli: "What you feared has happened. Cellarius, who is motivated by a true Anabaptist spirit, has tricked our Capito by his association with him." As a consequence, Bucer continued, hostility had broken out between himself and Cellarius, so much so that Cellarius, the dwarf, had nearly attacked Bucer, the giant, on the street.

There are reasons to suspect Cellarius' theological

conversion as well. It is true that by the time he had come to Strassburg the main outlines of this theological position had been worked out. That theology had immediately both drawn him to the Strassburg Reformers, as Capito remarked in his introduction to the *De Operibus Dei*, and put him in opposition to the Anabaptists. Nor was the crucial issue baptism—in this regard Cellarius continued closer to the Anabaptists than any other Reformers—it was the issue of free will versus predestination. On this issue he was clearly on Zwingli's side.

It appears, however, that he had not changed his opinion with regard to baptism. As Capito observed, Cellarius taught that it would have been better had infant baptism been eliminated, but that, according to the precept of charity, which regulated all externals, it should be retained for the time being. Nevertheless, as Cellarius wrote Oecolampadius in 1527, Zwingli was not pleased with *De Operibus Dei*. It was rumored, he wrote, that the little booklet had offended Zwingli precisely in that part in which he had asserted that infant baptism be retained out of charity. Indeed, Zwingli could not have been pleased with the way Cellarius had drawn the conclusion based upon a strict predestinarian approach he obviously believed Zwingli to share, that God's election was the only thing that mattered—baptism being one of those outward symbols which were not really important.

Luther and Melanchthon do not appear to have appreciated Cellarius' little booklet either. In a letter to John Hess in Breslau, of January 27, 1528, Luther remarked that Cellarius' "prophetic book" was filled with sedition and the spirit of Thomas Müntzer. Melanchthon mentioned Cellarius a few years later in a very different context. Referring to the quarrel regarding the Trinity which had erupted in Wittenberg as the result of Johannes Campanus's attack on that doctrine in 1529, he remarked that there was an inner connection between the opponents of the Lutheran interpretation of the Eucharist and anti-Trinitarianism. At first they had allegorized the communion service, but now Campanus, Cellarius, and Felinus were allegorizing other articles of faith. Not only Melanchthon, but the Calvinists too suspected Cellarius of being a follower of Servetus. Even Sebastian Castellio, in that part of his manuscript *Contra libellum Calvini (Against Calvin's Book)*, suppressed by none other than Cellarius himself, wrote that three professors at Basel were openly regarded by the Calvinists to be followers of Servetus. These were Martin Cellarius or Borrhaus, head professor of theology, and the two liberal arts professors, Coelius Secundus Curione and Sebastian Castellio. Then he went on to reveal that Servetus had sent his book in manuscript to Cellarius for the latter's judgment. Cellarius had replied in a friendly fashion that he approved of some parts, as he had indicated in his notes, that he disapproved of others, and that some he did not understand. But, Castellio concluded, the extent to which Cellarius was in agreement with Servetus could be gleaned from a careful reading of the former's *De Operibus Dei*, obviously implying that there was considerable agreement.

Nor does it seem that Cellarius completely gave up his belief in the New Jerusalem either. He may have become more cautious in his formulations of that concept, but those who shared these views seem to have read them either out of or into his writings. A particularly intriguing instance of this was Giocopo Brocardo. Born in Venice and educated there as an Aristotelian humanist as Cellarius was, Brocardo indirectly drew attention to this aspect of Cellarius' thought and its Joachimite overtones.

Early in 1527 Cellarius had married a woman of noble birth from the Uttenheim family who had inherited an estate and income from her parents. Praised by Capito as a particularly felicitous match, the marriage allowed Cellarius leisure and income enough to pursue his scholarly interests, all the while maintaining some contact with old friends in Strassburg. But when his wife died in 1536, he was deprived of her estate and income because the union had remained childless. So he decided to move once again, this time to Basel. Perhaps friendships in Strassburg had cooled off. Certainly Bucer was more hostile by this time, and an old friend, Simon Grynaeus, had just been appointed at the University of Basel.

But once in Basel, he was forced again to turn to glass blowing. Soon, however, he had access to the learned circles of the city even though some theologians continued to harbor suspicions against him. By 1538 he must have married again, apparently another woman of some means, for he was once again able to give up his menial lifestyle and be inscribed in the university where his friends hoped to find him an appropriate academic appointment. In the meantime, as Operinus wrote to Vadian, Cellarius had taken up a theme first discussed with Melanchthon in Tübingen. This led to the publication of a number of treatises on Aristotle, the first being *De censura veri et falsa (Concerning True and False Judgment)*, in which he applied the rhetorical method to the interpretation of two of Aristotle's writings. This was followed shortly, in December of 1541, by his appointment as professor of rhetoric to the university.

While Cellarius continued his work on Aristotle, he was not really satisfied until he succeeded Karlstadt as professor of Old Testament in 1546. By that time he had overcome most of the suspicions of his more conservative colleagues. So much was this the case that he was appointed university rector in that very year, and again in 1553 and 1564, the year of his death.

During his years in Basel, Cellarius, who now called himself Borrhaus, came to be highly regarded by his colleagues and revered by his students. But his interests continued to skirt the borders of heresy. His contact with

Servetus was already noted. One of his best friends in Basel came to be Curione, and together they formed a kind of sanctuary for many of the Italian Protestants, most of whom were not particularly compatible with the Genevan Reformers. He recommended Schwenckfeld and his old friend Gerhard Westerburg to Bullinger later on. He even became a close friend of David Joris, who was living incognito in Basel. When the latter died and his true identity was discovered, Cellarius, with the rest of his colleagues, was forced to condemn his ideas posthumously. For the man who defended Servetus' right to speak out, had helped many of the Italian refugees, and had himself repeatedly defied the established Reformers earlier in his life, this must have been a particularly distasteful task. On the whole, he seems to have maintained his own unique perspectives to the end.

The plague had intervened earlier in his life to lead him to Wittenberg and the reformed faith; it intervened again in 1564, and this time it was the ultimate intervention.

For further reading:

C. Gerbert, *Geschichte der Strassburger Sektenbewegung zur Zeit der Reformation 1524 bis 1534*, Strassburg, 1889.
B. Riggenbach, "Martin Borrhaus," *Basler Jahrbuch*, 1900, 47-84.
A. Hulshof, *Geschiedenis van de Doopsgezinden te Straatsburg van 1525-1557*, Amsterdam, 1905.
The Mennonite Encyclopedia, I, 538-539.

Jerome Friedmann

20. Michael Servetus

Advocate of Total Heresy

Michael Servetus, born in Villanueva de Sijena Spain in 1509 or 1511, was possibly the most celebrated and notorious heretic of the 16th century. For many orthodox reformers, Servetus represented the very essence of heresy, yet he was not a rabble-rouser nor a social revolutionary. Indeed, Servetus was not even a theologian by vocation and earned his living first as an editor and later as a physician living under the assumed name of Villanovanus.

Servetus was undoubtedly one of the great original thinkers of his age, demonstrating his genius in several diverse areas of accomplishment. He discovered and described the pulmonary circulation of the blood, contributed significantly to the infant study of comparative geography and demography, and laid an early foundation for modern scriptural exegesis. But the most controversial area of his accomplishment must remain his theological speculation. It is precisely this area which is least understood by historians because Servetus has traditionally been viewed strictly from the vantage point of his "anti-Trinitarianism" with little interest into why Servetus opposed the Trinity or other ideas and concepts found in his writings.

Treating Servetus in this single-issue fashion is as incorrect as approaching Anabaptism from the point of its views on immersion. In both cases, the alleged starting point is actually an end result of other views usually neglected or misunderstood. Consequently, rather than beginning our investigation with a Trinitarian discussion of the number of parts to the Godhead and their relationship, we must first understand that Servetus' overall religious system existed on two diverse levels of consideration. First, there was the cosmic and universal, and second, the personal and individual. Though separate and distinct, both considerations find their origin in Adam's act of disobedience to God. On a cosmic level, original sin permitted the evil forces of Satan, hitherto contaminating only the stars, to find a home on earth in the Garden of Eden. To avoid contamination, God withdrew from Eden and creation and an age of conflict between God and Satan ensued.

Servetus detected various stages in this cosmic battle between God and Satan for control over man and the world. By appearing to him under the guise of different and various names God tried to convince man of righteousness. Shaddai, Sabaoth, El, Elohim, Oz, and Yahweh were all names through which God communicated to man, each appelation granting progressively increasing knowledge of himself to an increasingly sophisticated mankind. Finally, to win man over, God appeared as Jesus Christ, a perfect representation of God's character. But when God sent Christ, his personification, Satan countered by sending the Antichrist, the very personification of evil.

Satan too attempted to win man to his evil ways and he too appeared under different manifestations and names. Baal, Bel, Moloch, Ashera, Bal Peor, Ashtoroth, and Queen of the Heavens were the names of Satan around which pagan religious practice dedicated to Satan developed. In the confrontation between Christ and Antichrist, the former was chased from earth when he was crucified by the forces of evil much as the Father was chased from Eden by Satan. Moreover, the very church founded by Christ was soon perverted by the Antichrist and Satan was soon firmly established as chief of the Church of Rome.

Fortunately for man, Christ sent his Spirit to the world to help guide man in his absence from an evil-saturated world. Unfortunately, most Christians followed Satan through obedience to Rome, but this situation would soon

Michael Servetus

change. By Servetus' computations the millennium would begin in 1585 when the archangel Michael would emerge to take up the battle against Satan. This time, however, God would vanquish Satan and the reign of the saints would begin.

What of man during this cosmic battle? Unlike conventional Christianity, Servetus did not believe that original sin left man naturally perverted, evil, and incapable of righteousness. On the contrary, the Old Testament was proof of the many instances where man followed God's will and the path of righteousness despite Satanic temptation. Servetus emphasized that man was created in God's image and was semi-divine. This natural human affinity to God was increased through the process of breathing, for God transmitted both grace and the life-giving substance to man through the air he breathed. Additionally, each new name of divinity God revealed to man, such as Yahweh or El Shaddai, facilitated greater righteousness and Servetus argued that the law of Moses as a whole led to even greater goodness and justification.

Christianity superseded the law, however, and promised a salvation whereby man was actually transformed into a god. This transformation was possible only after Christ's appearance, for Servetus envisioned the Son of God as a celestial being composed of the divine matter of the Father himself, which is passed on to man in the process of deification. Jesus was human in outward form and appearance only, but not in substance or essence, and along with the good news of the gospel, Christ gave man the path to deification and a return to the Father. Just as the God-given law of Moses led to righteousness, the Christ-given rituals of baptism and the supper led to deification.

Baptism granted man an inner illumination and divine understanding of such magnitude that only mature adults could participate in this ritual. Infants could not understand Christ and adolescents were too confused to appreciate the new illumination. Adults from the age of thirty might be initiated because they understood the cosmic nature of evil and their need for Christ to combat the serpentine wisdom of Satan in control of the Church of Rome.

The Lord's supper was not merely a commemorative ritual but a profound religious exercise. Though he rejected Catholic transsubstantiation as "too magical," Servetus' own views involved a real presence of Christ in the meal which once internalized by man began the process of transforming man into God. In time man would shed his outer human appearance and return to the Father much as Christ shed his human appearance some 1500 years earlier. In the meantime Servetus emphasized the beneficial nature of fasting, mortification of the flesh, and other ascetic practices to help liberate the soul from the crude matter of the body.

Historians intent upon describing how many persons Servetus envisioned in the Godhead in some form of divine arithmetic have neglected almost all of the above systematic considerations. Yet without the system as a whole, Servetus' anti-Trinitarianism makes little sense. For Servetus, the Father, Son, and Spirit were essentially different manifestations of the very same God. Moreover, the functions of all three were essentially the same—to fight the forces of evil and bring man to God through some appropriate form of worship. The only difference between these different manifestations were the circumstances and historical context in which they appeared. Consequently, if a voice spoke to Adam and Noah, the same God appeared in a burning bush when communicating to Moses. So too, God assumed a human form in Christ and was invisible as the Spirit. Rather than speaking of three separate persons eternally within God, Servetus preferred to identify various expressions of divinity. Each was predicated upon the temper of the times and the spiritual capabilities of man and together constituted a continuum of divine expression.

It is obvious that Servetus' understanding of Christianity was quite unusual. Had Servetus accepted a more orthodox notion of original sin, human depravity, and captivity to evil, he would also have necessarily accepted a partially human Christ to atone for a fallen mankind. In turn, a human Christ would have necessitated some conventional concept of the Trinity to account for how the same Godhead could consist of an unseen Father, a human Christ, and a phantom Spirit. Servetus' great departure from orthodoxy was that man did not need atonement but a divine ritual and a celestial Christ to transform man into God. Consequently, the key to Servetus' thought was soteriological and not theological; an elevated view of man simply made the Trinity unnecessary.

No doubt part of Servetus' radicalism can also be attributed to his unusual use of intellectual sources. Very knowledgeable in Hebrew and Greek, Servetus was heavily indebted to rabbinic exegesis and ante-Nicene patristic thought. Servetus cited over a dozen rabbinic sources though he was most influenced by David Kimchi, the Aramaic Targums of Onkelos, and Jonathan, and late medieval Spanish exegesis. And while Servetus cited no fewer than sixteen patristic sources, he relied heavily upon Irenaeus and Tertullian. Similarly, Servetus used a host of Platonic, Middle Platonic, and Neoplatonic sources, as well as Hermes Tresmegistus in constructing his cosmology. Additionally, Servetus was influenced by many ancient heretical systems ranging from Paul of Samosota, Sabellius, to Valentinian and Marcion, though he rejected Gnosticism. Servetus also rejected medieval Catholic tradition, Protestantism, and many contemporary radicals all of whom were understood as the rotten fruit of the Antichrist's church.

It was Servetus' genius and eclectic ability to combine these sources, approaches, and ideas into a complete amalgam, even if it was a terribly heretical Christianity. He was so controversial in his own day, however, that even his death caused a storm and furor. In 1553 Servetus was tried for heresy in Catholic Vienne and was condemned to death. Before the execution could take place, Servetus escaped from prison and attempted to make his way to Southern Italy by way of Geneva. Though he kept a low profile in that Protestant city, he was discovered, tried for heresy, and burned to death for holding the views outlined above. But Servetus proved as troublesome dead as he did when he was alive and John Calvin was soon heavily criticized and condemned for executing a man who broke no laws in Geneva and did not even attempt to preach his heretical views. Servetus' death was testimony to the intolerance and closed-mindedness of the times, but his life and accomplishments were a witness to creativity, originality, and uniqueness.

Yet Servetus the man remains something of a mystery and locating Servetus' place within the context of 16th-century life and society is no less difficult than determining his place within radical circles. Aside from specific facts, so little is known about his family, early education, sources of income, friends, and associates that Servetus remains an enigma for us today much as he was in his own times.

His family was petit Spanish nobility and his brother was a sometimes agent for the Spanish Inquisition, yet Servetus left Spain quite young, apparently had little contact with his family and disregarded the Inquisition though the latter did not disregard him or his Jewish sources. Servetus studied at Toulouse in the late 1520s but gained his strong background in Hermetica, Neoplatonism and Cabbalah from Symphorien Champier and his circle when working in Lyon as an editor for Trechsel during the late 1530s and early 1540s. Yet Servetus did not share Symphorien's passion for merging Plato and Aristotle or Cabbalah. Similarly, Champier first introduced Servetus to medicine but Servetus repudiated his teacher at the first opportunity and pursued an independent path which culminated in the discovery of the pulmonary circulation of the blood. Here too Servetus proves a curiosity for he was far more interested in the religious aspects of this discovery than in its medical significance.

For much of his life Servetus used the alias Michel de Villeneuve and attempted to conceal his true identity but the public record reveals little as well. Servetus corresponded with Erasmus and Calvin, knew Bucer, Capito and Franck, and lived in the house of Oecolampadius in Basel. Yet Servetus was both firmly anti-Protestant and anti-Catholic. Even the documents surrounding his controversial death are bereft of personal color, indicating only legal and theological concerns.

If Servetus appears curiously removed from all specific social and intellectual categories, this may reflect our ignorance but it may also reflect Servetus' position as a "one man clearing-house" of all ideas, movements, and concepts of his age which he filtered and distilled into his own creation. In his own time few readily conceded sharing his views and fewer still claimed him as a friend. Servetus was an intellectual compendium, synthesizing much of the thought of his age, but he was also a solitary figure whose legacy to us is as curious and puzzling as it is enticing.

For further reading:

E. M. Wilbur, ed., "Servetus: Two Treatises on the Trinity," *Harvard Theological Studies* XVI (1932).

J. Friedmann, "Michael Servetus: Exegete of Divine History," *Church History*, 43, 1974, 460-469.

H. J. Hillerbrand, *The Reformation*, New York, 1964, 275-290 (sources about Servetus).

R. H. Bainton, *Hunted Heretic. The Life and Death of Michael Servetus*, Boston, 1953.

J. F. Fulton, *Michael Servetus. Humanist and Martyr*, New York, 1953.

J. Fernández Barón, *Miguel Servet. Su vida y su obra*, Madrid, 1970.

C. Manzoni, *Umanesimo ed eresia. Michele Serveto*, Neapel, 1974.

J. Friedman, *Michael Servetus: A Case Study in Total Heresy*, Genève, 1978.

Hartmuth Rudolph

21. Theophrast von Hohenheim (Paracelsus)

Physician and Apostle of the New Creation

It is more difficult to justify the inclusion of Paracelsus (1493-1541) in this series of radical Reformers than any of the others. He was the innovator of medical science and reformer of the healing arts as well as of the practice of medicine in the age of humanism and Reformation. His verdict against the scholastic medicine of the time and his self-confident claim "Not you, but I lead; not I, but you follow" can create dissension among colleagues even in our own century. Is it also possible to describe and evaluate this "Luther of medicine" in the context of ecclesiastical controversies and developments of those decades and also from his stance toward that Reformation?

The attempt to answer these questions will encounter various difficulties of both form and content. Until a few years ago his theological and religio-philosophical writings, which would have to be consulted, were available almost only in handwritten copies, and are even today only partially available in printed form. They are in no sense inferior to the fourteen volumes of his works in medicine and natural philosophy. A number of writings, and especially those in which Paracelsus polemicized against the churches and the Christianity of his time, can for the time being not be dated. Extensive periods of his biography will, at least temporarily, and perhaps forever, remain unknown.

Even apart from these external problems there are circumstances of life and utterances of Hohenheim which make one skeptical of his inclusion here. Of all the "Reformers" included in this volume, Paracelsus was the only one who remained a member of the old Roman Church all of his life and was buried as such. Catholic prelates were precisely the ones who saw to preserving and spreading his writings. These facts may, however, not weigh very heavily in the balances since they need in no way compromise his nearness to and comparison with radical critics of the Reformation on the Protestant side.

Much greater difficulties are provided by observations which, in the works on medicine and natural science, but also in the religious writings, create the impression of a wide-ranging self-sufficiency of Hohenheim, and independence from relevant contemporary movements and ideas. This has on occasion led to a completely unhistorical glorification and exaggerated importance of Hohenheim which cannot be accepted. On the other hand, some have also unfortunately placed Paracelsus and his devotees into the realm of frivolity and charlatanism. This difficulty can be dealt with here only partially. During the past few years more careful investigations into the world view of Paracelsus, as well as of his underlying views in medicine, cosmology, and anthropology, have been carried out from the point of view of their traditional roots. However, apart from a few treatments of individual items, no comprehensive, accurate analyses have yet been done on the relationships of the lay theologian Paracelsus to inherited and contemporary formulations on theology and the church. As past experience has shown, every premature attempt to classify him which has not been sufficiently discriminating would only serve to strengthen the impressions described above.

With these reservations we will attempt to locate Paracelsus in the context of the Reformation and the distinctions and radicalizations caused by it.

He descended from a declining Swabian noble family, and was likely born toward the end of 1493 near the monastery of Einsiedeln into "poverty and hunger." Early in the new century the family moved to Carinthia, where his father became city physician in Villach. His father determined that the young Theophrast would become a physician. To his father also he owed his initial training in the "philosophia adepta," the knowledge of natural phenomena and their secrets. Later, as professor in Basel, he would oppose this arcane knowledge together with the practice and experience of the savant to all academic fakery and mere book knowledge. He also received instruction in monastic schools and in part from episcopal teachers. His university education was concluded with the doctor's degree in Ferrara, a school then characterized by the advance of Renaissance scholarship.

Like many a famed Renaissance scholar and humanist, perhaps like Agrippa von Nettesheim who bore considerable resemblance to him, Hohenheim "experienced" the Europe of his time for nearly a decade. He traveled from Portugal to Lithuania, from the Balkans to the Netherlands. Everywhere he hungrily gathered the treasures which were to be found in folk medicine and in that erudition about nature which existed outside scholastic systems. He sought them from scholars and magicians, at courts and from the common people, from gypsies and women with herbal lore.

About 1524 or 1525 Paracelsus seems to have ended his wanderings with the decision to settle down as a physician. He found an opportunity in Salzburg, but that quickly disappeared, for in 1525-1526 the archdiocese was caught in the flood of the peasant revolt and the decisions flowing from it. The Salzburg peasants, followed by the miners in Salzburg, Styria, and Carinthia, succeeded temporarily in their uprising against the prince-bishop. Paracelsus was drawn into the great social, political, and religious movement; for the first time we have some specific knowledge about him. His stance cannot clearly be determined. The authorities regarded him as an adherent of the insurgents, and even as one of their instigators. He participated in their gatherings, spoke publicly to the issues, and discussed them in drinking dens and taverns with peasants and other ordinary people as he had done during his travels. Apparently, however, he was able to defend himself against the charges on the ground that he had said only what agreed with the gospel. Undoubtedly he sup-

Paracelsus

ported most of the social and political demands of the peasants against the prince-bishop by appealing to "divine justice." He knew the life of the common people since child-hood.

During his youth in Carinthia he became acquainted with the dangers and adversities of the miners. He knew the living conditions of the people; he had often shared them on his wanderings.

However, providing a later reference of Hohenheim is dated correctly, he tried to be a mediator in the conflict. He tried to help the people understand the ecclesiastical authorities, and perhaps pilloried only their individual failures. In general, "while he was in the taverns he still had faith in them," that is, in the scholarly defenders of ecclesiastical authority. His rejection of the old church ("I am now a believer in Christ, and no longer in you"), and his characterization of the church as an antichristian devil's instrument, must be assigned to a later period. Nevertheless, Paracelsus was forced to flee from the city of prince-bishop Cardinal Matthäus Lang.

The Salzburg experiences were likely of the highest importance for the development of his social ethic with its communistic, democratic, and cooperative elements, as well as for his concepts of peace and toleration. Certainly, the hope which he cherished for a time that the emperor would be the representative and guarantor of a social and political reformation at the expense of the nobility, the hereditary rule of the princes, was one he shared with many contemporaries. It was virtually identical with the demand of the peasant insurrection, of rural as well as of urban Salzburg. However, this hope yielded later to a widespread skepticism concerning the emperor and then to his outright condemnation as when together with the *Mauerkirche* (the church as a socially established institution, subjected to worldly wealth and power) Paracelsus identified the emperor with "Antichrist," whose certain destruction he prophesied.

The first theological writings of Hohenheim must also

belong to the Salzburg time, for the later polemical style is missing, and they reflect the effort to gain dogmatic clarity on theological problems. In 1524 he published *De virgine theotoca* (The Virgin Mother of God) in which he defended not only the immaculate conception of Mary but also of her mother Anna. The Virgin Mary existed before the creation of the world and was taken, immortal, to heaven, for "God did not marry mortal flesh." In March 1525, Paracelsus is reputed to have addressed one of these earliest theological writings to the "Christian brothers" and "apostolic men" Luther, Bugenhagen, and Melanchthon.

Even if the letter of dedication is a later attempt to move Paracelsus into the proximity of Luther and at least partially to make him a partisan of the Reformation, it still reflects something of a historical relationship of the innovator and lay theologian to Luther. Hohenheim says that certain fetters kept him from his thirst "to drink with you at the fountain of truth." He submitted his work to the judgment of the Wittenberg pillars of the Reformation and asked them for critical evaluation. It may be that, like many critics of the old church, Paracelsus hoped for great things from Luther when the papal church with all its deficiencies, as well as Luther's own Reformation, was placed "into the searing presence of the gospel" (Heinrich Bornkamm).

The more specific Hohenheim's polemical utterances against the *Mauerkirche* (walled church) became, however, the more devastating were his judgments against the Reformation churches, Lutheran, and Zwinglian, and their kind, and Anabaptist. In his great commentaries on the Bible and polemical writings beginning soon after 1530, he called them the new proselytes, the followers of the Jewish Pharisees, scribes, and hypocrites, who were struck by the sevenfold curse of Christ (Matthew 23). Something of the coming separation from the Reformers may be indicated by the side comment in the letter of dedication: "It is better to walk in darkness than to have a faint but false light." At least Hohenheim's estimate of himself is audible here. He expressed it clearly in 1529-1530 to those who had called him a "Luther," that is, a heretic. "I am Theophrastus, not Luther. Luther is responsible for what is his; I will look to what is mine."

Hohenheim's flight from Salzburg (1525) led him first to Strassburg and then (1527) to the center of the humanism of the upper Rhine, Basel. Here, after a sensational medical treatment of Froben, he was appointed as city physician and at the same time professor of medicine at the university. The explanation for this appointment is to be sought not simply in the reputation which the medical skill of Paracelsus had by now achieved. Moreover, the humanists of Basel, including Erasmus, and even the humanistically oriented Swiss Reformation carried by Oecolampadius, Zwingli, and Leo Jud, perceived in this critic of scholastic medicine a supporter of their cause. In fact a number of indicators in Hohenheim's education permit the conclusion that he was intellectually close to Basel humanism. Several signs of this congruence in the external course of his life have already been mentioned. Completing the picture were the strongly personalized character of his writing, especially an array of autobiographical comments that served a certain urge to make his mark.

He had been in touch with the spirit of humanism already during his basic education in Carinthia. Kurt Goldammer has virtually established that the abbot of Sponheim, the highly educated and famous Trithemius, was his teacher. A connection with Perauldus mediated by one of his episcopal teachers also deserves mention.

The strong impulses of humanism upon Paracelsus also became visible in his attitude to the church situation of his time, which was characterized by a multiform Protestantism growing out of the old church. To be sure, his radical criticism of the papacy ("earthly Lucifer" and "Antichrist"), and his flogging of the *Mauerkirche,* as well as the highly developed apocalyptic character of his eschatology, was rooted in the apocalyptic, socially-critical, ascetic, and usually "heretical" reform movements of the Middle Ages. But alongside of this, typical humanistic motifs characterized his Christianity.

Paracelsus shared the interpretation of the history of the church as a progressively growing departure of the church from the integrity of its primitive status, the whole development coming to a climax in the present. He did not, however, draw the manifold conclusions which, for example, the radical wing of the Reformation, the enthusiasts, and Spiritualists drew from the same interpretation. Paracelsus did not struggle for the realization of a backward-looking utopia, nor did he remove the church into the realm of the invisible and spiritual. Moreover, he did not attack the church in its hierarchical form as such or in the multiplicity of its offices, but judged her to be the work of Antichrist on the basis of concrete phenomena. Chief among these were the social effects of the *Mauerkirche,* for example the prince-bishops who had become "ravening wolves" who deceived the people, and exploited them to an intolerable degree. With their dealings, their hypocrisy, whoredom, and luxury they had become "fat swine" and had turned themselves into heretics and representatives of Satan's divided and transient kingdom (Matthew 12:25). Those who were called heretics, on the other hand, belonged to the kingdom of Christ. The nature of the works determined whether or not one belonged to the true Christian church, which, however, did not exist in opposition, hidden in the visible form. Neither did it exist as the invisible or spiritual church, but rather in highly visible form: a good tree bears good fruit; an evil tree evil fruit.

This ecclesiological principle from Matthew 7:17 may not be understood simply as ethicism, but rather in the light of that which in his understanding Christians needed most. It is a theme which can be traced through both groups of the religious writings of Paracelsus. It is found in the tracts about the blessed life *De summo et aeterno bono* (The Sum of the Good Life), *De virtute humana* (Human Virtue), and *De felici liberalitate* (Blessed Liberality), to mention only a few. Even their titles point to the classical stoic theme which was an important aspect of humanism. Then there were the polemical writings which were under the spell of contemporary apocalypticism. They were distinguished apodictically between Luciferian and Christian, and came in the form of Bible commentaries, sermons, or dogmatic tracts. A certain internal unity based on this critical principle appears in these two groupings which seem so disparate. They have regularly presented editors and Paracelsus scholars with problems of chronological and biographical coordination and classification.

From the foregoing we get a portrayal of a reformed Christianity with the imprint of humanism, identified primarily by a socially extremely sensitive ethical rigorism. It grew out of the absorption of medieval apocalypticism, spiritual asceticism, and criticism of the church. We can be certain that the foregoing describes decisive elements in Hohenheim's religious activity.

However, one would fail to appreciate his uniqueness and importance if one simply sought to limit him to the synthesis of those elements which came from the then living streams of tradition, and to accomplish the definition of limits on the one side by drawing on the other. The singularity of the physician and lay apostle Paracelsus would not yet have been grasped. Nor would one have understood how his conceptions were bound to his time and person and, at the same time, his significance for the identification and preservation of what is humane today. Moreover, what has already been referred to, especially the alignment to "what Christians need," would be only partially understood. Characteristic of Paracelsus was the intimate union of his medical skill, his view of the world, and his cosmological and anthropological views with his theological and religious ethos. This connection becomes clear from the profusion of religious, philosophical, theological, and ethical ideas which appear in his works on natural history and medicine.

In the *Opus Paramirum* (Book of the Five Entities), which Paracelsus wrote in 1531, perhaps the theologically most important period of his life, he compared the function of the physician with the Christian apostolate. Christ's commands to go out and heal the lepers and give sight to the blind "concern the physician as well as the apostle." Although sometimes he refused to be considered an apostle, there are in his writings sufficient indicators of a consciousness of being sent. It is visible also in his life. Although he rejected any superiority of his "virginal" state over marriage, he nevertheless deliberately renounced marriage, following the example of Christ and the apostles.

The views of Parcelsus illuminate the inner connection between the medical and spiritual aspects of his sense of call in several ways. It is rooted primarily in his anthropology with its speculation about two bodies, one material-corporal and the other spirit-soul. This is not traditional philosophical dualism but an expression of the wholeness of the development of all creation in the history of salvation. It comes from an anthropocentrism based on divine governance which Paracelsus derived from the *philosophia adepta* (philosophy of the initiate), the highest possible knowledge of nature in his time, and from the biblical views of creation and salvation.

This combination of ideas is also the context of Hohenheim's evaluation of the sacraments (baptism and the Eucharist), the resurrection of the body and his Christology. His position is clearly distinguished from all rationalist, Anabaptist, and spiritualist conceptions of the sacraments. Participation in the sacraments, especially the Eucharist, produced the actual creaturely transfer of man from the "cagastric" (mortal) to the "iliastric" (transfigured), from the old to the new birth, from mutuable to eternal life. In contrast to the *devotio moderna* and other Christian schemes for restitution concentrating on pious living, Paracelsus' concerns with questions of the realization of Christian living and his concentration on "what Christians need" was not accompanied by an emphasis on ethical and Spiritualist interpretations that minimized the sacraments. On the contrary: Paracelsus understood them as *pharmakon athanasias*, the imparting of the immortal heavenly medicine to the earthly and mortal, of the sacramental to the elemental body.

Paracelsus frequently explained his life and intellectual pilgrimage, his writings, and specifically his legitimation to act in the authority of Christ against this backdrop. He understood himself as advancing from the "light of nature" to the "eternal light," and for this reason referred to himself from a certain time onward as a doctor of holy Scripture. Paracelsus' attempt to influence the ecclesiastical developments of his time by writing, preaching, and discussion without attempting to found another church, and without ever breaking with the old church, can best be understood from his self-assured sense of call and not from any variety of Spiritualism.

Many of the developments in the world of his thought were undoubtedly called forth by the external course of his restless life. Decisive breaks in it, however, can only be explained by his calling. The professorship in Basel did not last a year. The offense he created with his lifestyle was simply too great. He had regular association with the lower and despised strata of the people, and on the other hand proved to be unyielding in his demand for honoraria from wealthy patients. After a clash with a patrician, the city physician of Basel was able to escape persecution only by flight. The final turning point had arrived. The attempt to insist upon the practice of new medical arts within the structure of that society had conclusively failed.

Years of restless wandering in extreme want followed. His efforts to publish his books and other attempts to improve his lot failed. A failure, too, was his meeting with Vadian, the city physician and Zwinglian Reformer of St. Gall, on which Paracelsus had pinned high hopes (1531).

In the succeeding years Paracelsus traveled through the Alpine countries in bitterest distress as a medical and spiritual counselor of the "needy." In 1532-1534 he was in Tyrol at a time when the Anabaptists there were exposed to fierce persecution. There he sought to stem the ravages of the Black Death. After that his situation improved somewhat ("the snow of my distress has melted"). His fame as a physician even took him to the court of Ferdinand I. Johann von Lipa was one of his patients (1537), which can surely not only be attributed to his skill as a physician. The protector of the Hutterian Brethren may have seen Paracelsus as closely related to the Anabaptists. After the death of Matthäus Lang he returned to Salzburg.

His writings on medicine and natural science circulated rapidly. A first edition of the complete works was published in 1589. He had many followers, among them influential people and circles at a number of European courts. However, the development in church politics in the years of Protestant orthodoxy and Catholic reform prevented the printing of his religious and theological writings. The collection and tradition of his manuscripts shows that Paracelsus was by no means without influence in this area as well. Valentin Weigel's writings, more than any others, show the influence of the lay theologian Paracelsus. The Schwenckfelders felt tied to him and were among those who transmitted his manuscripts. This is true even when careful study shows today that Paracelsus stood at a greater distance to Spiritualism than formerly thought, as indicated by his teaching on the Eucharist. The influence of Hohenheim on Jacob Boehme is clearly visible. It was certainly not only the physician and cosmosophist but also the lay apostle Paracelsus who was transmitted to the *philosophus teutonicus* and harsh critic of the *Mauerkirche* by those circles. Perhaps these connections also provided for the spread of Paracelsian lore in England since the seventeenth century.

Taken as a whole, however, the religious and even more the social-ethical ideas of Hohenheim have had no recognizable influence until today. This is true despite the fact that, for example, the development of his thought on peace and toleration points beyond his own time.

For further reading:

K. Goldammer, *Paracelsus. Vom Licht der Natur und des Geistes. Eine Auswahl*, Stuttgart, 1979.

_____, *Paracelsus. Sozialethische und sozialpolitische Schriften*, Tübingen, 1952.

Jolande Jacobi, ed., *Paracelsus: Selected Writings*, New York, 1951.

K. Goldammer, *Paracelsus. Natur und Offenbarung*, Hannover-Kirchrode, 1953.

W. Pagel, *Das medizinische Weltbild des Paracelsus. Seine Zusammenhänge mit Neoplatonismus und Gnosis* (Kosmographie I), Wiesbaden, 1962.

_____, *Paracelsus: An Introduction to Philosophical Medicine in the Era of the Renaissance*, Basel and New York, 1958.

O. Zeckert, *Paracelsus. Europäer im 16. Jahrhundert*, Stuttgart, 1968.

H. Schipperges, *Paracelsus. Der Mensch im Licht der Natur*, Stuttgart, 1974.

S. Domandl, *Erziehung und Menschenbild bei Paracelsus*, Salzburger Beiträge zur Paracelsusforschung, Folge 9, Wien, 1970.

S. Domandl, ed., *Paracelsus. Werk und Wirkung Festgabe für Kurt Goldammer zum 60. Geburtstag*, Wien, 1975.

Paracelsus in der Tradition: Vorträge. Paracelsustag, 1978. Salzburger Beiträge zur Paracelsusforschung, Folge 21, Wien, 1980.

Cahiers de l'Hermetisme. Paracelse, par L. Braun, K. Goldammer, P. Deghaye, E. W. Kämmerer, B. Gorceix, R. Dilg-Frank, Paris, 1980.

Kreatur und Kosmos. Internationale Beiträge zur Paracelsusforschung. Kurt Goldammer zum 65. Geburtstag gewidmet, Stuttgart und New York, 1981.

Sources of Illustrations

There are no contemporary portraits of the figures described in this book. This is the reason for resorting to largely imaginary portraits produced in later years.

P. 30. Thomas Müntzer. Taken from Christophel van Sichem, *Het tooneel der hooftketteren, bestaand in verscheyde afbeeldsels van valsche propheten, naacktloopers, geest-dryvers, sectaristen en duyvelskenstenaren,* Middelburgh, 1677. Henceforth Sichem engraving. Engraving of 1608, perhaps following Hans Holbein the Younger. Cf. G. Franz, "Die Bildnisse Thomas Müntzers" *Archiv für Kulturgeschichte* 25, 1934, 21-37.

P. 49. The only known portrait of Andreas Bodenstein von Carlstadt. Basel, University Library. Taken from M. Steinmetz *et al., Illustrierte Geschichte der frühbürgerlichen Revolution,* Berlin (East), 1975.

P. 59. Hans Hut. Sichem engraving.

P. 78. Title page of The Twelve Articles. Pamphlet. Zwickau, 1525. Taken from Günter Jäckel ed., *Kaiser, Gott and Bauer. Die Zeit des deutschen Bauernkriegs im Spiegel der Literatur,* Berlin (East), 1975, 409.

P. 90. Michael Gaismair to the Royal Council in Innsbruck. Made available by Walter Klaassen.

P. 99. Title page of *The New Changes,* attributed to Hans Hergot, 1527. Taken from Hans Hergot und die Flugschrift "Von der Newen Wandlung eynes christlichen Lebens." Facsimile reproduction and transcription (foreword by Max Steinmetz and an appendix by Helmut Claus), Leipzig, 1977.

P. 109. Peasants from the hinterland of Zürich pelt the patrician Jörg Göldli with stones because he challenges their fishing rights in the name of the Zürich Council (March, 1525). Taken from a copy of the *Reformationsgeschichte* of Heinrich Bullinger. Made available by Heinold Fast.

P. 121. The Grossmünster in Zürich. A book illustration by Hans Leu, father and son, early sixteenth century in the Schweizerisches Landesmuseum, Zürich. Taken from Fritz Blanke, *Der junge Bullinger,* Zürich, 1942.

P. 135. Title page of the Schleitheim Articles 1527 taken from James M.

Stayer, *Anabaptists and the Sword,* Lawrence, Kan., 2nd edition, 1976, 115.

P. 149. Balthasar Hubmaier. Sichem engraving.

P. 161. A nocturnal Anabaptist gathering taken by surprise. Wick Collection, Central Library in Zürich. Taken from *Mennonitische Geschichtsblätter* 1974. Cf. Heinold Fast, "Die Aushebung einer nächtlichen Täuferversammlung 1574," *loc. cit.* 103-106.

P. 173. Arrested Anabaptists are led to Zürich. Taken from *Mennonitische Geschichtsblätter* 1974.

P. 180. Melchior Hoffman. Sichem engraving.

P. 195. Title page of the pamphlet "Newe Zeytung, die Widerteuffer zu Münster belangende," Woodcut, 1535. Taken from Günter Jäckel ed., *op. cit.*, 505.

P. 205. Menno Simons. Sichem engraving.

P. 219. Caspar von Schwenckfeld. Original portrait in the Schwenckfeld Library, Pennsburg, Pa. Taken from Selina G. Schultz, *Caspar Schwenckfeld von Ossig (1489-1561). Spiritual Interpreter of Christianity, Apostle of the Middle Way, Pioneer in Modern Religious Thought,* Norristown, Pa., 1946.

P. 229. "Franck's Face" by A. Luppius. Taken from Will-Erich Peuckert, *Sebastian Franck. Ein deutscher Sucher.* Munich, 1943. (In the legend Franck is obviously mistaken for Caspar von Schwenckfeld, the Silesian nobleman.)

P. 249. Michael Servetus. Sichem engraving.

P. 258. Paracelsus. Woodcut from the Görlitz Codex Th. VI. 146, 4° of 1567. Taken from J. Betschart, "Theophrastus Paracelsus. Der Magus vom Etzel." *Schweitzer Heimatbücher* 57, Bern 1953, 38.

The Authors

Willem J. de Bakker, born 1944, doctoral candidate at the University of Chicago. Taught Renaissance and Reformation History at the University of Saskatchewan. Publications: "De vroege theologie van Bernhard Rothmann. De gereformeerde achtergrond van het Munsterse Doperrijk," *Doopsgezinde Bijdragen*, n.r. 3, 1977, 9-20.

Klaus Deppermann, born 1930; PhD; professor, Historisches Seminar, University of Freiburg. Publications: *Der hallesche Pietismus und der preussische Staat unter Friedrich III*, 1961; co-editor of the annual *Pietismus und Neuzeit; Melchior Hoffman: Soziale Unruhen und apokalyptische Visionen im Zeitalter der Reformation*, 1979; research articles on Anabaptism and Pietism.

Heinold Fast, born 1929. ThD; pastor of the Mennonite church in Emden. Publications: *Heinrich Bullinger und die Täufer*, 1959; editor of *Der Linke Flügel der Reformation*, 1962; editor of *Quellen zur Geschichte der Täufer in der Schweiz*, vol. 2: *Ostschweiz*, 1973; articles on Anabaptism. He is an editor of the *Mennonitische Geschichtsblätter*.

Jerome Friedmann, born 1943; PhD; professor of Reformation history, Kent State University, Kent. Publications: *Confrontation and Conciliation: The Crisis of Reformation*, 1972; *Michael Servetus: A Case Study in Total Heresy*, 1978; articles on Radical Reformation and late medieval Hebrew studies.

Abraham Friesen, born 1933; PhD; professor of Renaissance and Reformation history, University of California, Santa Barbara. Publications: *Reformation and Utopia: The Marxist Interpretation of the Reformation and its Antecedents*, 1974; coeditor with Hans-Jürgen Goertz, *Thomas Müntzer*, 1978; coeditor and translator with J. B. Toews, P. J. Klassen, and H. Loewen, P. M. Friesen, *The Mennonite Brotherhood in Russia (1789-1910)*, 1978; articles on the historiography of the Radical Reformation.

Barbara B. Gerber, born 1952; doctoral candidate at the Historisches Seminar of the University of Hamburg, early modern section (Prof. Dr. R. Wohlfeil). Publications: with

Hans-Jürgen Goertz and Gabriele Wohlauf, "Neue Forschungen zum deutschen Bauernkrieg," *Mennonitische Geschichtsblätter* 1976, 24-64 and 1977, 35-64.

Hans-Jürgen Goertz, born 1937; ThD; professor in the Institut für Sozial- und Wirtschaftsgeschichte, University of Hamburg. Publications: *Innere und äussere Ordnung in der Theologie Thomas Müntzers,* 1967; *Die Täufer. Geschichte und Deutung,* 1980; *Geist und Wirklichkeit. Eine Studie zur Pneumatologie Erich Schaeders,* 1980; editor of *Die Mennoniten. Die Kirchen der Welt* vol. 8, 1971; editor of *Umstrittenes Täufertum 1525-1975. Neue Forschungen,* 1975; second edition, 1977; editor with Abraham Friesen, *Thomas Müntzer,* 1978; articles on Müntzer, Anabaptism, and Peasant Revolt. He is an editor of *Mennonitische Geschichtsblätter.*

Leonard Gross, born 1931; PhD; executive secretary of the Hispanic Committee of the Mennonite Church and director of its archives and historical research program. Publications: editor of *Mennonite Historical Bulletin;* editor with John A. Hostetler and E. Bender, *Selected Hutterian Documents in Translation 1542-1654,* 1973; *The Golden Years of the Hutterites,* 1980; articles on Anabaptists and Mennonites.

Martin Haas, born 1935; PhD; teacher at the Gymnasium in Winterthur, Switzerland. Publications: *Huldrych Zwingli,* 2. edition, 1976; editor of *Quellen zur Geschichte der Täufer in der Schweiz, vol. 4: Drei Täufergespräche,* 1974; articles on Anabaptism. Editor of *Zwingliana* 1970-1975.

Irvin B. Horst, born 1915; ThD; professor at the Theologische Fakulteit, University of Amsterdam. Publications: *The Radical Brethren: Anabaptism and the English Reformation to 1558,* 1972; *A Bibliography of Menno Simons, ca. 1496-1561, Dutch Reformer,* 1962; editor of *Bulletin voor de Uitgave van Documenta Anabaptistica Neerlandica 1-10* (1968-1978); editor with A. F. de Jong and D. Visser, *De Geest in Het Geding: Opstellen anngeboden aan J. A. Oosterbaan,* 1978; editor of *The Dutch Dissenters,* 1982; articles on Anabaptism.

Walter Klaassen, born 1926; PhD; professor of history, Conrad Grebel College, University of Waterloo. Publications: *Anabaptism: Neither Catholic nor Protestant,* 1973; *Michael Gaismair: Revolutionary and Reformer,* 1978; editor and translator, *Anabaptism in Outline: A Selection of Primary*

Documents, 1981; articles on Anabaptist and Mennonite history.

William Klassen, born 1930; ThD; professor and head of the Department of Religion, University of Manitoba, Winnipeg. Publications: *The Forgiving Community*, 1966; *Covenant and Community: A Study of the Life and Writings and . . . Hermeneutics of Pilgram Marpeck*, 1968; *Release to Those in Prison*, 1977; editor and translator with W. Klaassen of *The Writings of Pilgram Marpeck*, 1978; articles in Anabaptism, contributions to *Interpreter's Dictionary of the Bible*, 1976.

Steven E. Ozment, born 1939; PhD; professor of history and religious studies, Yale University. Publications: *Homo Spiritualis: A Comparative Study of the Anthropology of Johannes Tauler, Jean Gerson and Martin Luther*, 1969; editor of *The Reformation in Medieval Perspective*, 1971; *Mysticism and Dissent: Religious Ideology and Social Protest in the Sixteenth Century*, 1973; *The Reformation in the Cities: The Appeal of Protestantism to Sixteenth-Century Germany and Switzerland*, 1975; *The Age of Reform 1250-1550: An Intellectual and Religious History of Late Medieval and Reformation Europe*, 1980; articles on Reformation history.

Werner O. Packull, born 1941; PhD; assistant professor of history, Renison College, University of Waterloo. Publications: *Mysticism and the Early South German-Austrian Anabaptist Movement 1525-1531*, 1977; editor and translator with James M. Stayer, *The Anabaptists and Thomas Müntzer*, 1980; articles on Müntzer and Anabaptism.

Hartmuth Rudolph, born 1941; ThD; collaborator in publication of the complete theological and religious-philosophical works of Theophrast von Hohenheim (Paracelsus Edition) under the leadership of Professor Kurt Goldammer in Marburg. Publications: *Das evangelische Militärkirchenwesen in Preussen. Die Entwicklung seiner Verfassung und Organisation vom Absolutismus bis zum Vorabend des I. Weltkriegs*, 1973; "Fragen der Ostpolitik im Raum der Ev. Kirche in Deutschland," *Kirche zwischen Krieg und Frieden. Studien zur Geschichte des deutschen Protestantismus*, 1976, 460-540. Since 1977 he has published several articles concerning the religious writings of Paracelsus.

Gottfried Seebass, born 1937; ThD; professor of church history, University of Heidelberg. Publications: *Das reformatorische Werk des Andreas Osiander*, 1967; edited with G. Müller,

Andreas Osiander: Gesamtausgabe, 3 volumes published, 1975, 1977, and 1979; more than 30 articles on the history of the Reformation, the former imperial city of Nuremberg, and the Radical Reformation; unpublished Habilitationsschrift: *Müntzers Erbe: Werk, Leben und Theologie des Hans Hut*, 1972.

Ferdinand Seibt, born 1927, PhD; professor of late medieval history, Ruhr-Bochum University. Publications: *Hussitica*, 1965; *Die Zeit der Luxemburger. Handbuch der Geschichte der böhmischen Länder I*, 1967; *Bohemica*, 1970; *Utopica: Modelle Totaler Sozialplannung*, 1972; *Deutschland und die Tschechen*, 1974; *Karl IV*, 1978.

Ronald J. Sider, born 1938; PhD; professor, Eastern Baptist Theological Seminary, Philadelphia. Publications: *Andreas Bodenstein von Karlstadt*, 1974; *The Chicago Declaration*, 1974; *Rich Christians in an Age of Hunger*, 1977; *Karlstadt's Battle with Luther: Documents in a Liberal-Radical Debate*, 1977.

James M. Stayer, born 1935; PhD; professor of history, Queen's University, Kingston. Publications: *Anabaptists and the Sword*, 1972; Second ed. 1976; editor and translator with W. O. Packull, *Thomas Müntzer and the Anabaptists*, 1980; many articles on Anabaptism.

Horst Weigelt, born 1934, ThD; professor at the Institut für Evangelische Theologie, University of Bamberg. Publications: *Pietismus-Studien. I. Teil. Der spenerhallische Pietismus*, 1965; *Erweckungsbewegung und konfessionelles Luthertum im 19. Jahrhundert*, 1968; *Sebastian Franck und die lutherische Reformation*, 1971; *Spiritualische Tradition im Protestantismus. Die Geschichte des Schwenckfeldertums in Schlesien*, 1973. Articles in books and periodicals.

Christof Windhorst, born 1940, ThD; research assistant at the University of Tübingen, 1971-1975, and at the Kirchliche Hochschule Bethel in Bielefeld, 1975-1979. Now pastor at Gohfeld. Publications: *Täuferisches Taufverständnis: Balthasar Hubmaiers Lehre zwischen traditioneller und reformatorischer Theologie*, 1976; editor with J. Nolte and H. Tompert, *Kontinuität und Umbruch: Theologie und Frömmigkeit in Flugschriften und Kleinliteratur an der Wende vom 15. zum 16. Jahrhundert*, 1978; editor of *Die Vorstellung von Zwei Reichen und Regimenten bis Luther*

(first edition by V. Duchrow and H. Hoffman), second
revised edition, 1978; articles on Hubmaier, Luther,
Schwenckfeld, and Anabaptism.

Index of Persons